The Power
of Sales Analytics

Andris A. Zoltners

Prabhakant Sinha

Sally E. Lorimer

ZS Associates, Inc.

Published by ZS Associates, Inc.
1800 Sherman Avenue, Suite 700
Evanston, Illinois 60201

www.zsassociates.com

Text design, typesetting, and project management: Books By Design, Inc.

Library of Congress Control Number: 2014944108

ISBN: 978-0-9853436-3-7

United States Map [Image Number 167366684], Copyright chrupka (Chapter 5, Figure 5-6); Connecticut Map [Image Number 164533028], Copyright Rainer Lesniewski (Chapter 5, Figure 5-8), all used under license from Shutterstock.com.

Contents

Foreword

By Neil Rackham
Author of *SPIN Selling*

The Corporate Executive Board reports that 50 percent of all companies that have sales operations functions set them up within the last three years. Sales operations, and the analytic approach that goes with it, has become the newest sales "must have": a contender for the next big thing to follow after mobile customer relationship management (CRM). Yet the idea of sales operations, and the analytics that underpin it, isn't new. I first came across the concept at Xerox during the 1970s, when sales operations was the newly created group responsible for sales planning, compensation, forecasting, and territory design. J. Patrick Kelly, who ran sales operations at the time for Xerox, memorably described it as "all the nasty number things that you don't want to do but need to do to make a great sales force." When pressed further, he would explain, "It's about discipline: using numbers to keep sales on track." For the time, that wasn't a bad starting definition for *sales analytics*.

We can see that as early as the mid-1970s, leading sales forces like Xerox's were finding the traditional undisciplined, seat-of-the-pants sales approach used by most companies to be inefficient, wasteful, and unsustainable in the long run. But Kelly's vision of a disciplined sales force that, in his words, "used numbers to make its numbers" was many years ahead of its time. Why has it taken nearly 40 years for sales analytics to become widely accepted as an essential sales management tool? A primary reason is that in the early days, nobody knew what data to analyze. My own research in the 1970s provides a good example of the problem. We wanted to measure the skills most linked to sales success. Our purpose was to analyze the behaviors used by successful salespeople during sales calls and to use that information to train and coach the rest of the sales force. We needed to decide which behaviors to analyze. Hundreds of observable things happen in the average B2B sales call. We ended up measuring more than a hundred different possible behaviors before we found the half dozen trainable behaviors that we were looking for. Until we had built a valid success model, we didn't know what data we should be collecting for analysis. Initially, this work was just as wasteful and expensive as the seat-of-the-pants approach that we wanted to replace.

Models and Frameworks: The Cornerstone of Analytics

Analytics, whether in sales or in other areas of the business, are only useful if they make some activity, process, or decision more efficient or more effective. When the measurement theorist Daniel L. Stufflebeam wrote that "the purpose of evaluation is not to prove but to improve," he might just as well have been writing about sales analytics. To translate data into meaningful prescriptions for improvement requires not only the data itself, but also models and frameworks to give the data meaning and to guide decisions. This may sound very theoretical, but let me give you a practical example; it's a good one because the authors of this book made their reputation from it.

How do you decide how big a sales force should be? Traditionally, this has been a complicated exercise in guesswork. Into the mix went such factors as whether the market was expanding, the future product stream, the state of the economy, the available budgets, and—possibly above all these—the political clout of sales within the company. The whole process was so complex and arcane that I shuddered inside whenever a client asked me whether their sales force was the right size. It was pure guesswork; a variation on the classic and unanswerable question, "How long is a piece of string?" Then in the mid-1980s, I heard of a small consulting company, ZS Associates, founded by two professors from Northwestern University's Kellogg School of Management, that had come up with a method for sizing sales forces. I remember thinking at the time how very specialized and limited a market that was for a consulting company. Their approach to sizing rested on a rational analytic model. They had brought the same analytic, data-based thinking to size that my research team had brought to selling skills.

Beyond Sales Force Size

If ZS Associates had stopped there, they would have remained a small niche player with an important but limited offering. Fortunately for the sales world, they didn't stop there. Realizing that their special competence was the analytic method, they began to apply rigorous data-driven thinking to other sales problems. By the year 2000, they had applied analytics to develop models and frameworks in such areas as sales territory design, recruitment, quota setting, and compensation. In the process, they had grown to over 400 people, making ZS Associates one of the biggest sales consulting firms in the world at that time.

In 2001, Andris A. Zoltners and Prabhakant Sinha published *The Complete Guide to Accelerating Sales Force Performance*, which describes many of the analytic tools and frameworks that they have developed. I have a confession to make. I bought their book as soon as it was published, but I didn't read it for several months. I think that the word *complete* put me off. I didn't believe that any book about sales could live up to such a title. Left to myself, I might never have opened the book. It didn't sell particularly well and had disappointingly few reviews. Then one day, I was having coffee with the preeminent marketing thinker Philip Kotler, and he asked me what I thought of the book. He was astonished that I hadn't read it and brushed aside my feeble excuse that it was waiting on my shelf. "Read it," he said. "It's important." When Phil Kotler says that something is important, for me there's no higher endorsement. So the next day I read the book and was stunned that I had left such an important work unopened for months.

Questionable Best Practices

To understand why the frameworks and models in the *Complete Guide* had such a deep impact on me, you must go back to the prevailing best practices for sales data at the time the book was published. Companies were spending hundreds of millions annually on cumbersome CRM systems that were generally failing to live up to the vendors' promises. The cause of analytics was being seriously damaged by the enormous effort of CRM data collection set against its meager returns. Depending on whose survey you choose to believe, between 50 and 70 percent of CRM implementations in 2000 were judged by their unhappy customers as a failure. Sales managers were learning the hard way that data have no value unless they can be used to improve sales. Worse, the cynicism of most salespeople toward CRM meant that much of the potential for CRM analytics was being sabotaged by inaccurate, incomplete, or deliberately falsified information that salespeople had entered into the system. Electronic lies are no better than manual lies; they just arrive quicker. As one vice president of a New York bank told me, "Now that we've installed the new CRM system, we can make the wrong decisions faster than ever before." In this climate, many senior managers were justifiably cynical about whether analytics could deliver results.

Another difficult issue was the pervasive use of analytic models and frameworks that were disturbingly naive. Even today, many companies rely on simplistic activity models that use calls per day as a key metric in the B2B sale. Although the underlying assumption that "more calls equals more sales" has long been discredited, activity measurement is still alive and well.

So when I read the *Complete Guide*, I was delighted to see sophisticated, performance-related analytics. I wasn't the only one. The approach that ZS Associates had developed clearly resonated with leading companies everywhere. Propelled by a series of important books, such as *The Complete Guide to Sales Force Incentive Compensation* and *Building a Winning Sales Force*, ZS has gone from strength to strength. Today, ZS Associates has more than 2,500 employees worldwide, making it not only the preeminent authority on sales analytics, but also the world's largest sales consultancy by a whole order of magnitude.

About This Book

The Power of Sales Analytics is no ordinary sales book. It represents the culmination of many years of intense and thoughtful effort by many talented people, some of whom have contributed authoritative chapters here. It is a survey of the cutting edge of sales analytics and the state-of-the-art in sophisticated sales management. Many readers will find this book complex, and for that I make no apology and neither should the authors. It was Michael Kami who first said, "For every complex problem, there is a simple answer—and it is *wrong*!" Sales has grown up and has progressed far beyond the seat-of-the-pants "silver bullet" days. Simple answers just don't cut it anymore. If you want to be a player in the exciting future world of sales, you will need to master the frameworks, models, and methods in this book. Armed with these tools, you can make great strides forward in terms of sales effectiveness; without them, you'll fall ever further behind.

Neil Rackham
Visiting Professor of Sales, University of Sheffield

Introduction

The smart use of sales analytics and decision frameworks helps ensure that the right sales team is in place and is engaged in the right activities for driving success with customers and delivering results.

Andris A. Zoltners, Prabhakant Sinha, and Sally E. Lorimer

Today's World of Sales and the Role of Analytics

Gone are the days when running a sales force followed a three-step recipe:

1. Hire charismatic people and train them.
2. Point them toward customers and prospects.
3. Pay for performance.

Today's world of sales is more complex. Customers are better informed and far more demanding. Competitors are quick to seize an edge or close a gap. Salespeople need to step up with a higher level of knowledge. To be valuable, they need problem-solving and consultative skills; good products and relationships are only table stakes. As sales leaders ponder the challenges of structuring, sizing, deploying, hiring, developing, motivating, informing, and controlling their sales organizations, they are working with a new generation of technology-savvy workers and an explosion of data and technology that has several components:

- Escalating volumes of information on customers, sales transactions, market potential, competitors, sales activity, and salespeople
- Social networks such as Facebook, LinkedIn, and Twitter
- More powerful and fast-changing computer, storage, and mobile communication technologies
- Advanced models and analytic tools

All this creates opportunity, and *that* is the central theme of this book.

The opportunity exists, as never before, to leverage data and judgment with the help of decision frameworks. A decision framework is a structured way to think about an issue so as to minimize bias and enhance decision quality. But there are risks too. It's not easy to see clearly in the fog of too much information. And information can be used selectively to justify any preconception. *Far too often, we see new sales force technologies hyped before they are proved successful, and in many cases, the results have been disappointing.*

Take, for instance, what we call the *Long Path to CRM Success*. During the late 1980s, companies spent billions of dollars and millions of hours building and operating the first wave of customer relationship management (CRM) systems. As early as 1990, the Conference Board (a global, independent business membership and research association headquartered in New York City) cautioned that half of these companies regretted going down that path. In the second wave of CRM system implementation, led by software company Siebel Systems, companies spent tens of billions of dollars. Yet many surveys conducted around the year 2000 reported that 50 to 70 percent of these implementations failed. People who rolled out CRM systems at that time seemed to like the systems most just before they implemented them. Now in its third wave, recent CRM efforts are more successful; companies have learned from the early failures. Today's industry-tailored solutions are quicker to deploy and lighter to sustain. But it took more than 20 years to get to this point.

How This Book Can Help Your Sales Force

We are neither fad chasers with the latest silver bullet nor cheerleaders exhorting you to jump on the latest data and technology bandwagon. For over 30 years, we have been helping companies around the globe leverage the power of analytics to do the blocking and tackling for driving sales force success. We started our consulting firm, ZS Associates, in 1983, and by 2014 the firm had grown to more than 2,500 employees worldwide. Over 60 percent of ZS consultants' time is spent helping companies use data and technology to make and implement better, analytically based sales force decisions. Here are a few examples:

- How can salespeople identify the right customer opportunities? What sales activities best seize those opportunities?

- How can sales activities be organized into effective selling roles? How many people do we need in each role?

- What is the profile of a successful salesperson? Does our recruiting program acquire the best talent? Are we training and developing the right competencies?

- What information and tools does the sales force need to create value for customers?

- Are incentive programs, goals, and performance management processes aligned to motivate high achievement and drive results?

We have seen firsthand the tremendous potential that analytics and decision frameworks have to address these and other questions. We are convinced that sales forces that use analytics to approach sales decision making consistently outperform those that do not.

But we also know that realizing the potential is not easy. There are huge challenges to overcome, including these:

- **Proliferation of data.** It's challenging to sift through all the data that's available today to find the most relevant and accurate information for supporting sales force decisions. Some data sets have become so large and complex that traditional data processing methods won't work. It's also challenging to maintain objectivity and avoid using selected data to justify one's bias.

- **Getting the cooperation of many people.** Often, multiple company functions must collaborate to make sales analytics work, including sales, marketing, human resources, finance, and information technology. This requires people with different mind-sets and motivations to work together. The challenge becomes even greater when outsourcing partners, including offshore resources, are thrown into the mix.

- **Constant change.** Sales analytics must respond to ongoing change in the marketplace, evolving company strategies, and rapidly advancing technology. Change creates opportunity, but it also creates the challenge of keeping sales support programs, systems, and processes flexible enough to adapt. It requires that people who participate in the sales analytics function can learn and adapt.

This book can help you address these and other challenges. It provides dozens of practical insights that we've gained by working with Fortune 500 companies, as well as smaller entrepreneurial businesses, on how to tap into the power of analytics to drive sales success in today's complex world. Here are just a few of the many examples featured in the book:

- **Roche Diagnostics.** Guided by a vision and charter for using analytics to support sales decisions, this global healthcare leader achieved the ambitious goal of increasing the company's market share by 3 points in just a year and a half. Recognizing the importance of analytics to sales success, the company elevated sales analytics leadership to a vice president–level position (see Chapter 1).

- **Oakwood Worldwide.** An initiative led by the sales operations group at this leading provider of temporary furnished and serviced apartments transformed the company's sales process to emulate the best practices of top-performing salespeople. The sales operations group supported the new sales process with tools and metrics and proactively diagnosed opportunities and challenges on an ongoing basis. Win rates for deals tripled, sales cycle time dropped by over 50 percent, and salesperson turnover shrank to under 5 percent (see Chapter 3).

- **Novartis.** Annual sales force effectiveness reviews drove six consecutive years of double-digit, top-line growth for this global healthcare leader. The company identified high-priority sales force effectiveness projects each year, executed an improvement plan, and measured progress. One initiative, a performance frontier study for salespeople, was linked to improved customer perceptions of salespeople and better sales results. Based on its initial success in the U.S. market, Novartis replicated the approach globally (see Chapter 6).

Who Should Read This Book

The Power of Sales Analytics can help *sales leaders* (current and aspiring sales vice presidents and directors) take their sales organizations to the next performance level by using analytics to enable smarter sales force decisions. It can also help *sales analytics leaders* (current and aspiring directors of sales analytics or operations) discover new ways to add value to their sales forces and learn how to implement strategies for delivering that value.

How This Book Is Organized

The Power of Sales Analytics lays out a practical approach for using analytics and decision frameworks to boost sales force performance. We call the approach, which is described in detail in Chapter 1, the *support-diagnose-design-partner framework*.

- *Support* provides the data and analytics to keep the sales machine operating.

- *Diagnose* puts sensors in place to address concerns and identify improvement opportunities.

- *Design* uses analytics and decision frameworks to create or enhance the decisions and processes that drive sales force effectiveness.

- *Partner* provides advisory capacity to help leaders set priorities and direction and enact strategic and tactical sales force change.

After Chapter 1, the chapters are grouped into two main sections. Each section addresses a core question that you'll need to answer in order to realize the value of sales analytics in your organization.

- **Section 1:** How can analytics improve sales force effectiveness? We'll demonstrate what is possible in eight key sales force decision areas.

- **Section 2:** How do you build the capability to make it possible? We'll show you how to overcome some key implementation challenges and realize opportunities to make sales analytics work.

Section 1: How Analytics Improve Sales Force Decision Making

Section 1 (Chapters 2–9) demonstrates the potential benefits that the smart use of analytics can bring to your sales organization. It lays out a range of opportunities, organized around the support-diagnose-design-partner framework, and shares specific analytic techniques, decision frameworks, and examples. Each chapter in Section 1 demonstrates the power of analytics to improve decision making and enhance performance in one of eight key sales force decision areas:

- Customer potential estimation (Chapter 2)
- Sales process (Chapter 3)
- Sales force size and structure (Chapter 4)
- Territory design (Chapter 5)
- Hiring and training (Chapter 6)
- Incentive compensation (Chapter 7)
- Goal setting (Chapter 8)
- Performance management (Chapter 9)

Section 2: Building the Capabilities to Make Sales Analytics Work

Section 2 (Chapters 10–13) is for leaders who believe in the value of sales analytics and who want to build or improve capabilities to realize the opportunity. Capabilities include people and competencies, processes, and data and tools. Ultimately, those who are successful can build a partnership in which sales analytics leaders have the respect of top company leaders as key contributors to sales force success. Section 2 starts with an overview of how to build capabilities (Chapter 10). Then it discusses three special challenges and opportunities that can affect implementation success.

- Outsourcing and offshoring (Chapter 11)
- Achieving sales and information technology alignment (Chapter 12)
- Implementing sales analytics when launching a new sales force (Chapter 13)

The Ultimate Objective

We hope that *The Power of Sales Analytics* introduces you to several ideas that you can put to work immediately to drive sales force performance and build competitive advantage. The smart use of sales analytics and decision frameworks helps ensure that the right sales team is in place and is engaged in the right activities for driving success with customers and delivering results.

CHAPTER 1

Enhancing Sales Force Effectiveness Through Analytics and Decision Frameworks

The best sales organizations use analytics and decision frameworks for supporting sales force needs, diagnosing issues and finding opportunities, and designing and constantly improving the drivers of sales effectiveness.

Andris A. Zoltners, Prabhakant Sinha, and Sally E. Lorimer

Andris A. Zoltners is a professor emeritus of marketing at Northwestern University's Kellogg School of Management and a co-founder of ZS Associates. He has personally consulted for more than 200 companies in over 20 countries. He has spoken at numerous conferences and has taught sales force topics to thousands of Executive, MBA, and PhD students. He is a co-author of numerous academic articles and a series of books on sales force management. He received his PhD from Carnegie-Mellon University.

Prabhakant Sinha is a co-founder of ZS Associates and a former Kellogg faculty member, who continues to teach sales executives at the Indian School of Business and the Gordon Institute of Business Science in South Africa. He has helped over 200 firms improve sales force strategy and effectiveness. He is a co-author of many academic articles and a series of books on sales force management. He received his PhD from the University of Massachusetts and graduated from the Indian Institute of Technology, Kharagpur.

Sally E. Lorimer is a business writer. She is a co-author of numerous academic articles and books on sales force management. As a former principal at ZS Associates, she has helped clients in a range of industries implement strategies for improving sales effectiveness and performance. She has an MBA from Northwestern University's Kellogg School of Management and is also a graduate of the University of Michigan.

The authors thank former ZS associate David Vinca for his contributions to this chapter.

Sales Force Decision Making: Yesterday and Today

Leading a sales force to deliver profitable revenue growth in today's complex business environment is a big challenge. Not so long ago, when making critical sales force decisions, sales leaders relied primarily on their own judgment and experience, as well as on input from field sales managers and salespeople. Today, sales leaders need to do more. A perfect storm of data, technology, and analytic innovation is radically changing the dynamics of sales force management and allowing leaders to gain new insights for driving sales force success. Figure 1-1 summarizes key innovations affecting sales analytics today.

Explosion of Data	Enabling Technologies and Analytics
• Customer profiles • Direct sales transactions • Sales through distributors • Demographics/market potential • Competitive intelligence • Sales force activity data • Salesperson profiles • Social networks	• Mobile devices • Cloud computing • Business intelligence, sales force automation, and performance management systems • Advanced analytic and reporting tools • Descriptive, predictive, and optimization models • Decision frameworks

Figure 1-1. Innovations affecting sales analytics today

Whereas sales leaders were once piloting their sales forces with a set of tools comparable in sophistication to the cockpit instruments of the earliest airplanes, today they have available navigation tools comparable to those of the most modern jets.

In a transformed and turbulent world, savvy leaders can make better-informed sales force decisions. The examples shown in Figure 1-2 illustrate what is possible today, compared to yesterday.

Sales Analytics: A Powerful Tool

To compete more effectively today, companies need certain capabilities—a set of people and competencies, processes, data, and tools for using analytics and decision frameworks to *support* sales force needs, *diagnose*

Decision	Yesterday	Today

Should we expand the sales force?	• Ask sales managers how many people they need.
	• Calculate how many salespeople the company can afford.
		• Use market-based sizing models that:
		  – Segment customers according to needs and potential.
		  – Determine what sales process and effort level are required for each segment.
		  – Estimate the financial value of covering different segments.
		  – Determine the best size.
		• Deploy sales resources to match potential.

Should we change the incentive plan?	• Ask salespeople if they like the plan. • Check incentive costs versus budget. • Evaluate plan administration for accuracy and timeliness.	• Use analytics to test proposed plan designs, compare alternatives, and reveal unwanted side effects and financial risks. • Monitor payout distributions and metrics showing a plan's strategic alignment, motivational power, and costs. • Proactively make adjustments to keep the plan on track.
How can we reduce sales force turnover?	• Brainstorm with sales managers and Human Resources (HR) to discover ways to reduce sales force turnover.	• Integrate data on salesperson attrition with data about salesperson performance and potential. • Match solutions for reducing turnover to the needs of high, average, and low performers. • Conduct periodic reviews to track retention and diagnose and address problems early.

Figure 1-2. Examples of the changing dynamics of sales force decision making

problems and opportunities, and *design* solutions for major sales force decisions.

Sales analytics capabilities can reside in a dedicated internal function, such as a sales operations or analytics department. Capabilities can also reside in other company departments, such as Finance or Information Technology (IT), or with outsourcing partners. Regardless of where the capabilities reside, the best sales leaders view the sales analytics function as a *partner* in setting the right priorities for constantly improving sales force decisions and leading efforts for positive change.

The Power of Sales Analytics at Roche Diagnostics

Bill Lister, formerly the senior vice president and general manager at global healthcare leader Roche Diagnostics Corp., is a firm believer in the power of analytics for driving sales success. Bill focused relentlessly on building and sustaining an analytics-based decision-making culture within the sales force at Roche. He led by example, guided by a vision and charter for using analytics to support sales force decisions.

Bill recalls a time when he and his staff proposed that the organization achieve the ambitious goal of increasing the company's market share by 3 points in just a year and a half.

"The sales force thought the goal was impossible to achieve," he says. "We spent weeks analyzing the data using numerous statistical models. When we broke down opportunities by market segment and major customer, we discovered a targeting and customer coverage strategy that could work. It took many meetings to educate the sales force and get the commitment we needed.

"The data and analysis were critical to that process. We could show salespeople exactly what they needed to do to achieve their goals, and we could eliminate much of the emotion involved. The data and analysis contributed greatly to our ability to achieve the goal."

According to Bill, "Developing an analytics-based sales culture starts at the top. It takes persistence and discipline, but the benefit is huge." Bill used the following tactics, among others, to create and sustain an analytics-based culture:

- **Bring in the right people with the right skills.** "You'll need people with strong sales support skills, but you'll also need individuals who are strategic thinkers."

- **Put the right processes in place.** "Educate everyone on how to use data and analysis to run a business. Conduct meetings with the expectation that decisions must be supported by data; insist that people consistently back up their line of reasoning with analytics. Hold everyone accountable from meeting to meeting."

- **Monitor progress and demonstrate ongoing value.** "People may be skeptical at first, so put metrics in place for tracking success. For example, after we started using a data-based approach to setting sales goals, we hit some very challenging numbers on a consistent basis. Pretty soon, the organization started to believe."

- **Elevate the role of sales analytics.** "Make the sales analytics function highly esteemed within the organization. Demonstrate its importance by making the leader of sales analytics a vice president–level position."

The Sales Force Effectiveness Drivers

Many decisions and processes are required to operate a sales force. These decisions and processes are key determinants of sales performance; thus, we call them the sales force effectiveness (SFE) drivers. Figure 1-3 provides a

Sales Strategy	Organization
• Customer potential • Customer targeting • Sales process	• Sales force size • Sales force structure • Territory design

People	Activity Enablement
• Success profile • Hiring • Training and coaching	• Incentives and goals • Dashboards and information • Performance management

Figure 1-3. The principal SFE drivers

list of the principal SFE drivers organized into four categories: sales strategy, organization, people, and activity enablement.

The SFE drivers influence and determine the sales team and its activities. Strong SFE drivers, enabled by analytics and decision frameworks, ensure that the right people are in place and are engaged in the right activities for driving success with customers and ultimately delivering company results.

Sales Analytics: Beyond Customer Analytics

Frequently, when people think about using analytics in a sales force, they think about customer analytics — using data about buyer needs and behaviors to prioritize customers, develop customized offerings, and create sales. As important as customer analytics are, there are many, many more sales force decisions that can benefit from the power of analytics. Sales force members, ranging from top leadership (e.g., a sales vice president) to first-line sales managers (e.g., district or regional sales managers) to frontline salespeople, all have questions that analytics can help address. Here are just a few examples.

Some Questions from Sales Leaders

- **Sales force structure and size.** What are the right sales roles (for example, generalist, product specialist, technical specialist, key account manager, inside sales) for our company? How many salespeople should we have in each role?

- **Sales force recruiting.** What is the right profile for success in the sales job? How do we attract, find, and select the best sales talent?

- **Incentive compensation.** How do we design, implement, and improve an incentive plan that motivates and drives results?

Some Questions from First-Line Sales Managers

- **Sales territory design.** How should I assign responsibility for customers and prospects to salespeople to maximize coverage and give all salespeople a fair chance to succeed?

- **Sales training and coaching.** What guidance can I give salespeople? What instructional programs should I suggest to help salespeople acquire and improve their skills and knowledge?

- **Goal setting.** How can I determine territory-level sales goals that are fair, realistic, and motivational?

- **Performance management.** How should I assess and diagnose the performance of salespeople? How can I help them succeed?

Some Questions from Salespeople

- **Customer targeting.** Which customers and prospects should I focus on?

- **Value proposition.** What offering is best for each customer?

- **Sales process.** What is the best way to interact with each customer to maximize my chance of success and deliver value profitably?

- **Sales force tools and dashboards.** What information do I need to plan my time, help my customers succeed, and achieve my sales goals?

> *Analytics can improve the quality of decisions made by salespeople, sales managers, and top sales leaders.*

How Sales Analytics Add Value

Analytics and decision frameworks enable companies to enhance sales force decisions in four ways, as illustrated in Figure 1-4.

- **Support** ongoing needs to keep the sales machine operating.

- **Diagnose** concerns and discover new opportunities.

- **Design** SFE drivers that align sales effort with strategic goals.

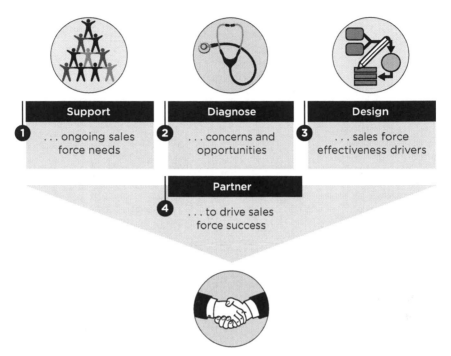

Figure 1-4. Four ways that sales analytics enhance sales force decisions

- **Partner** with sales leaders to set priorities and direction for the sales force and to enact strategic and tactical sales force change.

Partnership requires developing the full range of support, diagnosis, and design capabilities needed to meet critical sales force needs.

Supporting the Sales Organization

Supporting ongoing sales force needs keeps the lights on for the sales force. Here are some ways sales analytics can support the sales organization:

- **Sales process.** Support the tools that enable salespeople's interactions with customers (for example, pricing tools and proposal generators).
- **Sales reporting.** Distribute useful, timely, and accurate sales dashboards and reports to salespeople and managers.
- **Incentive plan.** Administer the sales incentive program and ensure accuracy and timeliness of performance data and incentive payments.

> ### Supporting Sales Compensation Plans
>
> A 1,200-person sales force is organized into four selling teams, each with its own sales compensation plan. The four plans share some common features (all plans are goal-based), but each plan also has unique features. For example, the key account team ties a small incentive component to achievement of qualitative objectives, and a specialty team has an added bonus for goal achievement on specific products. Supporting the sales compensation plan requires the participation of the company's technology group, a third-party software vendor, and two full-time company analysts. The technology group processes the sales and account assignment data. Using sales performance management software configured by a third-party vendor, the analysts execute the monthly processing, working to ensure that the process is efficient and error-free. The company spends about $1 million a year, or about 5 percent of sales compensation costs, supporting the sales compensation program.

Support responsibilities tend to recur regularly — for example, distributing sales dashboards and making sure quarterly incentives are accurate and are paid on time.

Supporting a sales force with analytics requires processes, data, and tools that enable accurate, efficient, and reliable delivery of what the sales force needs. It also requires detail- and process-oriented people and managers with an operational mind-set.

Diagnosing Sales Force Issues and Opportunities

The best sales organizations improve constantly. Sales analytics are pivotal to diagnosing issues and discovering opportunities to improve SFE drivers. Here are a few examples:

- **Customer valuation and targeting.** Assess the value of the sales effort by customer segment, and identify opportunities to reallocate effort for improved performance.

- **Territory design.** Evaluate the distribution of workload and opportunity across sales territories, and identify coverage gaps.

- **Goal setting.** Evaluate territory sales goals to determine if they are set at a level that challenges salespeople appropriately.

Diagnosis tells the sales organization how things are going and when a course correction is needed. Diagnosis often begins as an ad hoc request from the sales force:

- "Which high-potential accounts are not getting enough attention?"
- "Is our incentive plan paying for performance?"
- "Is the turnover of high-performing salespeople too high?"

When the sales force finds the response to these requests valuable, the requests become part of ongoing support:

- The list of high-potential accounts is produced every month to help salespeople focus their time more effectively.

- The pay-for-performance analysis is generated at the end of each quarter so leaders can make adjustments for the following quarter.

- The salesperson turnover analysis is conducted every year to ensure that hiring and performance management stay on track.

Diagnosing the Effectiveness of an Inside Sales Team

A financial services company had an inside sales team that sold credit and lending products to small businesses over the telephone. At first, the team drove sales growth by making outbound calls to high-quality leads. But as market growth slowed and lead quality declined, it became harder for salespeople to engage less-willing prospects. Over a three-year period, the productivity of the inside sales team had decreased by half.

Sales analysts looked at millions of records and listened to dozens of calls. The diagnosis broke down performance in a number of ways, revealing several insights for driving sales improvement.

- **Time of call.** Calls to prospects at certain times of day produced three times the level of sales that calls produced in less-effective time slots. Analysis suggested that profits could increase by 20 percent with no change in capacity simply by taking advantage of time zone differences and shifting more calls into time slots when customers were likely to buy.

- **Customer targeting and call frequency.** Average sales per call varied widely across industries; in 7 of 14 targeted industries, average profits per call were less than call cost. Analysis showed that profits could increase by 16 percent if the sales team expanded the number of calls to high-value, responsive industries and reduced or eliminated calls to low-value, nonresponsive industries.

- **Sales approach.** Average sales per call varied across salespeople; top salespeople were two to three times as effective as the average. By comparing the customer conversations of top and average salespeople, the company discovered that top salespeople used a more consultative sales approach: they engaged customers more often and asked questions that led to customer understanding and better product recommendations.

These insights prompted a redesign of the company's targeting and selling approach, eventually leading to increases in sales and profits.

Being good at diagnosis requires people with an insight mind-set, as opposed to the process mind-set needed to support a sales organization. Diagnosis also requires processes and tools that allow both proactive analysis and flexible, quick responses to sales force queries. Diagnosis often requires merging data from multiple sources. A monthly report showing sales by customer is an example of support. The report becomes a diagnosis when data on customer potential and call activity are integrated to reveal opportunities to improve coverage.

Designing Sales Force Effectiveness Drivers

Every SFE driver has to be *designed* in the first place, and then it has to be *redesigned* as the sales environment evolves and diagnosis reveals opportunities for improvement. Examples of SFE driver design include:

- **Sales force size and structure.** Determine the right number of salespeople and the right mix of generalist and specialist roles.
- **Hiring and training.** Create a new sales force hiring profile, and design sales force training programs that align with a new sales process.
- **Incentives and goal setting.** Design a fair and motivating goal-setting process and incentive plan.

Design requires processes for addressing new issues, as well as data and tools that enable flexible analysis and modeling. The people participating in design need creative problem-solving, project management, consulting, and change management skills. They must work collaboratively across departments. Often, sales forces outsource or use partners for design work because the need for such work is so infrequent that it's hard to sustain internal expertise.

Partnering with Sales Leadership

Achieving partnership means that the sales analytics function has earned the respect of top leaders and of other departments and has a seat at the executive table. Respect has to be earned through a proactive and comprehensive approach backed by a record of consistently delivering on sales force support, diagnosis, and design needs.

Designing a New Sales Force After a Pharmaceutical Merger

When two global pharmaceutical companies merged, the sales analytics team was a key participant on the sales integration task force. The company merged sales forces in 40 countries under tremendous time and cost pressure. Leaders sought to minimize customer and organizational uncertainty and avoid a drop in short-term performance.

Using the structured design process shown in Figure 1-5, a cross-functional merger team consisting of company participants and outside consultants completed the steps required for designing the new merged sales organization on schedule.

Figure 1-5. A process for merging two pharmaceutical sales forces

The implementation of the design process required:

- **Fact-based decision making.** The team collected and organized data on products, customers, geography, and the location of company personnel to help with each decision.

- **Speed.** Just three months after the merger deal closed and one month after the company began operating as a single legal entity, plans were in place for sales force integration around the globe, and plans were fully operational just a few months later.

- **Communication.** The merger team orchestrated more than 300 meetings with over 500 company managers, organized routine teleconference question-and-answer sessions, and published newsletters to keep the sales force informed.

In the end, the new sales force design worked for customers. The combined sales force achieved the much talked about but seldom realized merger synergy, without the performance dip observed with prior industry mergers. Company leaders attributed much of the success to careful project planning and execution by the merger team.

Proactive, Not Reactive, Approach

A partnering sales analytics function helps sales leaders set priorities for what to do, not only by answering the questions correctly, but also by proactively asking the right questions, developing a solution approach, and enlisting the support of other departments (for example, Marketing, HR, Finance, and IT) to ensure the work gets done well.

Figure 1-6 shows an example of how partnering can work for one SFE driver: sales force incentive compensation.

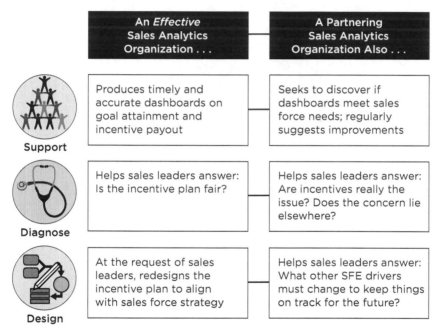

	An *Effective* Sales Analytics Organization . . .	A Partnering Sales Analytics Organization Also . . .
Support	Produces timely and accurate dashboards on goal attainment and incentive payout	Seeks to discover if dashboards meet sales force needs; regularly suggests improvements
Diagnose	Helps sales leaders answer: Is the incentive plan fair?	Helps sales leaders answer: Are incentives really the issue? Does the concern lie elsewhere?
Design	At the request of sales leaders, redesigns the incentive plan to align with sales force strategy	Helps sales leaders answer: What other SFE drivers must change to keep things on track for the future?

Figure 1-6. An analytics–sales force partnership for incentive compensation

Comprehensive Approach Linked to Sales Force Needs

For some drivers, such as incentive compensation, the opportunity to add value through analytics exists across the support-diagnose-design spectrum. For other SFE drivers, the opportunity to add value is more focused. For example, analytics enhance sales force size and structure decisions through diagnosis (How good is the current size or structure?) that is followed by a primary emphasis on design (What new size or structure can better meet

Ch. #	SFE Driver	How Sales Analytics Add Value*		
		Support	Diagnose	Design
2	Customer potential estimation	✓✓	✓	✓✓✓
3	Sales process	✓✓	✓	✓✓
4	Sales force size and structure		✓	✓✓✓
5	Territory design	✓✓✓	✓✓	✓✓
6	Hiring and training	✓	✓✓	✓✓
7	Incentive compensation	✓✓✓	✓✓✓	✓✓✓
8	Goal setting	✓✓	✓✓	✓✓✓
9	Performance management	✓✓	✓✓✓	✓

*The number of checkmarks reflects the typical relative value that sales analytics can add.

Figure 1-7. The typical emphasis of sales analytics value by SFE driver

customer needs?). Figure 1-7 summarizes the typical opportunity for value creation, although the opportunity varies with each selling environment. Chapter 10 includes assessment worksheets to help determine the best opportunities for each situation as well as the capability gaps that need to be filled to realize those opportunities.

For some SFE drivers, the opportunity for sales analytics to add value is well established. For example, many companies have used analytics for decades to improve decisions about SFE drivers such as territory design, incentives, and goal setting. Others SFE drivers are emerging areas of opportunity. For example, there are more opportunities to apply analytics in areas such as hiring and training. A partnering sales analytics function takes the lead in bringing analytics to both traditional and nontraditional sales management decision areas.

Figure 1-8 shows that the emphasis on support, diagnosis, and design also depends on whether sales force needs are episodic or ongoing. Episodic needs are event driven (for example, integrating two sales forces after a merger) and tend to have a large design component. Ongoing needs (for example, producing weekly sales dashboards) are more focused on support.

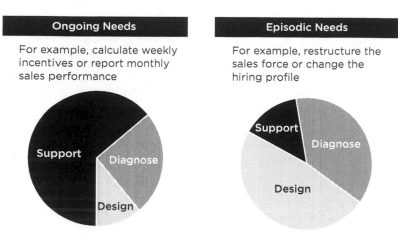

Figure 1-8. Focus on meeting ongoing and episodic sales force needs

Well-Developed and Proven Capabilities

To partner with the sales force, the sales analytics function needs people and competencies, processes, and data and tools for meeting the support, diagnosis, and design needs across the spectrum of SFE drivers. Only when these capabilities are functioning well can sales analytics begin to mature to the partnership level. Partnering also requires people with characteristics such as:

> *It takes time to earn trust and build the wisdom required to achieve a successful sales analytics partnership.*

- The ability to earn the trust of sales and marketing leaders
- The wisdom to identify vital priorities
- The courage to develop and proactively assert independent thought
- The aspiration and experience to lead and orchestrate change in the sales organization, not simply execute it

Partnership can't be developed overnight. The leaders of a partnering sales analytics function usually have a proven track record of several years of successfully supporting, diagnosing, and designing programs for the sales force.

The remaining chapters of this book show the possible benefits that sales analytics and decision frameworks can bring to an organization, and they provide advice for overcoming the challenges inherent in putting sales analytics capabilities to work.

How Analytics Improve Sales Force Decision Making

Section 1 explores a range of opportunities sales analytics have to improve sales force performance and build competitive advantage. Chapters share specific analytical techniques, decision frameworks, and examples that demonstrate the power of analytics to make improvements in eight key decision areas that drive sales force effectiveness.

■ **Chapter 2** Measuring Customer Potential
Learn how to develop estimates of sales potential for each customer and prospect, and deploy sales resources against the highest-potential opportunities.

■ **Chapter 3** Enhancing the Sales Process
Examine how sales processes, and the tracking of sales process metrics, can improve sales force activity and create better outcomes for customers, salespeople, and the company.

■ **Chapter 4** Sizing and Structuring the Sales Force
See how sales analytics and decision frameworks enable sales force size and structure decisions that improve customer coverage and company financial results, while supporting the company's sales strategy.

■ **Chapter 5** Designing Sales Territories
Learn how sales analytics can help a sales force create and manage territory alignments that allow effective and efficient customer coverage, while cultivating more satisfied salespeople and increasing revenues.

■ **Chapter 6** Shaping the People in the Sales Force
See how analytics can improve sales talent management by helping
companies hire and train more effectively, retain strong performers,
energize sales teams, and drive positive financial results.

■ **Chapter 7** Compensating the Sales Force and Paying
for Performance
Understand how analytics can help companies determine if an
incentive compensation plan is working or not, and can contribute
to designing and supporting plans that deliver desired sales force
behavior and performance.

■ **Chapter 8** Setting Motivating Sales Force Goals
Develop an analytically based sales force goal-setting process that
produces territory sales or profit goals that are challenging yet
achievable, leading to a more motivated sales team.

■ **Chapter 9** Managing Sales Force Performance
Learn how to put in place the right analytics for managing sales
force performance, while providing sales force members with the
information they need to drive continual improvement.

CHAPTER 2

Measuring Customer Potential

Sales force success starts with understanding customer needs and potential.

Andris A. Zoltners, Prabhakant Sinha, and Sally E. Lorimer

Andris A. Zoltners is a professor emeritus of marketing at Northwestern University's Kellogg School of Management and a co-founder of ZS Associates. He has personally consulted for more than 200 companies in over 20 countries. He has spoken at numerous conferences and has taught sales force topics to thousands of Executive, MBA, and PhD students. He is a co-author of numerous academic articles and a series of books on sales force management. He received his PhD from Carnegie-Mellon University.

Prabhakant Sinha is a co-founder of ZS Associates and a former Kellogg faculty member, who continues to teach sales executives at the Indian School of Business and the Gordon Institute of Business Science in South Africa. He has helped over 200 firms improve sales force strategy and effectiveness. He is a co-author of many academic articles and a series of books on sales force management. He received his PhD from the University of Massachusetts and graduated from the Indian Institute of Technology, Kharagpur.

Sally E. Lorimer is a business writer. She is a co-author of numerous academic articles and books on sales force management. As a former principal at ZS Associates, she has helped clients in a range of industries implement strategies for improving sales effectiveness and performance. She has an MBA from Northwestern University's Kellogg School of Management and is also a graduate of the University of Michigan.

The authors thank former ZS principal Ladd Ruddell for his contributions to this chapter.

Analytics for Customer Potential Estimation and Targeting

Successful selling starts with understanding what is valuable to customers (customer needs) and which customers are valuable to the company (customer potential). Potential—the amount that a current customer or prospect *could buy* from the company—is linked to a company's ability to understand and serve the customer's needs. If the company understands customer needs and potential, it can target customers whose needs the company can meet and can tailor value propositions and sales processes around those needs. The company can devote field sales effort to those customers with enough potential to warrant the effort. It can use cost-effective selling channels, such as inside sales or the Internet, to reach customers that don't have enough potential to justify field sales effort. And it can choose to eliminate coverage of customers with too little potential to justify any sales investment.

The familiar 80/20 rule states that 20 percent of customers produce 80 percent of sales. Yet all too often, sales forces ignore this principle. They spend too much time with easy and familiar accounts or with demanding customers with urgent needs. They call on too many unlikely prospects. Their activities prove true a less-well-known corollary to the 80/20 rule of sales: the overinvestment that many sales forces make in the bottom 30 percent of customers can cut profits by 50 percent over time.

> Too often sales forces are not discriminating enough when choosing which customers to focus on.

Figure 2-1 demonstrates the value of targeting accounts based on potential. If salespeople target accounts in their territory randomly, they will roughly cover a percentage of their territory potential equal to the percentage of accounts that they cover. For example, if they visit 20 percent of their accounts, those accounts will represent 20 percent of territory potential. But smart salespeople can do much better. In a "perfect targeting" scenario, salespeople target the accounts in their territory that have the most potential, and as a result, they cover a larger percentage of their potential. In the Figure 2-1 example, by selecting the right 20 percent of accounts to target, salespeople cover 80 percent of their territory potential. Alternatively, they could cover 20 percent of their territory potential by targeting a very small number of accounts—those that have the largest potential.

Measuring customer potential is not easy. A sales analytics function is front and center in creating the data and insight for understanding potential

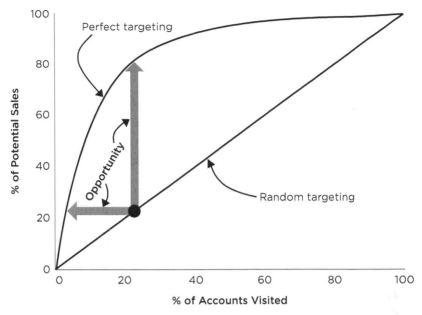

Figure 2-1. A conceptual view of the value of smart account targeting

at the account level. Customer potential estimation provides a foundation for building all of the sales force effectiveness drivers discussed in this book and listed in Figure 2-2.

This chapter focuses on how sales analytics can:

- **Design** and execute an approach for estimating account potential that enables effective customer targeting and enhances other sales force decisions.

- **Support** the sales force in targeting the right customers and keeping estimates of account potential up-to-date.

- **Diagnose** customer targeting effectiveness and the quality of account potential estimates.

Designing and Executing an Approach for Estimating Account Potential

Most companies know how much each customer *did buy*. But estimating how much each customer or prospect *could buy* can be challenging.

	Understanding customer needs and potential allows sales forces to . . .
Customer Targeting (Ch. 2)	Focus sales effort on those customers that are most likely to buy and have enough potential to justify investment.
Sales Process (Ch. 3)	Match the nature and quantity of sales activities to customer needs and potential.
Sales Force Size and Structure (Ch. 4)	Use the right sales channels, number of salespeople, and sales roles for meeting customer needs, while ensuring a good return on the investment.
Territory Design (Ch. 5)	Design territories that allow good customer coverage and have enough potential to allow all salespeople to succeed.
Hiring and Training (Ch. 6)	Match the hiring profile to customer needs and coach and train salespeople on the best ways to spend their time.
Incentive Compensation, Goals, and Performance Management (Ch. 7, 8, and 9)	Match sales goals to opportunity, evaluate salespeople fairly, and reward salespeople for true performance, rather than for a high-potential territory.
Sales Data and Tools (Ch. 9)	Help salespeople understand customer needs and potential and spend time more productively.

Figure 2-2. The impact of understanding customer needs and potential for SFE driver decisions

Companies that invest in sales analytics for estimating account potential consistently find the investment to be worthwhile.

An approach for effectively estimating account potential involves the following steps:

1. Build an integrated database.

2. Develop initial estimates of account potential.

3. Use sales force input to improve estimates and estimation methodology.

Using Estimates of Customer Market Potential to Focus Sales Effort and Meet Goals

GE Fleet Services, a business within GE that leases over-the-road trailers to trucking, retail, and manufacturing companies, used estimates of customer market potential to help the sales force focus effort on the most attractive opportunities and ultimately meet ambitious revenue growth goals. Customer profile characteristics such as fleet size and composition, company size, and industry were used to predict customer potential. The information allowed the business to redeploy several sales territories into more lucrative markets, to increase qualified leads by 33 percent in one year, and to increase sales productivity by 7 percent. The business gave back a budgeted $2 million for additional headcount because the productivity improvements allowed the sales organization to meet growth goals without adding salespeople.

Step 1: Build an Integrated Database

Developing a database for estimating account potential for each customer and prospect requires effort and creativity. Typically, it's necessary to merge data from multiple sources into a single integrated database that includes the types of information shown in Figure 2-3.

An integrated customer database might include the following data:

- **Customer master files:** Account profile data, such as the account name, location, and type of business
- **Customer sales data:** Historical sales by product
- **Financial data:** Product margins and sales forecasts

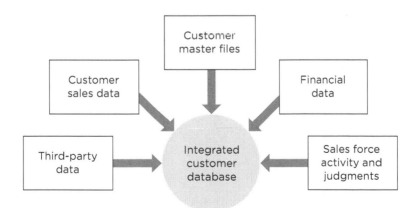

Figure 2-3. Examples of data required in an account potential database

- **Sales force activity and judgments:** Information captured in a customer relationship management (CRM) system about call history or observed account needs and decision-making processes

- **Third-party data:** Data that measure account potential directly (purchases of competitive products) or that provide a surrogate for account potential (business account profile and demographic data)

Sources of third-party data include the following:

- **Industry-specific data sources.** In some industries, third-party data companies sell information on the sales of all competitive products by account, thus providing a direct measure of account potential. For instance, IMS Health (headquartered in Danbury, Connecticut) provides this type of information to the U.S. pharmaceutical industry. Many industries, such as airlines, hotels, and hospitals, have industry-specific sources that provide business account profiles and demographics that are surrogates for account-level potential.

- **Cross-industry data sources.** Companies such as Dun & Bradstreet (Short Hills, New Jersey), Austin-Tetra (Irving, Texas), Infogroup (Papillion, Nebraska), Jigsaw (San Mateo, California), OneSource (Concord, Massachusetts), AccuData (Fort Myers, Florida), and Experian (Dublin, Ireland) can provide business account profiles that are relevant for many industries, including variables such as industry, number of employees, and revenues. Such sources can also provide contact information (such as email addresses) for key decision makers.

- **U.S. Census.** The Census Bureau provides a wealth of demographic data by geography.

Figure 2-4 shows some variables that sales forces in several industries have used to estimate account potential.

There are many challenges in building a database for estimating account potential. The first challenge is that market data sources track history, not the future. Data reflecting a customer's "wallet size," needs, or buying processes are rarely available. Second, many data sources use estimates or projections, with varying levels of accuracy. Finally, cleaning and matching data from multiple sources is always difficult. Multiple data sets often use different unique identifiers for accounts, making it necessary to develop algorithms for matching accounts on identifiers that may not match exactly, such as company name and address.

> *A good sales analytics team is well positioned to overcome the challenge of measuring account potential.*

Industry	Measures of Market Potential
Building materials	Number of households earning over $100K, housing starts, time of the year
Computer software and peripherals	Number of different types of computers installed, overall company revenue, and number of company locations
Education	School type (public or private), student population (full-time or part-time), student type (commuter versus resident), enrolled students (full-time equivalent)
Greeting cards	Population and average household income within a three-mile radius of each retail store
Health and beauty aids sold in retail stores	Type of outlet (mass merchandiser, drugstore, grocery store, etc.), all commodity sales volume, and square footage in each store Buying Power Index: census tract data on income, retail sales, and population
Insurance	Number of employees
Motorcycle financing	Customer demographics, competitors, presence of local credit unions, the onset of spring weather (which triggers an increase in motorcycle sales)
Office equipment	Number of white-collar workers by industry
Pharmaceuticals	Historical prescriptions written for a particular drug category in countries where pharmacy records are kept electronically Physician office size, physician specialty, size of patient waiting area, and patient demographics in countries where electronic pharmacy records are not available
Surgical instruments and supplies	Number of surgical procedures

Figure 2-4. Measures of account potential in several industries

Step 2: Develop Initial Estimates of Account Potential

A company with a limited number of customers and prospects, such as a first-tier supplier to automobile manufacturers, can estimate potential for each account individually. But most companies have many possible

---

Conducting Primary Market Research to Estimate Account Potential

If third-party data do not provide the level of accuracy and detail required for estimating account potential, companies can conduct their own primary market research to develop estimates. Here are two examples:

- A medical imaging company asked its salespeople to collect data on the type, manufacturer, and acquisition date of installed equipment at every hospital and imaging center in their territory. The information helped salespeople increase the impact of their calls by visiting prospects at a time when their imaging equipment was ready for replacement.

- A seller of contact lenses surveyed ophthalmologists to determine the size of their practices and their need for the company's products. The data allowed the sales force to pre-book appointments and to focus sales effort on high-potential customers and prospects. In the quarter after the sales force saw the customer/prospect potential data, sales that had been declining for two straight quarters grew by 7 percent, well above the market growth rate.

---

customers, so it's more practical to organize customers and prospects into market segments and to estimate potential by segment.

Customer segmentation is a complex topic. Examples of criteria for defining market segments can fall into the three categories shown in Figure 2-5.

Entire books have been written on how to segment markets, primarily for marketing purposes. For more information about customer segmentation approaches for sales strategy development, see Andris A. Zoltners, Prabhakant Sinha, and Sally E. Lorimer, *Sales Force Design for Strategic Advantage* (New York: Palgrave Macmillan, 2004).

With market segments defined, an effective approach to estimating account potential involves studying the historical sales to accounts in each segment and using this information to develop rules for estimating the level of sales that should be possible for all accounts in the segment. Analysis for

Demographic Criteria	Behavioral Criteria	Needs-Based Criteria
• Industry • Geography • Number of employees	• Historical sales or sales growth • Sensitivity to sales effort • Loyalty • Response to innovation	• Product criticality to buyer • Price, technology, or service? • Product, solution, or partnership? • Degree of centralization • Buying influences • Awareness

Figure 2-5. Three categories of criteria for segmenting accounts

developing these rules can range from simple heuristics to advanced statistical techniques.

Consider a company that sold educational products to high schools. The company segmented schools according to three criteria (the number of students, the type of classes offered, and student demographics) and used a heuristic approach to estimate the potential of the schools in each segment. Figure 2-6 shows the frequency distribution of sales to schools in one segment. The distribution includes the 100 high schools in this segment that had purchased from the company in the last year.

The height of each bar shows how many of these schools produced the sales levels identified on the horizontal axis. The company used these data and the following steps to estimate sales potential for the next year by account (for both current customers and prospects):

- The sales leaders started with the maximum sales that any account in the segment had achieved. In the example, the maximum sales at an account were $94,000.

- For each of the 100 schools that had purchased from the company last year (that is, all schools shown in Figure 2-6), leaders felt that next year the sales force had the opportunity to match last year's sales plus sell an additional 50 percent of the gap to the maximum. Thus, if an account

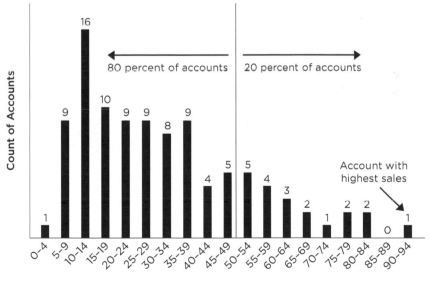

Figure 2-6. The frequency distribution of sales to high schools in one market segment for an educational products company

had sales of $30,000 last year, its potential for next year was estimated as $30,000 + .5 * ($94,000 − $30,000) = $62,000.

- For schools in the market segment that had not purchased from the company in the last year (that is, prospects), leaders hoped that next year the sales force would sell at least 15 percent of the maximum. Thus, the potential of each prospect was identified as .15 * $94,000 = $14,100.

The appropriate percentage of the gap to the maximum to use for estimating potential depends on the life-cycle stage of the product or customer. In the growth stage, a higher percentage is appropriate. In the mature stage, a lower percentage is appropriate. Different heuristic approaches may be appropriate for different customers and prospects or for low-penetration and high-penetration accounts. Heuristic approaches are approximate, yet

Using Regression to Develop Measures of Hospital Potential

To achieve ambitious revenue growth goals, the sales force at a medical instruments company needed to acquire many new hospital customers. The company did business with approximately half of the hospitals in the United States — leaving more than 3,000 hospitals as prospects. With a limited budget for adding salespeople, the company wanted to focus attention on the subset of prospects for which sales effort was most likely to pay off. The sales analytics team developed a measure of potential for every hospital using three steps.

1. **Merge the company's sales by hospital with a third-party hospital demographic database.** For each hospital, the data included 32 profile characteristics that were believed to predict potential. These included the number of admitted patients, beds, operating rooms, and surgical procedures. The sales analytics team consulted with the sales force to fill in some data for hospitals that were missing from the database.

2. **Use a regression model to analyze the merged data for hospitals that were current customers.** The regression analysis revealed three profile characteristics that best predicted sales, as well as an appropriate weighting of those characteristics. The sales analytics team vetted and refined the mathematically derived model through consultation with the sales force.

3. **Develop an estimate of potential for each hospital.** Using the profile characteristics and weights determined in step 2, the sales analytics team developed an estimate of potential for every hospital, including both current customers and prospects.

Having estimates of the sales potential of every hospital helped the sales force prioritize and target prospective new hospital accounts. It also helped identify hospitals that were current customers that offered even more opportunity for new business, and others that were getting too much sales force attention.

they can be extremely valuable to sales organizations that wish to develop meaningful estimates of account sales potential.

Statistical approaches, such as regression analysis, have also been used successfully by some companies for developing estimates of potential for their accounts.

Step 3: Use Sales Force Input to Improve Estimates and Estimation Methodology

Members of the sales team have detailed and practical knowledge of what determines opportunity with specific customers. By having the sales force audit the results of a data-driven model for estimating potential, it's possible to improve the database and estimation methodology. Sales force input about account potential not only helps ensure that the set of measures chosen for estimating potential is comprehensive; it also increases the likelihood that the measures selected will resonate with and be embraced by the sales force.

Monitoring Sales Force Feedback to Improve Account Potential Estimates

Sales analytics can use sales force and customer insight to improve measures of account potential. Here are some examples:

- Tracking wins and losses on major deals, following up with customers and salespeople to gain insight about why deals are won or lost, and using the learning to improve customer potential measurement and targeting.

- Following up with salespeople on the quality of leads, looking for common characteristics of good versus poor leads, and using the learning to improve customer potential measurement and targeting.

Supporting the Sales Force in Targeting the Right Customers and Keeping Estimates of Account Potential Up-to-Date

Sales analytics can provide salespeople with insight about customer potential. Companies can give salespeople tools for accessing and understanding the data useful for estimating potential. These data and tools help salespeople become smarter about how they allocate sales time.

Account potential rarely remains static. Account needs and situations are always changing. Some current accounts grow or decline in potential, others go out of business or relocate, and new opportunities emerge. If account potential data are not continuously maintained, they will quickly become outdated. The sales analytics function is uniquely positioned to oversee an

---

Improving Sales Manager Coaching with a Sales Coverage Tool

At xpedx (a distribution business within International Paper), the effectiveness of sales manager coaching improved when the company began providing first-line sales managers with new insight into salesperson performance through a sales coverage tool. The tool allowed managers to examine the details of each salesperson's territory to look at a breakdown of the business by account, product, and industry, presented in a concise and visually friendly format. The tool also provided data measuring account potential, calculated based on factors such as industry, account size, and past sales. With a benchmark for understanding potential, managers could have a more balanced discussion with their people about the best tactical territory plans and goals. They could point salespeople toward the best prospects and coach them on how to focus their time and energy on the best opportunities. The sales coverage tool and account potential data enabled managers to communicate better with their salespeople and take more meaningful action to improve performance.

Using Sales Potential Data to Enhance Sales Productivity at an Apparel Company

A family-owned work apparel company wanted a more analytically rigorous approach to sales management and sales effort allocation to help it compete against aggressive new competitors. Using Dun & Bradstreet data as a backbone, the sales analytics team built a customer database that included measures of retail outlet sales potential. The data helped the sales management team implement a more analytically based and fair approach to setting organizational and territory-level goals, and the data also helped the team increase productivity through better sales force sizing and geographic deployment. The data also provided a starting point for supporting salespeople in lead generation. The sales analytics team created a screen of six questions for qualifying leads and called over 20,000 stores in the database, focusing on key urban areas, to identify the best leads for salespeople. The effort generated a list of 2,000 high-potential retail outlet prospects to share with salespeople and sales managers. These leads helped the sales force achieve the key sales objective of increasing retail store acquisition in urban areas.

---

operational process for keeping account potential data up-to-date and for ensuring that the sales force is armed with the best possible information about opportunities at all times.

Diagnosing Customer Targeting Effectiveness and the Quality of Account Potential Estimates

Sales analytics can help address two key questions for diagnosing the quality of account potential data and targeting:

- How good are the measures of account potential, and how can they be improved?
- How effectively is the sales force targeting against potential?

How Good Are the Measures of Account Potential?

Measures of customer potential should be reevaluated periodically, and especially when any of the following occur:

- Changes in customer demographics, needs, or buying processes
- Changing economic conditions
- Advances in technology (such as Internet-enabled technologies and mobile devices) that can improve the timeliness of data provided to salespeople
- Changes in the competitive environment
- Shifts in the product portfolio
- Evolving company marketing goals and strategies
- A new sales process or sales force structure
- New or improved customer data sources
- Sales force feedback suggesting inconsistencies in the quality and usefulness of customer potential data
- Data analysis showing a weak correlation between account potential and account sales across the customer base

A reevaluation in response to events such as these will involve repeating some or all of the steps in the approach for estimating account potential

---

How Much Precision Is Needed in Measures of Account Potential?

The level of precision in account potential estimates has implications for how the data can be used to support sales force decisions. Although it is impossible to estimate account potential with 100 percent accuracy, data must have fairly high account-level precision to be useful for determining which accounts to target and what to offer each account. Data that are less precise at the account level can be useful for decisions that require aggregating data across multiple accounts, thus evening out the level of imprecision in the metric. For example, estimates of potential require only territory-level accuracy to be useful for territory design and goal setting. And market segment-level accuracy is enough for using the data for sales strategy development (for example, what markets and segments to target), as well as for decisions about channel design and sales force sizing.

described earlier in this chapter. Periodic reevaluation helps ensure that measures of account potential stay current and aligned with market needs.

How Effectively Is the Sales Force Targeting Against Potential?

Salespeople who have many customers too often spend more time than they should with low-opportunity accounts. With measures of account potential in place, sales analytics can regularly diagnose how effectively the sales force allocates effort against potential.

Analyzing Sales Effort Allocation at a Pharmaceutical Company

Sales analytics showed sales leaders that salespeople were not directing enough effort toward the top 30 percent of physicians (segments A and B) who wrote 90 percent of the prescriptions for the classes of drugs the company sold. The graph in Figure 2-7 compares ideal calls (derived by analyzing data on account potential) with actual calls by segment, revealing that salespeople were wasting a good deal of time with unprofitable physician segments.

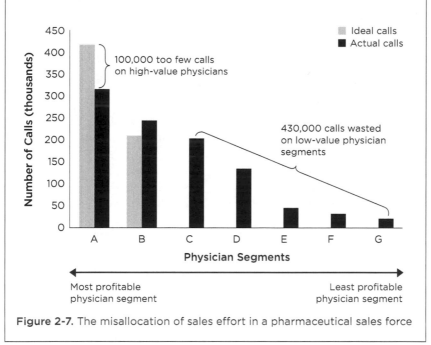

Figure 2-7. The misallocation of sales effort in a pharmaceutical sales force

Conclusion

The best sales forces use analytics to develop and continuously improve their understanding of customer potential. This understanding allows them to target customers who have needs the company can meet and who have sufficient potential to justify the investment of sales effort. Customer potential estimation enables the optimal deployment of sales resources against the best opportunities, while also providing a foundation for making better decisions about many sales force effectiveness drivers, including territory design, goal setting, and performance management.

CHAPTER 3

Enhancing the Sales Process

Analytics increase the effectiveness of the interactions that occur between a company and its customers.

Scott Sims

Scott Sims is the office managing principal of ZS Associates' Chicago office and the leader of the firm's Energy and Industrial practices, where he focuses on sales transformation, go-to-market, and incentive compensation issues. Scott has more than 29 years of sales and consulting experience and has worked with over 200 companies in the high tech, telecommunications, and industrial and professional services markets. Scott holds an MBA and a BSBA in marketing from the University of Denver.

The author thanks former ZS associate Karianne Gomez for her contributions to this chapter.

The Sales Process: Where the Rubber Meets the Road

A sales process defines how a company finds and understands, acquires, and serves and grows its customers. For each of these three selling stages, the sales process specifies:

- The *activities* required and the *milestones* that demonstrate progress
- The *participants* from the company, its selling partners, and the customer
- The *enablers* needed, including data, tools, and resources

A sales process is, clearly, where the rubber meets the road.

Figure 3-1 provides an overview of the sales process used by a manufacturer of industrial automation products. The sales process defines critical activities and advancement milestones, the participants involved in each activity, and the tools and resources needed to enable the activities.

Analytics are a critical element of an effective sales process. Analytics help with designing, diagnosing, and supporting the interactions that should occur between a company and its customers in order to create customer value and drive company results.

Activities	Find and Understand			Acquire		Serve and Grow
	Identify and develop opportunity	Create custom solution	Develop proposal	Negotiate and close	Implement solution	Reinforce ongoing value
Milestones	Customer assessment complete	Value proposition presented to customer	Proposal and terms submitted to customer	Contract signed by customer	Customer solution in place	Ongoing support processes in place
Participants	• Market analyst • Industry specialist • Account executive	• Account executive • Industry specialist • Finance	• Account executive • Industry specialist • Finance • Sales manager	• Account executive • Others, as needed	• Account executive • Implementation team	• Account executive • Account service specialist • Others, as needed
Enablers	• Customer profile data • Needs-assessment tool	• Offer design tool	• Proposal generator • Pricing tool	• Proposal generator • Pricing tool	• Implementation support tools	• Financial review data and tool

Figure 3-1. The sales process for a manufacturer of industrial automation products

How a Sales Process Creates Value

Sales processes, and the tracking of sales process metrics, improve sales force activity and create better outcomes for customers, salespeople, and the company. The impact of a defined and tracked sales process is summarized in Figure 3-2.

Almost all sales force decisions are affected at some level by the sales process.

A sales process helps salespeople take a more disciplined approach to selling, create more value for their customers, and produce better and more consistent results. A sales process also provides focus for aligning and improving other sales force effectiveness (SFE) drivers. For example, a sales process can allow:

- A more effective and efficient sales force structure due to greater clarity about roles and sales activities that require specialized skills and knowledge

- Better training and coaching by the sales manager, enabled by a common language and understanding of what it takes to succeed

- A better understanding of the success profile for sales process participants and therefore a better sales force recruiting process

- More accurate sales forecasting through a better view of the sales pipeline

- A more effective sales compensation design by aligning incentives with the sales process

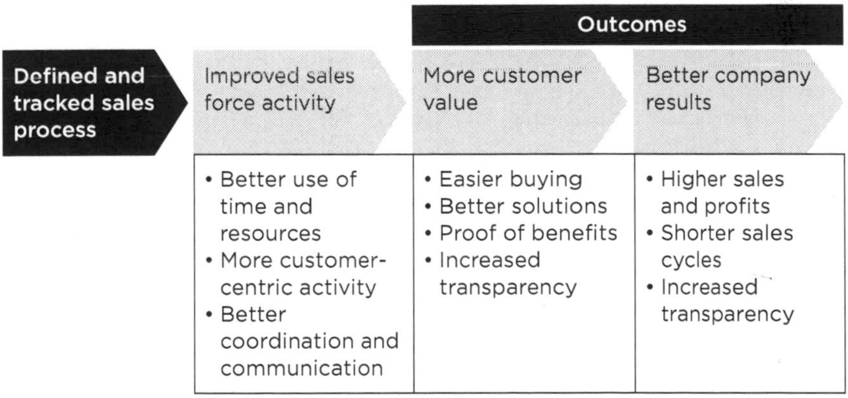

Defined and tracked sales process	Improved sales force activity	More customer value	Better company results
	Outcomes		
	• Better use of time and resources • More customer-centric activity • Better coordination and communication	• Easier buying • Better solutions • Proof of benefits • Increased transparency	• Higher sales and profits • Shorter sales cycles • Increased transparency

Figure 3-2. The impact of a defined and tracked sales process

Transforming the Sales Process at Oakwood

In 2006, there was significant variation in performance across the sales team at Oakwood, a leading provider of temporary furnished and serviced apartments headquartered in Los Angeles, California. A few top-performing salespeople had adapted to the increased sophistication of their customers, but most seasoned salespeople were having trouble changing the way they sold. Oakwood's past sales success had been based on relationships:

- With individual buyers
- At branch locations of corporate customers
- In an environment with little competition

The company's sales force was dealing with a changing landscape that included:

- A move to centralized, corporate-level decision making with buying committees
- Buyers seeking financial value
- Many competitors, some very much in tune with the new realities of the market

To help Oakwood improve sales performance, Ken Revenaugh, the company's Vice President of Sales Operations, led an initiative to:

- Document the best practices of top-performing salespeople who had adapted well to the new centralized corporate buying model.
- Design and implement a formal sales process with milestones and metrics.
- Support the sales process with tools and metrics.
- Diagnose the sales process on an ongoing basis to bring key opportunities and challenges to the leadership team's attention before it was too late.

The sales process, or "playbook," had eight crucial steps: identify, qualify, explore, solve, propose, negotiate, win, and strengthen. Each step was enabled by tools, processes, training, and other support programs. The holistic transformation was achieved through a tight partnership between Oakwood and its sales effectiveness and training partners.

But the switch was not without its trauma. About half the sales force did not survive, but all the top performers did. The results were nothing short of dramatic. The win rate for deals tripled in a year, and the length of the sales cycle dropped by over 50 percent. Salesperson turnover shrank to under 5 percent.

Oakwood's success did not go unnoticed. The initiative was recognized with two Stevie Awards (described by the *New York Post* as "the business world's own Oscar awards"). Oakwood was awarded Sales Process of the Year in 2010, and Revenaugh was honored as Sales Operations Leader of the Year in 2011. He also received the first ever SAVO Pioneer Award for demonstrating vision, leadership, and stewardship as a sales enablement trailblazer.

Despite the many benefits of a sales process, sales force members often say they don't need one.

- A sales manager said, "Sales is an art; it can't be a process. We need to just go out there and sell."
- A sales leader said, "Our best people already do this."
- A salesperson said, "My manager uses the sales process to micromanage me. He starts breathing down my neck at the end of the quarter to rush big deals through."

The last statement reflects a legitimate concern and illustrates the potential dark side of formalized sales processes. Too often, sales managers try to use sales process tracking to control the sales team. If managers harass salespeople to close sales quickly before an incentive period ends, and doing so is not in customers' best interests, salespeople will likely stop providing accurate data about how far along they are in the sales process with specific customers so they can avoid undesirable pressure from management.

The best sales processes are rigorous and complete and are used as a guide for salespeople to create value for customers, not as an instrument of control for management.

This chapter shares several examples of sales processes and illustrates ways that sales analytics can contribute to the design, diagnosis, and support of a sales process.

> *A sales process will fail if it's used by managers to control salespeople without adding enough value to salespeople and customers.*

Subsequent chapters in Section 1 show how to enable the sales process by aligning other SFE drivers around it.

Designing (or Redesigning) a Sales Process

Sales analytics can help the sales organization design and implement a formal sales process for the first time. Analytics can also help with redesigning an existing sales process as customer needs and the company's products and strategies evolve. Although the sales process can be tweaked regularly, major sales process design or redesign is typically episodic and infrequent. It is often prompted by a significant event, such as a shift in the customer buying process or a major new product launch. It can also come about after diagnosis reveals that the current sales process (or lack of a process) no longer serves customer and company needs.

Requirements for Sales Process Design

Designing a sales process requires defining the activities and milestones, participants, and enablers (reports, tools, and resources) that make up the process.

Sales Process Activities and Milestones

Figure 3-3 shows sample activities for each of the three main stages of the sales process: (1) finding and understanding, (2) acquiring, and (3) serving and growing customers.

The nature of sales process activity varies across selling situations. Some situations—for example, capital equipment sales—are primarily "deal" focused. The sales process in these situations consists of discrete activities through which a sale is won or lost, and a seller can get eliminated at any stage. In such cases, the sales process includes milestones, or objectives for advancing from one stage to the next. Other situations—for example, sales of consumable goods—involve more continuous activity. Sales process activity focuses on serving ongoing customer needs, maintaining relationships with customers, and looking for new opportunities to escalate mutual value.

Find and Understand	Acquire	Serve and Grow
• Create awareness • Generate and qualify leads • Map buying process • Identify purchase influencers • Listen and probe to understand needs	• Provide information • Craft detailed solution • Prepare bid • Write proposal • Persuade and negotiate • Finalize terms and close • Deliver and implement	• Train and support • Provide customer service • Place reorders • Nurture relationship • Reinforce value • Look for new opportunities

Figure 3-3. Examples of activities for the three main stages of the sales process

Sales Process Participants

The sales process goes beyond the sales force. It defines the playbook by which all company participants (and outside selling partners) design, communicate, prove, deliver, and reinforce value to customers. Examples of participants involved in each stage of the sales process are listed in Figure 3-4.

Find and Understand	Acquire	Serve and Grow
• Marketing • Lead generation team • Salesperson • Product or technical specialist	• Salesperson • Product or technical specialist • Contracting • Manufacturing • Finance • Engineering	• Salesperson • Installation and training team • Customer service

Figure 3-4. Examples of participants in each stage of the sales process

The best sales processes explicitly define the roles, responsibilities, accountabilities, coordination requirements, and authorities of all sales process participants.

Sales Process Enablers

Figure 3-5 lists examples of enablers, including data, tools, and other resources, for supporting each stage of the sales process.

Find and Understand	Acquire	Serve and Grow
Find • Target lists • Estimates of account potential *Understand* • Account demographics and purchase history • Tools for probing customer needs, mapping the buying process, and identifying decision influencers	• Data and tools that demonstrate value to customers • Tools that generate collateral, proposals, or contracts • Pricing support	• Data and tools that demonstrate ongoing value to customer

Figure 3-5. Examples of enablers for each stage of the sales process

How Sales Analytics Contribute to Sales Process Design

Sales leaders usually take the lead when designing or redesigning the sales process. The sales analytics function can contribute to designing sales process activities, milestones, and participants, but its most important role is in designing the enabling data and tools. Sales analytics add value to sales process design by:

- Sharing learning from top-performing salespeople
- Mapping the customer buying process to enhance understanding of customer needs

An analytics function can also help facilitate change management to build the commitment of the sales team and customers to a new sales process.

Sharing Learning from Top-Performing Salespeople

One of the best ways to enhance sales process design is by learning from the company's top-performing salespeople. Using techniques like performance frontier analysis (described in Chapter 6), sales analytics can identify the salespeople with the best sales performance after accounting for differences in territory potential. By interviewing and observing these top performers, as well as average performers, it's possible to compare the two groups

---

Using Successful Salespeople's "Critical Moves" to Improve the Sales Process

A pharmaceutical industry study used observation and analytics to determine the "critical moves" of top-performing salespeople — that is, the specific actions that top performers used (and that average performers did not use) to drive success with customers. These critical moves were used as input for improving every stage of the sales process, including the following:

- **Find and understand customers.** The best salespeople excelled at navigating each customer's network by maintaining a customer organization chart and a decision influence diagram. These activities were added to the sales process.

- **Acquire customers.** The best salespeople engaged in thorough call preparation by reviewing notes from prior visits and by planning goals, scripts, and materials for current visits. These activities were added to the sales process.

- **Serve and grow customers.** The best salespeople could articulate where they wanted to take each customer over the next 12 months. Developing a specific long-term plan for each major customer became part of the sales process.

Adding these critical moves to the sales process helped average salespeople improve their execution and even enhanced the success of the best performers. This led to improvements in both customer ratings and sales performance.

and discover what the top performers do differently to drive success with customers.

Insights from top performers can improve the sales process itself as well as the tools and data that support the process. Top performers often develop their own tools and processes that enable them to better assess and address customer needs. If the sales force has a collaborative culture in which salespeople are willing to share ideas, a sales analytics function can replicate these tools and

> *Enhance sales process design by learning from top-performing salespeople.*

processes on a broader scale, making them part of a recommended sales process so that all salespeople and customers benefit.

Mapping the Customer Buying Process

Sales analytics can help sales leaders enhance their understanding of the customer buying process to enable better sales process design.

When one industrial sales force redesigned its sales process to increase customer value and drive performance, sales analysts interviewed customers and mapped the buying process for each customer segment. They then worked with the sales organization to develop a sales process mirroring the customer buying process, as shown in Figure 3-6. They equipped salespeople with tools to support each buying and sales process stage. The participation of both customers and the sales force in the design ensured commitment to the process and regular use of the tools by salespeople. At the same time, customers felt that their time was valued.

Facilitating Change Management to Implement a New Sales Process

Getting the sales organization to embrace a new sales process is perhaps the greatest challenge associated with sales process redesign. Salespeople, especially those who have been selling for many years, may have deeply entrenched work styles and views on how to sell. Many sales process design initiatives have been derailed by a prevailing sentiment among salespeople that "we already do that." Three ways to break down the barriers to change when implementing a new sales process are:

- Involving an early experience team in designing and advocating for the sales process
- Engaging first-line sales managers in coaching to the sales process
- Aligning other SFE drivers around the sales process

Customer Buying Process and Questions

Problem Recognition and Information Search		Evaluation of Alternatives and Purchase Decision		Postpurchase Evaluation	
What problem are we solving?	What are possible solutions?	What does each solution offer?	Which solution is best?	Did we make the right decision?	Should we change?

Sales Process

Find and Understand		Acquire		Serve and Grow	
Generate and qualify leads	Develop opportunity	Tailor and communi- cate offering	Negotiate and close	Support ongoing needs	Reinforce value

Supporting Tools Help with . . .

• Account profiling and planning • Customer needs assessment	• Proposal and contract generation • Demonstration of value to customer	• Demonstration of ongoing value to customer

Figure 3-6. A sales process matched to customer buying needs

Involving an Early Experience Team. A small and influential early experience team can partner with leaders to co-design, validate, and refine a new sales process. Typical teams include a few well-respected salespeople and managers, along with representatives from non-sales functions such as Marketing and Human Resources. These individuals not only help shape the design of the sales process and its enabling tools; they also serve as advocates of the new approach to the rest of the sales force and can share with their peers proof points of its success with customers.

> *If change is driven by leadership mandate alone, sales process redesign is likely to fail.*

Engaging First-Line Sales Managers. First-line sales manager (FLM) coaching and support are in many ways the "secret sauce" in enabling salespeople to develop the skills and enthusiasm for making a new sales process work. FLMs play a pivotal role in implementing sales process change.

Manager training programs, best practice sharing sessions, and coaching by sales leaders can help FLMs build the expertise and motivation they need to coach their people effectively. These programs can also help build awareness among FLMs about the downside of using the sales process as an instrument of control for the sales team. A sales process that is used to control rather than enable salespeople is likely to be rejected by the sales team.

Aligning the SFE Drivers. The lasting success of a new sales process requires the alignment of other SFE drivers around the new approach. This starts with a new competency model (see Chapter 9) and role expectations that define and reinforce the desired behaviors of sales team members. Then hiring processes, training programs, coaching, performance management, and rewards can be aligned accordingly to reinforce the competency model and role expectations. In addition to contributing to the design of a new sales process, the sales analytics function adds value by working with sales leaders to ensure that all SFE drivers are aligned to support that new sales process.

Diagnosing and Improving Sales Processes

The sales process provides a framework for diagnosis to help with:

- Assisting salespeople with identifying problems and capitalizing on opportunities before competitors do

- Revealing pain points where salespeople need coaching, support, or assistance

- Assessing the value that customers and salespeople get from the sales process enablers that the company provides

Where Are the Problems and Opportunities in the Sales Pipeline?

With a sales process in place, sales analytics can provide tools for enabling the sales force to track the sales pipeline and assess key metrics, such as wins and losses, and reasons for success or failure at different stages of the sales process. For example, analytics provided visibility into what was happening in the "find and understand" and "acquire" stages of the sales process for an industrial products sales force. Figure 3-7 shows an analysis from a pipeline tracking tool that allowed salespeople to track their leads through the sales

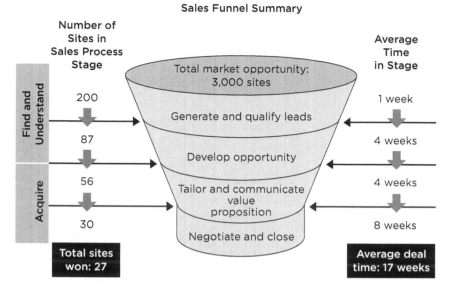

Note: Data on a 12-month rolling average.

Figure 3-7. Pipeline tracking analysis for an industrial products sales force

process and to document reasons for wins and losses. This visibility helped all sales force members in the following ways:

- *Salespeople* could track their progress and plan more effectively.
- *Sales managers* could pinpoint areas for improvement and identify coaching opportunities by drilling down to review the performance of specific salespeople.
- *Sales leaders* could track the overall pipeline and compare metrics to historical benchmarks. They could make timely strategic and tactical adjustments, rather than waiting until the end of the quarter to identify performance issues.

Pipeline tracking also helped marketing people understand where opportunities were lost so they could provide solutions.

Pipeline tracking helped this sales force achieve higher win rates and values, shorter sales cycle times, and higher sales and profits.

Ensuring That Sales Process Support Data and Tools Add Value

A periodic review of the data and tools available to support the sales process helps ensure that they continue to create value for salespeople and customers. For example, when leaders at an office products company assessed their homegrown sales tool portfolio, they discovered that although more than 20 tools were available to the sales organization, only one of those tools was used consistently across the organization's 100 autonomous sales regions. In the past, the Information Technology (IT) department had tried to please everyone by creating a new tool to satisfy every request. Old tools were rarely, if ever, eliminated. Eventually, the company had many disparate tools that didn't link to one another, creating confusion among salespeople and unnecessary work for IT. Working together, sales leaders and IT "cleaned house," dropping tools that no longer met sales force and customer needs and identifying others that needed improvement. The project resulted in a smaller set of focused tools. Salespeople could master all of the tools and use them more effectively to enhance the sales process. And the work required by IT to support the tools declined dramatically.

Sales Process Audit

Sales analytics can play a role in auditing the design and execution of the sales process to reveal improvement opportunities. Use the list in Figure 3-8 to evaluate the quality of a sales process.

Valuable to Customers	Rigorous and Complete	Implemented Well
• Focused on customer needs and value • Tailored to buying processes • Not a one-size-fits-all solution • Makes salespeople more than information providers	• Emulates approach of top performers • Details activities, advance metrics, participants, roles, and enablers • Addresses all decision influencers • Includes all company resources, not just sales	• Adopted consistently by sales and other roles • Supported with detailed call planning • Enabled by tools and information • Used to help salespeople, not just as an instrument of management control

Figure 3-8. Characteristics of a good sales process

Supporting the Sales Process

Sales analytics can provide the support salespeople need to continually find and keep customers. The following examples show how sales analytics can support various elements of the sales process.

Supporting Lead Generation

At a large distribution company, salespeople had to generate their own prospect lists by searching the Internet and scanning lists of local businesses. Occasionally, the Marketing department would provide a prospect list from a third-party database, but many of the entries on those lists were outdated or irrelevant, and there was no information about the sales potential of prospective accounts. When one analytically savvy salesperson created a spreadsheet tool that allowed her to update and manage her own prospect information, news of the tool spread quickly through the sales ranks. A sales analyst started helping other salespeople use the tool and eventually took over its maintenance. Lead generation improved when the sales analyst and the sales and marketing teams worked together.

Analytic sales process support comes in the form of data, tools, and other resources for enabling execution of each stage of the sales process.

Sales analytics can help sales organizations prospect more efficiently and effectively, especially in the absence of a standardized process in which sales and marketing work together. When the sales analytics function at one company began to play a liaison role in managing leads across marketing and sales, using the process shown in Figure 3-9, lead generation improved considerably.

Supporting the Sales Process with CRM

Customer relationship management (CRM) systems support many aspects of the sales process. CRM enhances sales force understanding of customer needs. In team sales environments, it adds value by providing an integrated view of company-customer interactions, so that if multiple sales team members interact with a customer, no one in the company is blindsided by what someone else may have said, done, or promised. Capturing information about customers in one place also helps create institutional knowledge of customers and facilitates transition of customer responsibility when salespeople are reassigned or replaced.

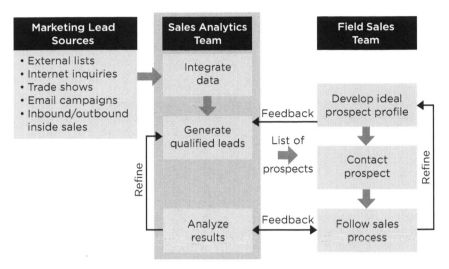

Figure 3-9. The role of sales analytics in lead generation at one company

CRM can also help sales forces acquire customers, for example, by providing software for developing custom sales collateral or configuring products.

Some sales forces use CRM to manage the overall sales process. For example, systems can track the sales pipeline and provide dashboards showing salespeople how they can improve.

Supporting the Sales Process with Mobile Technology

Many companies arm their sales forces with mobile technologies and tools that allow salespeople to share information in real time to help them

---

CRM Creates More Coordinated Sales Activity for Allied Signal

Allied Signal, an airplane parts supplier, was a pioneer in using CRM to improve the coordination of its sales effort. By the mid-1990s, Allied's sales organization had become very large and complex. Major customers had as many as 50 different contact points within Allied Signal to support the company's broad, technical product line. A lack of coordination among salespeople who shared accounts frustrated customers, many of whom were turning to lower-cost suppliers. To improve coordination, the company developed a company-wide CRM system that provided a single source of customer information for sales reps, field service engineers, product-line personnel, and response center agents across three business units. This allowed quick access to customer information and better coordination of the sales process for customers.

execute the sales process more effectively. Chapter 9 provides more information about how these technologies enable a more effective and more efficient sales process.

Supporting the Sales Process for a Business Logistics Provider

A global logistics provider has a suite of tools to help the sales force make the buying experience more effective and more efficient for customers. A sales analytics team worked with the sales and marketing teams to develop the tools described in Figure 3-10 for supporting each stage of the sales process.

Find and Understand	Acquire	Serve and Grow
Account Profile Tool	**Offer Design and Deal Builder Tools**	**Business Review Tool**
• Captures customer information • Helps salespeople match offering to needs	• Creates custom sales materials and proposals • Automates pricing	• Helps salespeople communicate value delivered

Figure 3-10. Support tools for each stage of the sales process at a business logistics provider

The *account profile tool* helps the sales force find and understand customers. It assists salespeople with customer interviews to determine account needs. Based on the customer's answers, the tool classifies the customer into an appropriate segment based on needs and helps the salesperson tailor the offering. Alternatively, customers can use an online tool to complete the interview on their own without the help of a salesperson.

The *offer design tool* helps the sales force acquire customers. It links to the account profile to help salespeople create tailored sales materials and proposals in less time and with a more unified look and feel. The *deal builder tool* also assists with customer acquisition. Developed with input from the finance and contracting teams, it helps salespeople expedite the pricing process and ensures that deals are attractive to customers and profitable to the company.

The *business review tool* supports the "serve and grow" stage by helping salespeople structure a quarterly account review for major customers. The tool captures feedback from the sales team, the service team, and customers and allows salespeople to share performance and cost-savings data. It facilitates a meaningful business-focused discussion to increase customer value and retention.

Conclusion

For a sales process to be effective, it must be consistently used by the sales force to develop, communicate, demonstrate, and reinforce customer value. A strong partnership between analytics and the sales force contributes to an effective sales process enabled by tools and information for enhancing salespeople's interactions with customers. An analytics partnership can span across a range of design, diagnosis, and support needs, with particular emphasis on providing analytics for *designing* and *supporting* a sales process that creates ongoing value for the sales organization and its customers.

CHAPTER 4

Sizing and Structuring the Sales Force

Decision frameworks and analytics can help companies size, structure, and allocate sales resources to match customer needs and potential.

Ty Curry and Pete Masloski

Ty Curry is a managing principal in ZS Associates' San Francisco office. He has more than 20 years of experience helping companies develop and implement sales strategies and improve sales force performance and productivity. His industry expertise includes high-tech, media and publishing, and life sciences. Ty has an MBA from Northwestern University's Kellogg School of Management and is also a graduate of the University of California at Los Angeles.

Pete Masloski is a principal in ZS Associates' Evanston, Illinois, office. He has more than 15 years of experience helping clients improve their marketing and sales efforts in areas such as sales process design, sales force strategy, competency assessment, territory design, and incentive compensation. Pete has an MBA from Northwestern University's Kellogg School of Management and is a graduate of Princeton University.

Sales Force Resource Decisions and the Impact of Analytics

Companies change the size, structure, and allocation of their sales forces for many reasons. They expand sales forces to penetrate new markets, support new products, or increase their coverage of existing customers. They downsize sales forces to reduce costs. They restructure sales forces to increase effectiveness (for example, adding industry specialists for expertise and focus) or to increase efficiency (adding inside salespeople to cover certain sales activities or customer segments). Consider some recent headlines pulled from the business press:

- "Medical device manufacturer eliminates 50 sales jobs to reduce costs."

- "Financial services company adds 100 salespeople and reorganizes around industry verticals to drive growth."

- "Computer manufacturer reorganizes direct sales force and partner channels to increase penetration of small businesses."

Addressing sales resource questions such as those listed in Figure 4-1 is both challenging and rewarding. The ultimate payoff is higher profits through increased sales, lower costs, or both.

Despite the significant impact of sales resource decisions on company performance, many companies still rely on the wisdom and experience of sales leaders for making such decisions. Those who make these decisions based on intuition alone are unlikely to optimize sales performance. Sales analytics and frameworks enable a more objective, structured, and data-driven approach to sales resource decision making. Using

> *Good sales force size, structure, and allocation decisions can often produce revenue growth double that of baseline expectations.*

analytic approaches increases the odds that the appropriate sales resources are placed against the best opportunities for maximizing customer value and company profitability.

However, sales force size, structure, and allocation changes are disruptive in nature and invariably lead to changes to existing customer relationships, creating risk to a company's base business. Such changes can also result in the relocation or severance of salespeople. Finally, these types of changes can affect the skills required to perform the job, the sales force's perception of the job, and salespeople's income potential and motivation. In short, it is critical to get these sales resource decisions right.

Decision Area	Key Questions
Sales force size	How many salespeople do we need to appropriately and profitably cover our customers and prospects?
Sales roles and structure	Should salespeople be generalists, or should they specialize by product, market, or sales activity?
Sales resource allocation	Are we devoting the right amount of effort to each customer segment, product line, and sales activity?

Figure 4-1. Sales resource questions

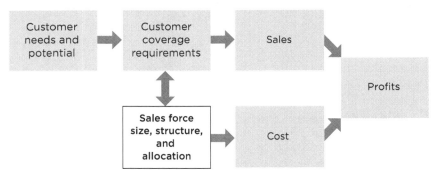

Figure 4-2. A sales force size, structure, and allocation decision framework

Given the business impact of optimizing sales resources and the potential downside of poor decisions, best-practice companies use frameworks and analytics to support their decision making. Using a process like the one shown in Figure 4-2, they link the needs and sales potential of each customer to the type and amount of sales force coverage each customer or segment requires and to the sales and profit consequences of that coverage. They examine multiple sales resourcing scenarios and choose the one most likely to produce the best combination of customer coverage and financial results.

The sales analytics function can and should be instrumental in helping companies make better-informed sales resource decisions, going beyond the role of support provider to deliver capabilities that enable the company to:

- *Diagnose* issues and opportunities with the existing sales force size, structure, and allocation

- *Design* a sales force with the right number of salespeople in the right roles engaged in the right allocation of sales effort across customers, products, and selling activities

This chapter shares ideas for using data, decision frameworks, and analytics to improve sales force size, structure, and resource allocation decisions. First, it discusses how to *diagnose* sales resource issues. Second, it discusses how analytics and decision frameworks contribute to the *design* of a sales resource plan that optimizes customer coverage and company performance.

Diagnosing Sales Resource Issues

Sales analytics can help companies identify sales resource problems and opportunities. Four performance diagnostics can evaluate where, how, and how effectively the sales force is spending its time.

Four Sales Resource Diagnostics

The following diagnostics can provide insights about the quality and quantity of customer coverage achieved with the current sales force size, structure, and resource allocation.

Customer Diagnostic: Is the Sales Force Meeting Customer Needs?

Customer survey results, when combined with profile and transactional data for those customers, can provide insights into potential sales force size, structure, and allocation issues. Surveys measure the quality of customers' interactions with salespeople versus that of competitors, customer awareness and knowledge of products, the degree of sales force responsiveness, and the reasons for recent wins or losses.

Figure 4-3 shows the results of a customer survey that an energy company conducted. The findings are broken down into mature versus growth customer segments. On almost all dimensions, customers in growth markets perceived gaps in sales organization performance when compared to customers in more mature markets. One such gap, in technical expertise, pointed to a possible sales resource solution for the company: add salespeople in growth markets to increase capacity and consider adding technical specialists to increase expertise for addressing technical issues.

Sales Skills Diagnostic: Are Salespeople Proficient in Key Competencies?

Sales force competency assessments made through manager observation, structured interviews, and self-ratings can uncover sales resourcing concerns and opportunities. Assessments can focus on salespeople's knowledge of markets and products and on their competency with key selling activities. Comparing competencies across groups of salespeople with different performance levels (for example, high versus low performers based on sales results) can provide additional insights.

Figure 4-3. Customer satisfaction survey results at an energy company

Figure 4-4 shows the results of a sales force competency self-assessment performed at a business services company. The assessment showed that many salespeople felt they lacked strong knowledge of several important industry vertical markets. For two of these verticals—energy and government—less than a third of salespeople felt they had strong knowledge. Even among salespeople with a high overall performance rating, self-rated knowledge of these markets was low. The company felt it was underperforming in these markets. Thus the analysis prompted the company to consider adding specialized sales roles to focus on the energy and government verticals. Industry specialists could bring greater expertise and could better capitalize on the opportunity in these segments.

Sales Activity Diagnostic: Do Salespeople Spend Time Wisely?

How salespeople spend their time across products, customer segments, and activities can provide clues about the sales force's effectiveness (customer impact) and efficiency (smart use of time). Companies can gather activity data through sales force observation, sales force activity surveys, and call reporting or pipeline tracking tools.

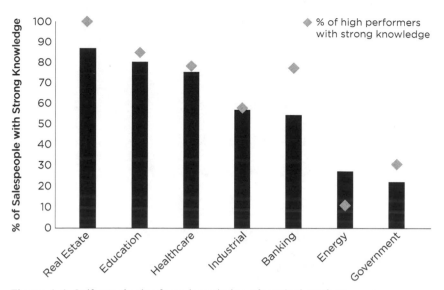

Figure 4-4. Self-rated sales force knowledge of vertical markets

Too often, salespeople spend too much time selling to small customers and prospects that have limited sales potential. Analytics for understanding sales potential at the account level (see Chapter 2) can help companies identify sales efforts that are placed against low potential opportunities, leading to inflated sales costs and missed opportunities with higher potential customers.

Another common problem identified through a sales activity diagnostic is role pollution, that is, salespeople engaging in activities that are not core to their job of selling. Figure 4-5 shows results from a sales activity analysis that an industrial products company did to uncover role pollution in its sales force. In this case, 45 percent of customer-facing time was spent on technical service and support as opposed to proactive selling. The company identified a sales force structure change as the solution, creating a lower-cost technical support organization to address customer issues more efficiently and enabling salespeople to spend more time selling.

Competitive Diagnostic: Does the Sales Force Get Sufficient Share of Voice?

Competitive benchmarks, in and of themselves, cannot provide answers to sales resource questions. Yet they can provide insights that highlight

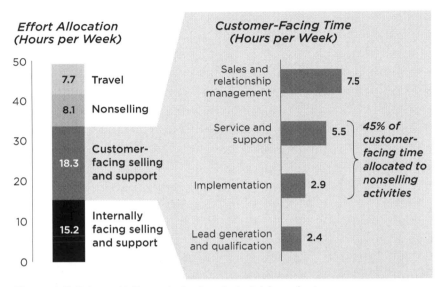

Figure 4-5. Sales activity analysis at an industrial products company

the need for deeper analysis about sales force size, structure, and allocation. Given that share of voice with customers will almost certainly have an impact on sales results, it's useful to consider the implications of a sales force sizing decision on the likely level of selling effort achieved versus the competition.

Figure 4-6 shows a competitive benchmarking analysis for a pharmaceutical company. The analysis shows that if the company hopes to become a major player in a specific therapeutic category, it will need at least 300 salespeople for product launch and 200 salespeople on an ongoing basis to achieve a competitive share of voice.

When using competitive share of voice to evaluate sales force sizing requirements, keep in mind that different companies and products have unique characteristics that influence what sales force effort levels are needed. It's a mistake to make sales force sizing conclusions based on share of voice alone. Supplement competitive diagnostics with other analyses described in this chapter.

Historical Results Analysis for Assessing Sales Resource Issues

Examining historical sales results can enhance understanding of the consequences of sales force size, structure, and allocation decisions.

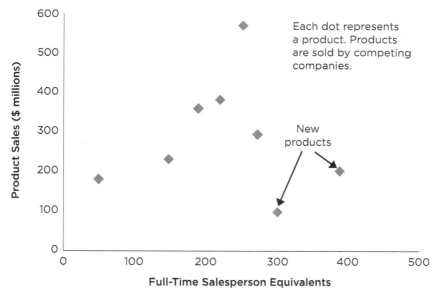

Figure 4-6. A competitive benchmarking analysis for a pharmaceutical company

Gaining Insight Through Market Penetration Analysis

Many companies know quite a bit about larger accounts but have much less information about the next tiers of potential accounts. Using analytics like those described in Chapter 2 to understand account sales potential, a company can identify gaps in account penetration that may indicate sales resource issues and can use analytics to uncover potential solutions. For example, one technology reseller conducted an assessment of sales potential across hundreds of thousands of possible business customers, segmented the accounts based on sales potential, and then mapped the accounts to its sales history to create the market penetration analysis shown in Figure 4-7. The analysis showed that the reseller had sold to 82 percent of large businesses but to a much lower percentage of small and medium-size businesses. It considered expanding its sales force to reach more opportunities with accounts that were not current customers, especially in the medium-size business segment. Additionally, the reseller's "share of wallet" (that is, actual sales divided by sales potential of current customers) varied by segment. Share of wallet was 53 percent in the small business segment, but was much lower for medium-size and especially for large businesses. Selling to large businesses involved different dynamics than selling to small businesses. For example, small businesses typically worked with just one or two

Segment*	Current Customers	Share of Wallet
Large business	82%	5%
Medium business	25%	21%
Small business	6%	53%

*Segment by potential based on number of employees.

Figure 4-7. Market penetration analysis for a technology reseller

suppliers, while large businesses would buy from many more suppliers. But even after accounting for this fact, the company felt that there was significant opportunity to increase share of wallet at large accounts. It considered adding product specialists for large accounts to increase sales focus on more products in its portfolio.

Gaining Insight About Sales Force Size and Structure Through Natural Experiments

Natural experiments occur in every sales force due to differences in customer coverage across territories, account segments, or markets. Some territories may have a large number of accounts with low coverage per account; these territories show what would happen with a smaller sales force size. Other territories may have a small number of accounts and high coverage per account; these territories show what would happen with a larger sales force size. Some territories may get coverage from sales specialists; others may get little or no specialist coverage. By acknowledging territory coverage differences and observing how these differences correlate with performance, it is possible to develop additional sales resource insights.

An apparel company that was losing retail store customers performed the analysis shown in Figure 4-8, which looked at the change in number of customers across sales territories. The company discovered that territories with a high number of retail stores to cover had suffered the greatest customer attrition; those with fewer stores, in fact, were gaining customers. Salespeople in territories with fewer accounts had higher sales effort per account, leading to better customer retention and higher prospect conversion rates. The company determined that it likely had too few salespeople to manage its existing customer base.

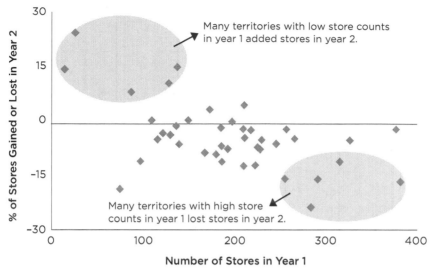

Figure 4-8. Gain/loss in retail stores by territory at an apparel company

Gaining Insight by Analyzing the Sales Pipeline

By tracking progress across different stages of the sales process to understand where and why deals are stalling, it's possible to reveal trends that tie back to sales force size and structure issues.

A software company analyzed its pipeline using the process shown in Figure 4-9. It recognized that, at current success rates, it would need to start with 555 qualified leads for the sales force to achieve its goal of winning 50 deals for the period. Either it would have to add field salespeople

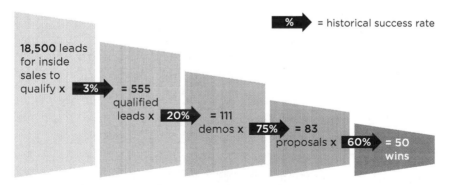

Figure 4-9. Sales pipeline analysis for a software company

to manage this volume of leads, or it could change the role of the inside sales team, asking it to both qualify leads and generate commitments for software demonstrations. With the inside team becoming accountable for more of the sales process, the field sales force would be able to focus on the downstream activities in the sales process, making it more likely to reach its goal of 50 wins without any additional head count.

Designing the Sales Force

Sales analytics and decision frameworks can play a central role in making decisions about the size, structure, and resource allocation of the sales force.

Sales Force Sizing

Sales analytics should go beyond commonly used financial decision rules for determining sales force size. A customer-focused approach that examines the linkages between customer coverage and sales results leads to better-informed and more profitable sales force sizing decisions.

Problems with Commonly Used Financial Decision Rules

The financial decision rules that many companies use to determine sales force size fail to explicitly recognize the most fundamental driver of sales resource needs: the customer. They also treat the sales force as a cost rather than an investment, often leading to suboptimal decisions.

Simple Financial Ratios. Ratios such as sales per salesperson and sales costs as a percentage of sales (cost-to-sales ratios) are straightforward metrics that companies commonly evaluate relative to company or industry benchmarks. However, these metrics are disconnected from customer coverage requirements and provide little insight into the profit implications of adding or cutting sales personnel. Although it's seemingly counterintuitive, when a sales force is undersized, adding salespeople increases the cost-to-sales ratio but also increases profitability. A company can always reduce the cost-to-sales ratio by cutting personnel, but the impact on profitability is positive only if the sales force was too large to begin with. Maintaining an industry average cost-to-sales ratio is especially damaging to small-share companies that want to grow. Sustaining a historical ratio can also result in excessive downsizing during a business downturn, leaving a company poorly positioned for success when business conditions improve.

Figure 4-10. The financial consequences of alternative sales force sizes at a pharmaceutical company

Earn Your Way or Pay as You Go. This "wait and see" approach views the sales force as a cost item justified by sales, rather than as an investment that drives sales. An earn-your-way, pay-as-you-go strategy is sometimes necessary in markets with high uncertainty or when a company is cash-strapped. But when companies take this conservative

> *Look at financial ratios (such as sales force cost-to-sales ratios) as a check for affordability, but don't rely on them as the primary criterion.*

approach when they have a high likelihood of success and available financing, they undersize their sales forces and forfeit opportunity. A pharmaceutical company's overly cautious expansion strategy, shown in Figure 4-10, resulted in too little support for a new product launch, costing the company 17 percent of profits over three years.

Using a Customer-Focused Approach

Effective sales resource analytics establish the relationship between sales force effort and the incremental sales and profit that will likely result. By understanding the relationship between the costs to cover a given customer or prospect and the likely revenue and profit stream driven by that selling effort, companies can determine which customers are profitable to cover and what type and amount of sales resource will be optimal. These analytic approaches examine the two key linkages shown in Figure 4-11:

1. How customer needs and sales potential affect customer coverage requirements and therefore costs of coverage

2. How customer coverage impacts sales results

Combining these two linkages allows companies to estimate the overall customer coverage achieved and the profit impact of different sales force sizing decisions.

A Four-Step Approach. Determining how much to invest in the sales force and how to allocate that investment across customer types, products, sales roles, and activities involves the following four steps:

1. **Determine account sales potential and segment accounts.** Start by developing an understanding of account level needs and sales potential for existing customers as well as prospects, and segment accounts into meaningful groups (see Chapter 2). The accounts in each group should be similar in terms of how the company should approach them from a sales resource standpoint. In addition to having comparable sales potential, accounts within each segment should require similar types of sales activities and levels of sales effort.

2. **Determine coverage requirements and the sales force sizing and cost implications.** Next, understand the baseline effort required to execute the sales process for each segment. Start by evaluating historical sales efforts or data obtained through sales force activity surveys. Then incorporate expert judgment that acknowledges the coverage impact of future changes to the selling environment. Evaluate linkage 1 in Figure 4-11 by estimating

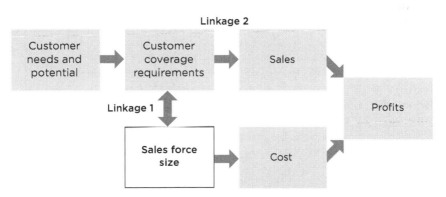

Figure 4-11. Two key linkages that determine sales force size

the average selling capacity expected per salesperson and calculating how many salespeople are required to meet coverage requirements. Then translate coverage requirements into costs using financial data that reflect fully loaded estimates for the average cost of a salesperson.

3. **Estimate revenues and gross profits.** Next, estimate expected revenues for each customer segment and product (linkage 2 in Figure 4-11) by looking at average historical deal sizes in each segment and historical advance rates through the sales process. An account segment that has very large deals but infrequent wins may be less attractive to cover than a segment with moderate-size deals but a high win rate. Again, historical analysis can provide insight into future revenue opportunities, but it will not address anticipated changes to the market and competitive environment. Accordingly, it is imperative to collect structured judgment from experts about how win rates and deal sizes will evolve going forward. Translate revenue estimates into gross profits by factoring in product costs.

4. **Construct financial models.** Evaluate the economic outcomes of different coverage scenarios across products and account segments. The key factors driving model outcomes are the estimated revenues and gross profits from account coverage and the selling costs associated with coverage. The bottom line is that some customer segments will be profitable for certain products but not others, some segments will be profitable across the portfolio, and some segments will just have too little opportunity to justify sales force coverage. Any decision to eliminate field coverage of accounts should be made purposefully, based on the economics. Shifting select customer segments to more efficient channels, such as inside sales, often substantially improves financial performance.

Two examples illustrate this analytic, customer-focused approach to sales force sizing.

Example 1: Activity-Based Analysis for a Retail Merchandising Sales Force. A retail merchandising sales force conducted an activity-based analysis to determine the right sales force size. The merchandisers performed a well-defined set of service-focused activities. The analysis focused on linkage 1 in Figure 4-11: determining how many salespeople were needed to produce the levels of service that customers required.

As shown in Figure 4-12, the company segmented accounts according to their sales volume (a good predictor of merchandising needs), determined the annual requisite coverage time for accounts in each segment (calls per

Segment: Retail Stores	No. of Accounts	Calls/ Year	Hours/ Call	Total Hours	Sales-people Needed
Over $75K	112	12	2.0	2,688	2.0
$35–75K	784	6	2.0	9,408	7.1
$15–35K	2,543	4	2.0	20,344	15.4
Under $15K	6,559	3	1.0	19,677	14.9
Total retail	9,998	—	—	52,117	39.4

Hours per salesperson per year = 1,325

Figure 4-12. Activity-based sizing analysis for a retail merchandising sales force

year times hours per call), and estimated the number of salespeople required to perform the work. By summing the call time across segments and dividing by the average number of calls a salesperson can make in a year, the company determined how large the sales force should be.

Example 2: Profit-Based Pipeline Analysis for a Medical Device Sales Force. Most sales forces will want to supplement activity-based analysis with analysis acknowledging linkage 2 in Figure 4-11: the impact of customer coverage decisions on sales and ultimately on bottom-line results.

The sales force sizing analytics illustrated in Figures 4-13 and 4-14 are for a sales force that sells medical devices to hospitals. The approach involved four steps:

1. Segmenting accounts according to their sales potential and coverage needs and mapping out the sales process steps for each segment.

2. Determining the number of leads entering the sales pipeline each year and estimating the time required and the success rate for each step.

3. Summing the time required to execute all steps to produce an estimate of the number of salespeople required to cover each customer segment.

4. Evaluating deal sizes and advance rates to determine the sales and profit implications of covering each customer segment.

In combination, these analytics enabled the company to evaluate the return on investment (ROI) impact of different sales force sizing scenarios.

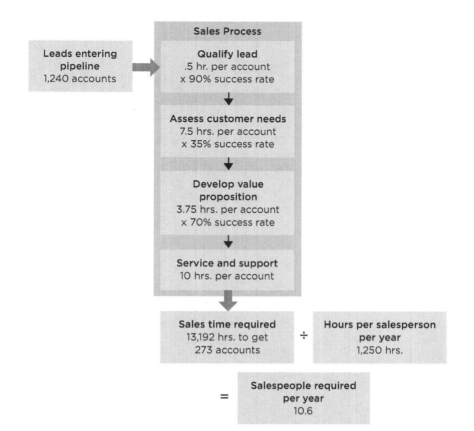

Figure 4-13. Sales force sizing analysis for one customer segment (segment A) of a medical device company

Customer Segment	Field Salespeople Required to Cover	Value of Field Sales Coverage ($ thousands)	Cost to Cover with Field Sales ($ thousands)	Profit with Field Sales Coverage ($ thousands)	ROI of Field Sales Coverage
A	10.6	24,706	2,650	22,056	832%
B	2.6	3,972	650	3,322	511%
C	5.8	4,882	1,450	3,432	237%
D	1.6	832	400	432	108%
E	1.6	420	400	20	5%
All segments	22.2	34,812	5,550	29,262	527%

Field salesperson cost ($ thousands): $250
ROI target: 200%

Figure 4-14. Financial sizing analysis for a medical device sales force

ROI for segments A, B, and C (see Figure 4-14) exceeded the company-set threshold of 200 percent; these segments were assigned to the field sales force for coverage. For segments D and E, ROI to cover with field sales fell short of the threshold; these segments were assigned to more efficient inside sales and Internet channels, which would produce a more favorable ROI.

The columns in the table in Figure 4-14 are calculated as follows:

- Field salespeople required to cover = (results from analysis in Figure 4-13)

- Value of field sales coverage = (number of accounts closed from analysis in Figure 4-13) times (average deal size) times (product margin percentage)

- Cost to cover with field sales = (field salespeople required to cover) times (field salesperson cost)

- Profit with field sales coverage = (value of field sales coverage) minus (cost to cover with field sales)

- ROI of field sales coverage = (profit with field sales coverage) divided by (cost to cover with field sales)

Sales Force Investment Dynamics

The best sales force sizing and allocation analytics acknowledge the following sales force investment dynamics:

- **Sales force investment has diminishing returns.** Greater investment drives more sales, but at a diminishing rate as the marginal salesperson hired will have to dig deeper into the universe of customers to drive sales.

- **Sales force investment has multiyear impact.** This year's sales force effort affects sales this year—and in future years. It is critical to consider the future revenue stream resulting from sales force effort. Otherwise, a financial model will understate the optimal sales force investment.

- **Sales force investment can be optimized through resource allocation.** Analysis that looks at economics across an entire product portfolio enables understanding of the optimal allocation of sales effort across products, as well as customer segments and sales activities, at any given sales force size. Often, it's possible to significantly improve financial results simply by reallocating sales effort to the right products,

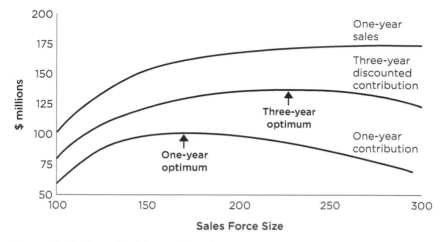

Figure 4-15. Financial sizing analysis for a pharmaceutical sales force

customer segments, and sales activities without changing the size of the sales force.

A pharmaceutical company conducted a sales force sizing analysis that acknowledges all of these dynamics. Figure 4-15 shows the results. The analysis involved analyzing historical data to understand the relationship between sales force effort and sales for each of the major products the sales force sold, estimating product and sales force costs, and measuring year-to-year carryover sales for each product. The analysis provided insight about the one-year and three-year profit impact of alternative sales force sizing decisions.

These examples of sales force sizing approaches are among the many approaches that are appropriate in different situations. For more detail on how to implement these and other customer-focused sales force sizing methods, see *Sales Force Design for Strategic Advantage* by Andris A. Zoltners, Prabhakant Sinha, and Sally E. Lorimer (Palgrave Macmillan, 2004).

Sales Force Structure

Designing a sales force structure requires determining what sales roles and responsibilities are appropriate for meeting customer needs effectively (with high impact) and efficiently (for less cost). Structures can include many different sales roles, including field salespeople who are generalists, product specialists, or technical specialists, as well as inside salespeople and key account teams.

Determining the right sales force structure is complicated. It's easy to make costly mistakes that create unnecessary customer disruption, reduce morale, and increase sales force turnover. Companies increase the odds of choosing the right sales force structure when they use decision frameworks to organize and reduce bias in their thinking. Frameworks can help companies engage in rigorous scenario analysis and debate about the customer coverage and financial consequences of structure alternatives. In addition to helping with designing a structure, analytic frameworks can help with understanding the costs and benefits of structure modifications and with managing any of the disadvantages inherent in a given structure.

Generalist or Specialist Sales Roles?

Should salespeople be generalists who sell all products and perform all activities for all customer types? Or should they specialize by product, market segment, or selling activity? The decision framework shown in Figure 4-16 can help companies answer this fundamental sales force structure question.

Whether and how to specialize depends on two factors:

1. **Bandwidth of salespeople relative to the diversity of customer needs and sales process complexity.** Consider the sales process at IBM. Many complex and diverse competencies are required for selling the company's broad line of computer hardware, software, and services to a wide range of businesses all over the globe. A single salesperson, no matter how intelligent or hardworking, could never master all of these competencies. To deliver the needed expertise to customers, IBM must have a highly specialized sales structure that includes dozens of types of market, product, and activity specialists.

2. **Company strategy.** A strategy to drive growth and penetration within an industry segment might suggest the use of industry specialists. A strategy calling for focus on one product within a broad line might suggest the use of product specialists. A growth strategy that requires developing many new customers might suggest a "hunter" specialist role. A strategy calling for maximal efficiency may suggest using generalists. A solution selling strategy may be best served by using account managers who have overall customer responsibility plus specialists to provide focus and specific expertise.

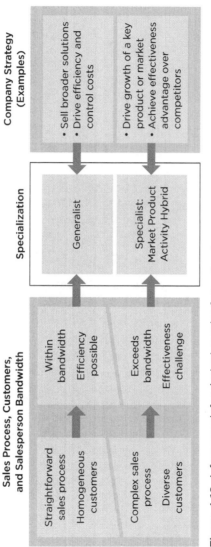

Figure 4-16. A framework for designing sales force structure

The questions listed in Figure 4-17 can help companies assess sales force structure considerations. The assessment will help the company evaluate sales force structure alternatives on different dimensions to help determine the right combination of generalists and specialists to effectively and efficiently execute the critical selling activities for each target segment.

Key Account Management and Inside Sales Roles

Over the past several years, increasing complexity of the sales function has contributed to growth in the magnitude and importance of two specific types of sales roles: key account management and inside sales.

Control and Motivation

- Will important products, customer segments, and selling activities receive sufficient selling effort?
- Does the structure have attractive roles that enable talent acquisition and retention?

Effectiveness

- Does the structure align with the company's sales strategy?
- Does selling certain products require specialized skills and knowledge?
- Will customers get the expertise they need for addressing their business needs throughout the buying process?
- Does the structure align the best talent to the highest-value opportunities?
- Does the structure enable effective sales coaching?

Complexity

- Does the structure encourage role clarity and clear reporting relationships and accountabilities?
- What coordination requirements and execution complexities does the structure introduce?

Efficiency

- Does the structure increase the cost of sales, e.g., multiple salespeople calling on the same customers?
- What are the territory size and travel implications of the structure?
- Are there specific products, customer segments, or selling activities that could be performed by lower-cost channels, such as inside sales?

Flexibility

- How much disruption to customer and sales organization relationships will the structure create? How can the disruption be managed?
- Is the structure adaptable to future events?

Figure 4-17. Key questions for evaluating sales force structure

Key Account Management. Large, strategically important, and typically complex customers require and warrant focused attention from the sales organization. These customers represent a disproportionate percentage of company revenues and are commonly major drivers of sales growth. Key account sales structures vary widely across companies based on a number of factors such as account needs, buying processes, geographic span, and sales potential. Several objectives can underlie key account approaches:

- Assign the best salespeople to strategically important customers.

- Achieve better coordination for the highest-potential customers who value a streamlined purchasing process and a single point of contact.

- Develop more comprehensive solutions for customers who have broader needs spanning a seller's full product and service portfolio.

- Develop strategic partnerships with key customers, often including joint business planning, mutual investments to create innovative solutions, and shared accountability for success.

When the objectives involve broader solution development or strategic partnerships with key customers, key account management is much more than a sales force structure decision; it is an organization-wide business strategy for driving growth. Given these stakes, it is critical to address key account management through fact-based, comprehensive approaches.

Sales analytics and decision frameworks can contribute to the design of key account management teams by:

- **Selecting key accounts.** Companies need consistent criteria and an objective process for deciding which customers to include in a key account program and occasionally which ones to remove. Decision criteria such as account potential, purchasing history, customer needs and buying processes, and geographic footprint are useful for determining which accounts are truly "key."

- **Articulating and supporting the key account team structure.** Given the added complexities of key account selling, it's critical to think comprehensively about the details underlying the key account team structure (including reporting relationships, accountabilities, coordination requirements, and authorities) and to provide the planning tools, processes, and metrics for supporting that structure.

Inside Sales. Increasingly, companies see inside sales as an important component of the sales force structure decision. Inside sales has always been an efficient structure option and has more recently proven to be an increasingly effective channel in certain situations. Three primary factors are behind the momentum inside sales has gained in recent years:

- Sellers feel competitive pressure to cut costs and thus are seeking more efficient ways to sell.

- Buyers are becoming more comfortable purchasing and collaborating remotely; they use the web to research product information, are comfortable communicating and collaborating with sellers through email and conference calls, and in fact prefer these methods over face-to-face communication for some sales tasks.

- Technologies such as easy-to-use online web conferencing and video tools make it possible for inside salespeople to create customer intimacy without field interaction.

Inside sales teams can drive improved sales force performance in the following ways:

- By executing the entire sales process at accounts that don't justify field sales coverage due to low sales potential, a remote geographic location, or a preference for buying over the telephone or Internet.

- By performing select stages of the customer engagement process. With certain types of accounts, inside sales may execute activities at different stages of the sales process (for example, lead generation or customer renewals), allowing more expensive field sales and key account team resources to focus on activities that benefit most from a face-to-face approach.

- By selling select products or services. Certain offerings and solutions with lower buyer risk lend themselves to more transactional selling that can be accomplished by inside sales, allowing more expensive field sales and key account team resources to focus on more complex products and services that require a consultative approach and customization.

The sales analytics function can play a key role in identifying those customer segments, selling activities, and products that can be moved to inside sales to drive efficiency improvements, often with little or no loss of effectiveness.

Increasingly, field salespeople are leveraging email, social media, and web and videoconferencing to maximize their own productivity and enhance the customers' experience. In this regard, the line between field sales and inside sales is blurring, and the sales analytics group is in a position to help the sales force adapt to optimize its efficiency and effectiveness.

Using Analytics to Evaluate Sales Force Structure

Every sales force structure has costs and benefits. Developing a scorecard that evaluates the sales productivity impact of these costs and benefits helps narrow down the choices and highlight the best one. A medical device company developed the scorecard shown in Figure 4-18 to evaluate the expected costs and benefits associated with moving from a generalist to a specialist sales structure. In this case, the company expected the benefits of the specialist structure to more than offset the increased costs.

Following implementation of a new sales force structure, it is useful to track metrics that reflect the extent to which anticipated costs and benefits are realized. Figure 4-19 shows some sample metrics.

Managing the Disadvantages of a Sales Force Structure

Every structure carries with it some advantages, but also some disadvantages. Companies must recognize this and can use analytics-enabled support systems and processes to sharpen and leverage the advantages while

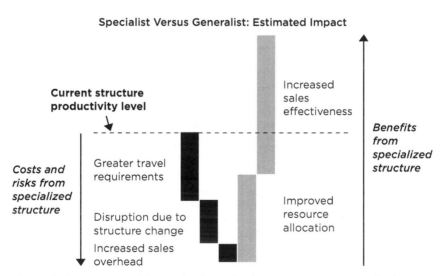

Figure 4-18. A scorecard for evaluating sales force structure at a medical device company

Benefit or Cost	Activity Metric	Customer Impact Metric	Company Result Metric
Customer disruption due to structure change	Implementation of relationship transition program by targeted account	Customer satisfaction in disrupted accounts	Sales change in disrupted accounts
Increased focus on product A due to product specialists	Increase in sales effort for product A	Greater awareness and knowledge of product A	Sales growth for product A
Greater success with segment B due to industry specialists	Increase in sales effort on segment B accounts	Greater awareness and interest among segment B accounts	Sales growth in segment B
Lack of coordination across specialist roles	Number of joint planning sessions	Customer satisfaction in accounts with multiple sales specialists	Products sold in accounts with multiple sales specialists

Figure 4-19. Metrics for assessing the impact of a new sales force structure

reducing the impact of the disadvantages. For example, a risk in a generalist sales structure is that salespeople may undersupport a key product that is difficult to sell. A well-designed sales compensation program (see Chapter 7) and a dashboard with key metrics for the product (see Chapter 9) can reduce this risk and keep sales effort appropriately focused. Figure 4-20 on page 82 shows some common sales force structure disadvantages, along with strategies for minimizing their impact.

Conclusion

Sales force size, structure, and allocation are high-stakes decisions that have significant impact on customer coverage and on a company's financial results. Sales analytics and decision frameworks can play a key role in the

Structure	Common Disadvantages	Ways to Minimize the Impact of the Disadvantage
Generalist	Nonoptimal effort allocation to products or customer segments	• Goals, incentives, metrics, and coaching aligned with strategy • Information and tools to improve customer targeting
	Insufficient product expertise	• Better product training, information, and sales tools
Product or activity specialists sharing customers	Customer confusion and lack of coordination	• Joint planning sessions with sales-people who share customers • Clear team roles and responsibilities • Sales specialists reporting to common managers • Information and tools (e.g., CRM) to support coordination • Territories aligned to facilitate coordi-nation (e.g., mirrored alignments) • Team-oriented salespeople and a teamwork culture
	Lack of cross-selling (with product specialists)	• More cross-selling incentives and team rewards • Better cross-product training
	Poor geographic coverage	• Inside sales, generalist, or hybrid roles for outlying areas
Any	Disruption (with change)	• Realignment of territories using a structured process that builds sales force commitment • Customer relationship transition program • Bridge compensation for salespeople

Figure 4-20. Sales force structure disadvantages and strategies for minimizing their impact

diagnosis of sales resource issues and the design of a sales force that supports the execution of the company's sales strategy. Sales analytics can help advance the sales organization from intuition and gut feel to fact-based, data-driven, and comprehensive decision making that will lead to increased sales effectiveness and higher sales and profits.

Designing Sales Territories

*Analytics enable companies to keep sales territories
aligned with ever-changing customer and company needs.*

Sandra Forero and Jason Brown

Sandra Forero is a principal in ZS Associates' Princeton, New Jersey, office and is a leader in the firm's Pharmaceutical Sales Solutions and Territory Alignment practices. She was recognized as one of *Consulting Magazine*'s Top 25 Consultants in 2012 for her distinguished work in client services. Sandra has an MBA from the University of Virginia's Darden School of Business and is a graduate of Universidad de los Andes in Bogotá, Colombia.

Jason Brown is a principal in ZS Associates' Boston office and leads the firm's Financial Services practice. He has more than 17 years of experience helping marketing and sales organizations with go-to-market strategy and implementation, market research, sales process design, compensation design, and sales force sizing and deployment. Jason has an MBA from the MIT Sloan School of Management and a BA in economics and statistics from the University of Chicago.

The Impact of Sales Analytics on Territory Design

Many circumstances necessitate changing a sales force's territory design or alignment, which is the assignment of accounts and selling activities to salespeople. You will need to design a new alignment if:

- You create a new sales force.
- You expand, downsize, or restructure an existing sales force.
- A merger necessitates bringing two or more sales forces together.

You *may* need a new alignment if:

- Customers or customer needs change.
- Your portfolio of products changes.

- The competitive environment changes.
- The sales process changes.
- You have not audited the quality of your alignment in the last two years.

Optimizing territory alignment by itself can increase sales by 2 to 7 percent[1] without any change in total resources or sales strategy. Although the impact of territory alignment grows with the size and complexity of a sales organization, even small, single-role sales forces can boost sales productivity by improving territory alignment.

A good alignment reinforces a customer coverage strategy by matching the capacity of salespeople with the need to execute specific sales activities at a local level. Sales analytics can play a key role in managing territory alignments to realize many benefits. The right territory alignment is:

- **Good for customers.** It encourages effective and efficient customer coverage and strengthens customer relationships.

- **Good for salespeople.** It ensures manageable territory workload and provides all salespeople with the opportunity to succeed.

  > *Alignment is a short-term, high-impact, tangible opportunity for sales analytics to drive top- and bottom-line results.*

- **Good for the company.** It aligns sales effort with company strategy and increases revenues through better customer coverage and more satisfied salespeople.

Sales analytics can help a sales force create a territory alignment that accomplishes three objectives:

- Optimizing customer coverage
- Enabling effective and efficient sales activity
- Supporting performance management

Optimizing Customer Coverage

A good territory alignment matches customer workload to sales force capacity. Consider the case of a cosmetics sales force of 300 people who sell to buyers, stock shelves, set up displays, and take inventory at retail

[1]Andris A. Zoltners and Sally E. Lorimer, "Sales Territory Alignment: An Overlooked Productivity Tool," *Journal of Personal Selling and Sales Management* (Summer 2000): 139–50.

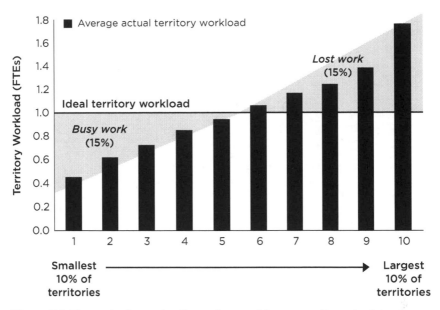

Figure 5-1. The cost of poor territory alignment in a cosmetics sales force

stores. The company estimated how long these tasks should take in each type and size of store, calculated the workload for each territory, and compared that workload to the capacity of a full-time equivalent (FTE) salesperson to reveal gaps in coverage (Figure 5-1). The largest 10 percent of territories averaged 75 percent more workload than an FTE could handle, while the smallest 10 percent of territories averaged just 44 percent of the ideal workload.

Two metrics reveal opportunities to improve the alignment:

- **Busy work** is unprofitable work that salespeople do in territories that are undersized. Salespeople spend time on unproductive tasks because they don't have enough "profitable workload" to fill their day (15 percent of the workload for the cosmetics company).

> *Too often, sales forces that are the right overall size have deployed territories suboptimally, resulting in lost productivity and lower sales.*

- **Lost work** is profitable work that salespeople can't deliver because their territories are oversized with more work than an FTE can manage (15 percent of the workload for the cosmetics company).

Deploying Generalists and Specialists for Efficiency and Effectiveness

A sales force sells employers of all types and sizes a range of customized payroll and human resource administration solutions. Some salespeople are specialists who have expertise with certain customer segments, products, or selling activities. Others are generalists who have a broad understanding of all customer segments, products, and selling activities. The company seeks to effectively meet each customer's specialized needs but, at the same time, wants to be efficient and use resources wisely. A good territory alignment is essential for achieving these goals. In Manhattan, for example, where customers and prospects are located close to one another, sales specialists focus on particular industries, products, or selling activities (hunting for new customers versus sustaining and expanding business with existing customers, for example). Multiple industry specialists visit customers in the same zip code or even the same building. By contrast, in Maine, where customers are spread out across a larger area, generalist salespeople sell all products and perform all selling activities for all customers in assigned zip codes. The generalists do not have the same depth of knowledge and expertise that the specialists in Manhattan have, but they are more efficient because just one individual travels to each customer site. To create additional efficiencies, an inside sales team covers customers in the farthest reaches of northern Maine. The alignment matches selling responsibilities to the skills and capacity of salespeople in a way that optimizes efficiency and effectiveness.

By identifying opportunities to realign and reduce customer workload in oversized territories while adding workload to undersized territories, sales analytics can help the sales force capture more revenues and profits.

Enabling Effective and Efficient Sales Activity

A good territory alignment enhances both effectiveness (impact with customers) and efficiency (smart use of sales resources). A good territory alignment on its own cannot make salespeople achieve their maximum potential; but a *bad* territory alignment can prevent such achievement.

Supporting Performance Management

Territory sales potential is often a stronger predictor of territory sales than is any other characteristic, including the salesperson's ability or effort. In fact, vacant territories with high sales potential frequently have higher sales than fully staffed territories with low potential. Similarly, territories with low potential tend to have low sales but high market share.

Frequently, sales leaders do not place enough emphasis on differences in territory potential when they evaluate, compensate, reward, and

---

Inequity in Territory Potential Fuels Turnover at a Computer Hardware Reseller

A computer hardware reseller paid its salespeople entirely through commissions on sales. The philosophy was "you eat what you kill" — salespeople kept their accounts permanently after making a sale. Many tenured salespeople had amassed large territories and earned several hundred thousand dollars a year, mostly by selling to longtime customers who provided a continuous and stable source of revenue and income. These veterans had so many customers that they didn't have enough time to cover all their accounts thoroughly. They felt no urgency to develop new business and refused to give up any accounts because of the negative impact on their income. New salespeople got small "starter" territories with just a fraction of the potential of the established territories. With market growth slowing, new salespeople found it impossible to build a sufficient book of business to earn a living. It became harder for the company to attract and retain new salespeople. Annual sales force turnover shot up to 57 percent, mostly because of inequity in sales territory opportunity.

---

acknowledge salespeople. When leaders underestimate the importance of these differences and treat salespeople as if their territories were identical, sales force morale can suffer. Few salespeople will be content with what they feel are inferior account assignments while colleagues of comparable skill and tenure make more money and get more recognition with less effort because they have "rich" territories. Territories with low potential,

> *Sales analytics can help a sales force create territories with equitable potential so that the right salespeople get rewarded.*

intense competition, or too many small accounts, but a high quota, lead to low job satisfaction and low motivation for salespeople, which often leads to salesperson turnover.

If sales force rewards (incentives and nonmonetary recognition, such as award trips) are tied to territory sales volume without controlling for territory potential, and territories *do not* have equal potential, you may reward the wrong salespeople. And territory equity is a *must* for those companies that publicly publish a forced ranking of salespeople from best to worst on any sales metric.

Sales Analytics at the Center of Good Territory Alignment

The sales analytics function is often the curator of territory alignment. In this role, it can leverage expertise with alignment issues, data, analytics,

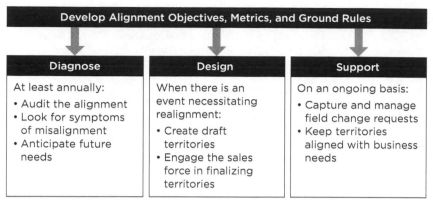

Figure 5-2. How sales analytics add value to territory alignment

tools, and processes to diagnose, design, and support alignments that enable effective and efficient customer coverage, as shown in Figure 5-2.

Developing Alignment Objectives, Metrics, and Ground Rules

Sales analytics can lay the groundwork for diagnosing, designing, and supporting productivity-enhancing territory alignments through three activities:

- Creating alignment objectives that support sales strategy
- Developing metrics for profitable territory workload
- Establishing ground rules that ensure consistency

Creating Alignment Objectives That Support Sales Strategy

Examples of territory alignment objectives include:

- Give salespeople a sales and service *workload* that enables them to serve customers well.
- Encourage *continuity of relationships* between salespeople and customers.
- Give salespeople enough territory sales *potential* to succeed.
- Control *travel time and costs* by creating territories that allow efficient customer coverage.

A Part-Time Consumer Products Merchandising Organization	A Chemicals Sales Force That Pays Salespeople on Commission
Objective: Build compact territories with manageable workloads while minimizing sales force travel costs.	**Objective:** Equitably distribute sales opportunity across territories while minimizing account assignment changes.
Rationale: Allows salespeople to perform their duties at stores without exceeding the weekly hour limit for part-time personnel.	**Rationale:** Allows salespeople to drive value and have a fair opportunity to succeed, while keeping sales force relationships intact, a key source of competitive advantage.

Figure 5-3. A comparison of alignment objectives for two sales forces

Territory alignment objectives should support business strategy. Figure 5-3 shows how the objectives varied across two sales forces facing realignment.

Developing Metrics for Profitable Territory Workload

Evaluating how good an alignment is requires metrics that measure achievement of the desired objectives. The most important metric is *profitable territory workload*—that is, the amount of sales activity that should take place, based on the potential and profitability of the accounts in a territory. A good alignment matches profitable workload in each territory to the capacity of the salesperson or sales team assigned to cover that territory. Some industries have data available for creating measures of profitable territory workload directly. Companies in other industries will need to rely on approximations and surrogates.

Sales forces in industries that lack extensive data can approximate profitable territory workload in two ways:

- Estimating profitable account workload based on observation and experience of the sales activity typically required to cover different types and sizes of accounts (see the cosmetics company example in Figure 5-1).

- Developing an "index" that combines multiple surrogate measures of account workload and potential. *Workload metrics* can include counts of customers and prospects by market segment, weighted according to the relative importance of each segment. *Potential metrics* can include existing customer sales, demographics, or market research–based projections (see Chapter 2 for more information).

Measuring Optimal Account Workload in the Asset Management Industry

An asset management wholesale company sells mutual funds through a variety of intermediaries, including financial advisers, broker-dealers, and banks. The company's salespeople call on individuals at these intermediary accounts to share product knowledge and drive market share. The company has data that allow estimation of optimal account workload. Salespeople keep records of their call activity by account in a sales automation system. The company also knows sales (assets under management) by account by month. Using these data, the company statistically estimates the relationship between selling effort (time spent with individuals by account) and sales results (changes in asset flows by account). By factoring in the cost of sales effort, the company can identify an effort level at which the incremental return from a sales call equals the incremental cost of that call — in other words, an optimal account workload. Using these data, it designs sales territories that match the profitable account workload in each territory to the capacity of the salesperson assigned to cover the territory.

Members of the sales and marketing organizations can provide input for developing a list of workload and potential metrics that reinforce sales strategy. Then by gathering and analyzing data that reflect those metrics, it's possible to recommend a subset of accurate, differentiating, and strategically aligned metrics for evaluating alignment quality.

Territory alignment metrics do not have to be perfect to add value. Because territories are built by aggregating multiple accounts, imprecision in the metrics usually evens out across many accounts, and therefore it does not significantly affect overall territory design.

It is especially difficult to find metrics for designing territories for key account teams that

> When it comes to evaluating territory alignments, using estimates of profitable territory workload — even imperfect ones — is much better than using no estimates at all.

cover relatively few customers. In these circumstances, territory alignments are often built through an account-by-account review.

Whatever metric you choose for evaluating alignments, it's important to get sales force input and agreement. If the sales force does not support the methodology, it may call the whole territory alignment into question. Ultimately, settling on the right metric for evaluating an alignment requires a mix of analytics and negotiation with sales and marketing leadership.

Establishing Ground Rules That Ensure Consistency

Sales analytics add value to alignment diagnosis, design, and support by laying out ground rules for consistent alignment decisions across the sales force. These ground rules can include answers to the questions listed in Figure 5-4.

Some sales forces allow exceptions to alignment ground rules for top performers. They reason that top performers are more efficient, can take on more work, and can extract more value from each dollar of opportunity; thus they deserve "richer" territories. This strategy should be used with caution for two reasons:

- When a top performer gets promoted or leaves the company, the "rich" territory that is vacated may be inappropriate for that person's replacement; sales leaders must make alignment adjustments following sales force turnover.

- When territories have unequal potential, it is difficult to evaluate salespeople fairly; sales leaders must use performance metrics that account for differences in territory potential and isolate the impact of the salesperson's effort and ability from the impact of the "rich" territory.

Ranges on key metrics	• What range in opportunity and workload is acceptable across territories? • What are the minimum opportunity and workload required for a viable territory?
Geographic rules	• Will we split metropolitan areas across territories? • Should we adhere to state (or other) boundaries? • Can customers who have multiple geographic locations be covered by multiple salespeople?
Allowable disruption	• To minimize short-term sales loss, how much disruption to customer relationships is acceptable?
Exception policies	• Under what conditions will we allow exceptions to the ground rules? • How will we approve exceptions?

Figure 5-4. Questions for establishing territory alignment ground rules

Too often, sales managers give top performers territories that are too rich; these territories exceed even the most highly talented and skilled salesperson's bandwidth. Sales are lost, and talent is attributed to the salesperson when in fact the success is due to the territory.

Diagnosing Alignment Issues and Opportunities

Sales analytics can help sales leaders identify and anticipate alignment issues and opportunities and can proactively suggest ways to keep alignments matched to changing market and company needs.

Looking for the Symptoms of Misalignment

Some simple signs of imperfections in territory alignments include:

- Wide variability in sales results across people in similar roles
- Wide variability across territories in the number of customers and prospects
- Salespeople who exhibit poor selling skills consistently delivering above-average sales results
- Some salespeople traveling so much that they get paid more through travel reimbursement than through the incentive program
- Consistently high turnover among newly recruited salespeople when those people are assigned "starter" territories

Sales forces that diagnose alignments regularly and make ongoing adjustments require major realignments less frequently.

Anticipating Future Sales Force Needs

Major events affecting the sales force can create a need for territory realignment. By anticipating upcoming events, sales organizations can capitalize on opportunities to realign territories for enhanced effectiveness.

Establishing a Yearly Planning Process

By performing an annual audit of the territory alignment, a sales organization can identify opportunities early and detect problems before they become serious.

Improving Performance in Rural Territories Through Realignment

A business services outsourcing company sold successfully to businesses in metropolitan areas, but in rural areas, its revenues were disproportionately low relative to the opportunity. The analysis shown in Figure 5-5 suggested that poor alignment contributed to low market share and high salesperson turnover in rural territories.

Metric	50 Urban Territories*	50 Rural Territories*
Target prospects (#)	140	250
Opportunity per prospect	$60,000	$50,000
Opportunity per territory	$8.4 million	$12.5 million
Sales contacts per prospect	4.0	2.8
Sales per territory	$1,100,000	$1,150,000
Market share	12.2%	8.8%
Incidental travel expenses (annual)	$9,680	$21,700

*Territory average.

Figure 5-5. Key metrics of urban versus rural territories at a business services outsourcing company

Rural territories had more opportunity than urban territories, but rural salespeople converted opportunity at a lower rate. Salespeople in rural territories also had higher travel expenses and made fewer contacts per prospect. Sales leaders concluded that salespeople in rural territories were stretched beyond their capacity. They reduced the size of many rural territories by assigning some prospects to new field salespeople or to inside sales. This led to increased market share, reduced travel costs, and improved sales force retention.

Supporting a New Product Launch Through Territory Redeployment

To launch a significant new product line, salespeople at one company would need to shift their efforts away from older product lines. This shift affected the distribution of workload and potential across territories. Potential for selling the older product lines was stronger in the Northeast, Midwest, and Southeast regions, while potential for the newer line was stronger in the South and West. Thus to match sales effort with potential for the revised product portfolio, the company would need to redeploy regional sales head count, as shown in Figure 5-6. Conducting the analysis several months before the new product launch allowed the sales force to begin managing attrition so that head count could be redeployed without costly relocations or layoffs.

Figure 5-6. The recommended redeployment of sales head count for a new product launch at one company

Optimizing Current and Future Coverage with an Annual Alignment Audit

Every year in May, sales analysts at a healthcare company lead a project called "Sales Strategy Review." The review includes an assessment of salespeople's account workload for the company's current product portfolio, along with an assessment of how that workload will likely change as the product portfolio evolves over the next three years. The analysts work with the sales force to implement territory alignment changes that optimize coverage for the current year, with an eye toward additional changes that will likely be required down the road.

Designing New Alignments as Sales Strategy Changes

When events or major changes necessitate a full-scale redesign of the territory alignment, sales analytics are a key source of value for the sales and marketing organization. By managing the territory redesign and implementation process, a sales analytics function helps ensure that the alignment is done right and that disruption to customer relationships is managed carefully.

With alignment objectives, metrics, and ground rules in place, the sales analytics function can help a company design and implement a major alignment through two main steps:

- Creating draft territories that reinforce sales strategy

- Engaging the sales force in refining the territories to create commitment

Creating Draft Territories That Reinforce Sales Strategy

There are many viable, reasonable alignments for any sales force. In fact, from a mathematical perspective, there are trillions of ways to assign 20 accounts to just five territories. Territory design and optimization software, which has been developed and improved over the last 40 years, greatly accelerates the process of finding a good territory alignment, while allowing easy comparison across alternatives. Sales analytics provide alignment data and tools to create an "optimal" draft territory alignment. This draft alignment acts as a benchmark for comparing all subsequent territory alignment adjustments.

Engaging the Sales Force in Refining the Territories to Create Commitment

Draft territories, no matter the quality of construction, are rarely the best territories for the sales force. Members of the sales or service organization will always recommend adjustments. The "feet on the street" may have better information about local nuances than headquarters does. For example, managers can adjust account workload and potential estimates based on direct knowledge of the opportunity at hand or the effort and travel required to service specific accounts. Managers understand decision-making influences within accounts and know the strength of the relationships that their salespeople have with buyers.

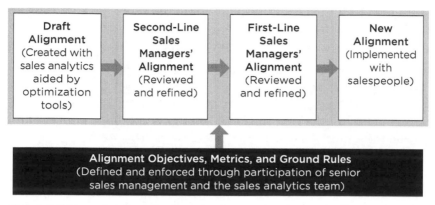

Figure 5-7. Engaging the sales force in alignment review and refinement

Field review and refinement of a draft alignment has an added benefit: it helps create sales force buy-in to territory alignment changes. When sales managers have the opportunity to review and refine territories for their direct reports, they feel more in control of alignment decisions. Their participation enhances ownership of the alignment and enables them to explain the rationale for alignment changes to their salespeople.

The best organizations implement major realignments by employing a cascading territory alignment "rollout." Figure 5-7 shows a process through which field sales managers can review and refine draft territories for their direct reports.

Participants from senior sales management, sales analytics, and other functions with a stake in the outcome also take part in these rollout sessions. The sessions are guided by a set of predefined "ground rules" and are best served by an atmosphere of openness and experimentation. Ultimately, the first-line sales managers make the final decisions, subject to an approval process. The sessions leverage mapping technology (an example is provided in Figure 5-8) and can be conducted either in person or using web-enabled technology.

Supporting Ongoing Alignment Processes

Neither the accounts that comprise territories nor the people who are assigned to the territories remain static. Alignments are always changing; the first change requests are likely to be generated the day after a new

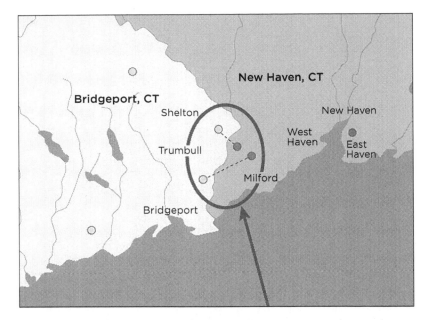

During a territory rollout session, a sales manager identified four accounts that were managed by a single ownership group in New Haven. The manager assigned all of these accounts to the New Haven salesperson. Customer coverage improved with minimal impact to territory fairness, illustrating the benefits of the rollout process.

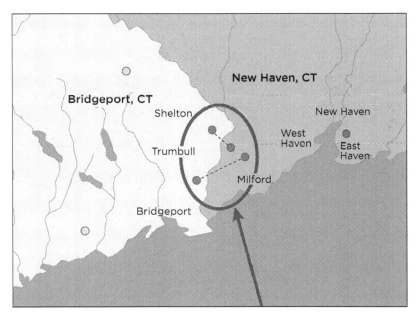

Figure 5-8. Mapping technologies for enabling territory alignment review sessions

alignment is deployed. An alignment that goes unchecked, where salespeople and managers make changes without oversight, runs the risk of quickly becoming out of sync with market needs—within as little as one year.

When it comes time for alignment maintenance, the sales analytics function is often the last one left at the party. It is uniquely positioned to oversee an operational process that accomplishes the following tasks:

> *A well-operated alignment maintenance process keeps alignments in tune with changing market needs while reducing sales force support costs.*

- Capture and manage alignment change requests from the sales force.

- Evaluate whether change requests are consistent with alignment objectives, such as the appropriate distribution of workload and potential.

- Implement small changes with limited delay.

- Document alignment changes in an alignment management system and implement changes in downstream systems (such as incentive compensation and sales reporting).

Ultimately, much of the value of territory alignment depends on its ongoing maintenance. Sales forces in dynamic markets or with sales or service teams that experience high turnover have the most to gain from an effective alignment management program.

Supporting Coordinated Alignments

In coordinated or mirrored alignments, sales territories for two or more types of sales specialists are geographically in sync with one another. For example, one technology company's sales force and telephone service organization have territories that overlay one another in a four-to-one ratio. Each telephone service rep provides support for all the customers covered by four salespeople, allowing each salesperson to coordinate with just one service rep and each service rep to coordinate with just four salespeople. This encourages teamwork between the sales and service organizations and provides salespeople with greater awareness of customer support issues so they can manage customer expectations better. It also provides customers with a more coordinated sales and service effort.

Supporting maintenance of a coordinated alignment is complicated. There is less flexibility to realign territories because a change proposed by a single salesperson or manager affects all layers of the overlay. More people need to be involved in evaluating and approving changes, inhibiting the ability to keep alignments in tune with market needs. Well-defined processes for handling changes, as well as alignment tools that can handle the complexity of coordinated alignments, enable effective and efficient support.

Supporting Alignment When the Customer Base Changes Often

At an office supply company, a dispatcher controls the ongoing assignment of new accounts to salespeople. Every time the inside sales team qualifies a new lead, the dispatcher decides which salesperson has the right skills, is in the right location, and has enough time to follow up on the opportunity. The dispatcher considers the needs and potential of the new account and strives to make an assignment that results in the best overall company outcome. The dispatcher also considers the impact on salespeople. Because salespeople are paid on commission, new accounts increase their earnings opportunity. It's important to keep top producers happy by providing them with new opportunities, but at the same time, not to overload them with so much work that their repeat business suffers. New salespeople also need opportunities that give them experience and the chance to succeed. The dispatcher uses tools and data that help him accomplish the objectives listed in Figure 5-9 when assigning accounts.

Objective	Data Required
Assign each new account to a salesperson well qualified to meet the account's needs.	• Mapped location of the account and nearby salespeople • Assessment of account needs and opportunity from the inside sales team • Assessment of salespeople's skill and experience level
Ensure that the needs of other customers are not neglected.	• An estimate of the current account workload assigned to each salesperson
Ensure that all salespeople have a fair opportunity to succeed.	• An estimate of the current sales opportunity assigned to each salesperson

Figure 5-9. Alignment objectives and data requirements at an office supply company

The right information and tools help the dispatcher balance the needs of the company, its customers, and its salespeople.

> ### Improving Alignment Maintenance Drives Cost Savings
>
> Instead of allowing sales managers to submit territory alignment change requests through email and phone communications, a large pharmaceutical company uses a web-based alignment maintenance system. Sales managers can review alignments and submit changes by a deadline before each new selling cycle. The system provides maps and feedback on key metrics (such as territory workload and potential) and lets managers know when their requested changes violate established alignment business rules. After first-line managers submit change requests, second-line managers review and approve those requests, making sure the changes are in the best interests of customers and the company. The system efficiently informs teams in information technology, sales automation, incentive compensation, and sales reporting about changes to keep all sales systems in sync. And it eliminates errors and delays in communicating alignment changes.

Conclusion

Analytics play an important role in helping sales organizations diagnose, design, and support territory alignments that enhance sales productivity and drive sales results. Analytics can ensure that the right objectives, metrics, and ground rules are in place for creating and maintaining the best possible alignments. By building and constantly improving alignment capabilities (including alignment experts, processes, systems, and tools), companies enable quick and effective response to alignment needs, including:

- Diagnosing alignment quality to identify opportunities to improve sales effectiveness and efficiency as markets and company strategies evolve

- Designing new alignments when markets or strategies change, using processes, supported by data and tools, to create territories that achieve business objectives while ensuring sales force commitment

- Supporting the sales organization in responding to ongoing customer or sales personnel changes by using processes and tools for efficiently implementing territory adjustments while maintaining alignment quality

Sales analytics add value to territory alignment decisions across the full support-diagnose-design spectrum. Yet often, the biggest opportunity for analytics comes in providing excellent *support* to ensure that territories stay continually aligned with market needs.

CHAPTER 6

Shaping the People in the Sales Force

Most sales forces have a huge opportunity to use analytics to diagnose talent management effectiveness and to improve approaches for acquiring, developing, and retaining their people.

By Tobi Laczkowski

Tobi Laczkowski is an associate principal in ZS Associates' Evanston, Illinois, office and was previously based in the firm's Zurich, Switzerland, location. For more than 10 years, he has worked with clients primarily in the medical products and services industry, helping them improve their sales force effectiveness, go-to-market strategy, organizational design, and talent management. Tobi has an MBA from Northwestern University's Kellogg School of Management and also a BS in chemical engineering from Northwestern University.

The author thanks former ZS principal Angela Bakker-Lee for her contributions to this chapter.

The Case for Using Analytics to Shape the Sales Force

In a sales organization, people are unquestionably the company's most important asset. That's why it's critical to shape the sales force by acquiring, developing, and retaining the best talent.

Many organizations have overlooked the opportunity for sales analytics to contribute to shaping sales force talent. Working closely with the sales force and the Human Resources (HR) department, the analytics function can play a critical role in improving the management of sales talent. In most organizations, HR focuses largely on supporting talent management. A big opportunity for sales analytics comes in *diagnosing* the effectiveness of talent management and discovering insights for *designing* better processes, programs, and systems.

This chapter shows how sales analytics can help shape the sales force across the stages of the talent management funnel, which are shown in Figure 6-1.

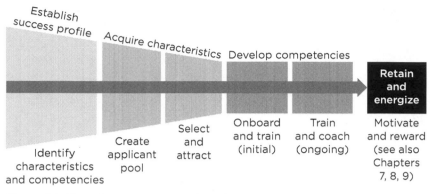

Figure 6-1. The talent management funnel

Establishing a Success Profile

Sales analytics can help with creating and sustaining a sales success profile that guides talent management and ensures that the sales team has the right characteristics and competencies.

What Is a Success Profile?

A success profile starts with the job requirements for a specific sales role and defines the *characteristics* (personal qualities) and *competencies* (skills and knowledge) that are needed for individuals to be successful in that role. A good success profile distinguishes characteristics from competencies. Job *competencies* can be learned and developed, but an individual will only be successful if the right personal *characteristics* for the job are inherent in the candidate's personality, character, and aptitude. Here are some characteristics and competencies included in one sales job success profile:

Sample Characteristics for a Sales Job:

- Motivated to succeed
- Empathetic
- Resilient

Sample Competencies for a Sales Job:

- Understanding customer needs and decision processes
- Call planning and preparation with consistent follow-up

- Adapting the message for each customer and focusing on customer value
- Enlisting the help of other company experts in meeting customer needs

To get the right characteristics, it's necessary to hire the right people. Then it's possible to develop and nurture the required competencies by providing developmental programs that train, mentor, coach, support, manage, and motivate around those competencies.

Bruce Nordstrom, former chairman of the department store known for its impeccable service, once described the importance of distinguishing between characteristics and competencies when hiring salespeople: "We can hire nice people and teach them to sell, but we can't hire salespeople and teach them to be nice."

Sales analytics can help support, diagnose, and design the sales force success profile.

Supporting the Profile

The sales analytics function can partner with HR to support the sales success profile by:

- Ensuring that recruiting, training, performance management, and other sales force programs stay aligned with the profile
- Ensuring that any changes to the profile are communicated effectively to the sales force
- Monitoring ongoing market and company changes and watching for events that could trigger a potential redesign of the profile

Diagnosing and Designing the Profile

Analytics can help a sales force identify which attributes (characteristics and competencies) belong in the sales success profile. Perhaps the best source of information about success attributes, and one that is too frequently overlooked, comes from within a company's own sales force: its best salespeople. The challenge is to *identify* who the top-performing sales team members are and to *select* and *classify* the attributes that drive their success. Then it's possible to *align* hiring, development, and other programs accordingly. The three-step approach shown

> *The top-performing members of the sales team likely possess characteristics and competencies that belong in the success profile.*

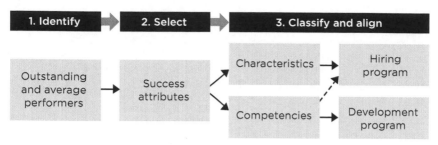

Figure 6-2. Three steps for discovering and leveraging the attributes of the best salespeople

in Figure 6-2 can help a company discover and leverage the attributes of its best salespeople.

Step 1: Identify. Start by identifying a group of outstanding performers and a group of average (not poor) performers for comparison. When identifying salespeople for these groups, go beyond performance rankings, competency model assessments, and sales manager input. Most sales leaders think that they know who their best performers are. Yet when they factor market opportunity into the equation using techniques such as performance frontier analysis, they sometimes discover that the success of a "star" salesperson is in fact driven largely by the environment (i.e., a good territory) and not necessarily by skill and effort.

Step 2: Select. Create a list of the attributes that enable sales success. Look at published lists from academics, consultants, and research-based recruiting and training organizations, and ask customers and company sales leaders, managers, and HR experts for input. Observe and gather data on the selected attributes for salespeople in the outstanding- and average-performance groups. Compare the results across the two groups to select the attributes that discriminate the best performers from the average performers.

Step 3: Classify and align. The list of discriminating attributes will likely include both characteristics (inherent traits such as high energy level and intellectual capability) and competencies (learned abilities such as selling skills and product knowledge). Classify each success attribute as either a characteristic or a competency, and then align the sales hiring and development programs accordingly. It's possible to hire for or develop competencies, but characteristics can only be acquired through hiring. The list of success attributes will depend on the sales role.

Performance Frontier Analysis for Identifying Top Performers

Performance frontier analysis uses historical territory-level data to isolate the impact of the salesperson on territory performance metrics such as sales, sales growth, and market share. The analysis accounts for territory differences that are outside the salesperson's control—such as territory market potential, starting customer base, or competitive intensity. The approach can include multiple dimensions of territory differences, but for simplicity, the example shown in Figure 6-3 is in two dimensions. Each dot represents a sales territory. Territory sales are determined in part by territory potential, which is measured, in this case, by a combination of account-level estimates provided by salespeople and business demographic data. The best-performing territories are those on the "performance frontier"—they have the highest sales relative to their potential. Many companies use a range to define the outstanding performer group. In this example, the 95th percentile and above is the performance frontier range.

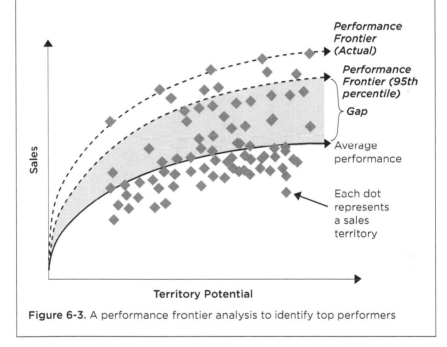

Figure 6-3. A performance frontier analysis to identify top performers

Sales analysts at a manufacturing company isolated success attributes of top performers by following these steps:

1. Analysts worked with sales leaders to identify a list of attributes believed to lead to sales success. The list included characteristics such as assertiveness, responsiveness, and versatility, and competencies such as call planning and territory knowledge. Salespeople were rated on these characteristics and competencies using a Myers-Briggs social style evaluation and sales manager input.

2. Sales success measures were gathered for each salesperson, such as sales, share, and quota achievement by product.

3. The analysts statistically examined the relationship between the attributes and the success measures across salespeople.

The success attributes that drove performance (sales and market share) varied by product. Salespeople with above-average assertiveness scores had more success selling a commodity product, while those with above-average territory knowledge and planning scores performed better on a now highly differentiated product. The results shown in Figure 6-4 helped the company hire the right people and develop the right competencies for selling each product.

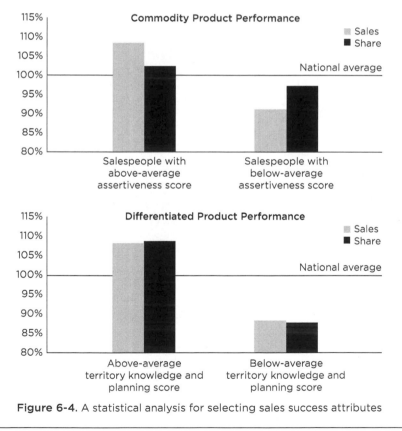

Figure 6-4. A statistical analysis for selecting sales success attributes

> **Novartis Leverages the Habits of Its Performance Frontier Salespeople**
>
> Global healthcare company Novartis has been a pioneer in using the performance frontier approach to identify top-performing salespeople, selecting their success attributes, and then aligning sales force hiring and development programs to create the needed characteristics and competencies. Working first with the U.S. sales force over a period of several years, Novartis identified a group of outstanding performers and selected a set of "success principles" that differentiated their performance. The company then aligned the sales process, sales hiring, development, and other programs around the success principles. The initiative led to a more favorable perception of the company's salespeople among customers and contributed to six consecutive years of double-digit top-line growth, well above the industry average. Based on its success in the United States, Novartis replicated the approach globally.

Acquiring Characteristics Through Recruiting

Although some sales leaders feel that their own experience and intuition make them good at identifying the best candidates for sales positions, experience and intuition alone are not enough to ensure consistently strong results when recruiting salespeople. The best companies use a purposeful selection process that includes the components shown in Figure 6-5.

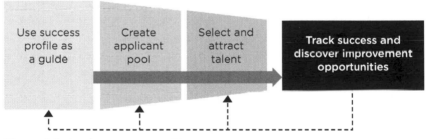

Figure 6-5. A salesperson recruiting process

Supporting the Recruiting Process

At most companies, HR provides support for sales force recruiting. Additional support from sales analytics can help ensure that the unique needs of the sales force are addressed. Support activities include:

- **Managing the applicant pool and recruiting channels.** There are many software options (broadly called *applicant tracking systems*) for streamlining the recruiting process and reducing the cost associated with tracking candidates.

- **Supporting sales force members in finding candidates.** Often the best candidates are *not* actively looking for a new job. By helping sales force members leverage referrals, for example by using tools such as LinkedIn, it's possible to identify many high-potential, passive candidates.

- **Providing behavioral interview questions.** Unstructured interviews often lead to poor hiring choices. Standardized screening criteria and structure for interviews, including questions that probe for examples of situations in which candidates have used the competencies identified in the success profile, dramatically increase the odds of selecting the right person for the job.

- **Testing candidates.** Testing can include online assessments and case study exams.

Diagnosing and Designing the Recruiting Process

A big opportunity for sales analytics is to diagnose what's working and what's not working with sales force recruiting and to use this insight to improve the design of the recruiting process.

Tracking the Recruiting Process to Reveal Opportunities

A company can track metrics such as those shown in Figure 6-6. By comparing to historical or industry benchmarks, companies gain insights into potential problems and opportunities for improving sales force recruiting.

Many companies collect these statistics, but those that analyze them in detail, track them over time, and use them to improve the hiring process can capitalize on a significant opportunity.

Analyzing the Backgrounds of the Best Sales Candidates

Using statistical modeling, the sales analytics group at a healthcare company analyzed five years of historical sales performance data and résumé data to determine what kind of prior job experience and educational background was most correlated with sales success. Analysis revealed that many successful salespeople came from nontraditional backgrounds, such as teaching, and had little or no experience in healthcare or life sciences. The company changed the criteria for screening candidates for the applicant pool, accelerating the rate at which it filled open positions during a major sales force expansion.

Statistic	Diagnosis
Number of applicants	If low or decreasing, possible explanations include a poor company image, low awareness of the position, and an unattractive job description.
Percentage getting an offer	If low or decreasing, possible explanations include poor prescreening of candidates and a low number of applicants.
Percentage accepting an offer	If low or decreasing, possible explanations include noncompetitive compensation and poor company or job image after interviewing.
Percentage retained 2+ years with good performance record	If low or decreasing, possible explanations include problems within the recruiting process and problems with programs for developing, motivating, and rewarding people. See "Diagnosing Talent Retention" later in this chapter.

Figure 6-6. Metrics for evaluating sales force recruiting

Using Analytics to Improve the Applicant Pool

Analysis can reveal opportunities to improve candidate screening by identifying the best sources of candidates for the applicant pool. Good sources provide many candidates who possess the characteristics identified in the success profile. Because it is difficult to assess characteristics at this early stage of the recruiting process when most information about a candidate comes from a résumé or job application, companies use screens to narrow down the pool of candidates to those whose backgrounds are most likely to suggest the presence of success characteristics.

Companies can break down key metrics by recruiting channel to learn more about which channels produce the best candidates. A useful template is shown in Figure 6-7.

Selecting Talent

To help with candidate selection, sales forces use many tools, including interviews, background checks, and assessment tests. Sales analytics can track and evaluate the effectiveness of different screening tools.

One company analyzed the validity of a psychological assessment test used for screening candidates for sales positions. The analysis shown in Figure 6-8 looked at current goal attainment of salespeople who had been

Candidate Source	Number of Applicants	Percentage Getting an Offer	Percentage Accepting an Offer	Percentage Retained 2+ Years with Good Performance
Campus Recruiting				
Employee Referrals				
Internal Placements				
Job Fairs				
Agencies				
Internet Postings				
Other Sources				
TOTAL				

Figure 6-7. A template for tracking recruiting metrics by channel

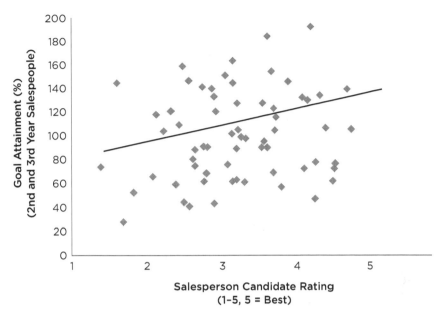

Figure 6-8. Analysis of psychological test validity for salesperson recruiting

with the company two to three years versus the assessment scores they had received as candidates for the job. Not all salespeople with high scores on the assessment test turned out to be strong performers. By studying the outliers, sales leaders identified characteristics that the test under- or over-emphasized. They worked with HR to determine whether to drop the test or to adjust it to improve applicant screening.

Developing Competencies Through Learning and Development

Sales analytics can support, diagnose, and design training, coaching, and other learning and development programs to help salespeople acquire and continuously improve key competencies.

Supporting Learning and Development

Many companies have a sales training group or a team within HR that supports sales force learning and development. Additional support from sales analytics can help ensure that the unique needs of the sales force are addressed. Support activities can include:

- **Delivering and tracking sales force learning and development programs.** Aided by software-based learning management systems, companies can provide and administer online training in many forms to deliver learning when and where it is needed while greatly reducing the need for personnel to travel.

- **Conducting in-person learning sessions.** In-person sessions are particularly effective when part of the objective is to bond with peers, develop social networks, and cultivate a common culture.

- **Supporting sales managers' coaching.** This involves providing data, tools, and analytics that enable sales managers to help their people.

Diagnosing and Designing Learning and Development Programs

Sales analytics can contribute to the diagnosis and design of sales force learning and development programs that:

- Help new talent get on board successfully
- Allow existing talent to continually learn and grow

Analytic Support Enhances Sales Manager Coaching at Oakwood

Temporary housing provider Oakwood uses a prescribed coaching process called Oakwood Associate Review (OAR). The process is based around a four-part strategy: plan, coach, execute, and win. Sales managers sit down with their people and engage in a dialogue structured around a dashboard of key metrics. The metrics reflect results (for example, sales versus quotas and top 10 wins or losses), potential (for example, number of prospects in the pipeline and top 10 active opportunities), and activity measures. Guided by the metrics, managers and salespeople can discuss what happened and understand cause and effect. Managers get guidance on how to have the most productive discussion, and they have an annual performance objective for the amount of coaching they should do. The entire organization is embedded in the OAR process. Surveys indicate that salespeople get significantly more coaching by way of OAR than at other companies surveyed, and they want even *more*. Customers say they have observed a positive difference as a result of OAR.

On-boarding and Coaching New Talent

Diagnosis focusing on the effectiveness of sales force on-boarding and coaching of new salespeople can reveal improvement opportunities. For example, a manufacturing company tracked territory performance data to understand how quickly different segments of new salespeople became effective and why. The analysis revealed that the quality of a new salesperson's first-line manager (FLM) had the biggest impact on how quickly a salesperson's performance improved. Salespeople reporting to top-performing FLMs performed much better in their first 20 months on the job compared to salespeople working with average-performing FLMs. The analysis is summarized in Figure 6-9. Top-performing managers did two things that contributed to the performance difference:

1. They did more field coaching during the on-boarding period.
2. They arranged for and encouraged mentorship from other team members.

Based on these findings, the company set new coaching expectations for FLMs and implemented a tracking system to ensure accountability.

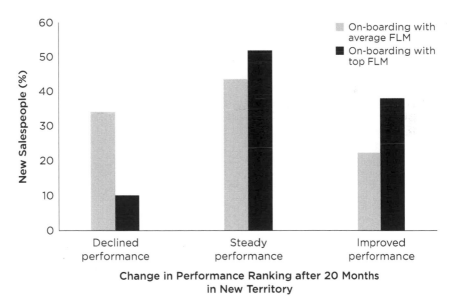

Change in Performance Ranking after 20 Months in New Territory

Figure 6-9. The impact of FLM quality on the performance of new salespeople

Ongoing Training and Development of Talent

Diagnosis can help identify training and development priorities for existing sales force talent. For example, leaders at one company wanted to prioritize training and development needs for first-line sales managers so they could focus limited training time on the highest-impact topics. A team gathered performance assessments on critical competencies for all managers. They used input from competency model ratings, sales leaders, each manager's direct reports and peers, and manager self-evaluations. The team also gathered input on the importance of each competency to the business from company leaders and external experts. The team created the matrix shown in Figure 6-10 to see a snapshot of current performance across FLMs and the importance of each competency to business success. The snapshot revealed gaps in competency levels versus expectations and helped leaders define a new training curriculum.

Measuring Training Impact

Training impact is hard to measure. Sales analytics can measure training impact at four levels using the four types of measures shown in Figure 6-11.

Leaders are especially interested in results measures, particularly sales and profit increases due to training. But it's hard to disentangle the variables that have an effect on results in order to isolate the impact of training. Training only has lasting impact on results when it is continuously reinforced by other sales force effectiveness (SFE) drivers.

Alignment of SFE Drivers Reinforces Training at Novartis

The principles taught in a performance frontier selling skills training program at Novartis were reinforced with changes to many sales force programs, including the sales competency model, coaching expectations and tools, and performance management. The changes had impact on sales performance, but it was impossible to isolate the impact of the training alone.

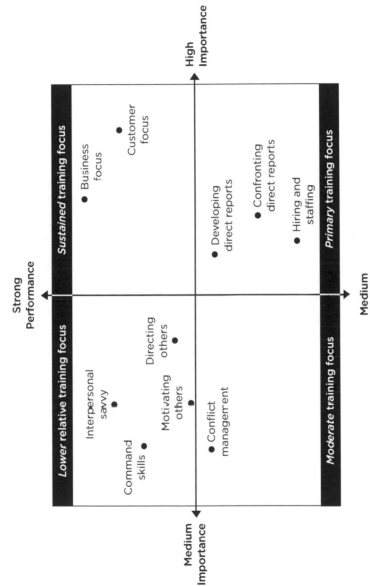

Figure 6-10. A matrix for prioritizing FLM training needs

115

	Cognitive Effect	Attitudinal Effect	Behavioral Effect	Results
What to ask	• What do learners know?	• How do learners feel?	• What do learners do?	• How do learner changes affect the organization?
What to measure	• Knowledge of course content	• Perceptions of training • Organizational climate	• Skills • Job performance • Absenteeism • Turnover	• Job satisfaction • Customer satisfaction • Sales, profits, and ROI
How to measure	• Exams • Self-assessments • Interviews	• Course and instructor evaluations • Surveys • Interviews	• Observation • Managerial assessments • Self-assessments	• Surveys • Experiments • Managerial judgment
When to measure	• At completion of training and at points in the future	• At completion of training	• Over the first year	• After a year

Figure 6-11. Measures of training effectiveness

Source: Based on research from Donald Kirkpatrick, *Evaluating Training Programs: The Four Levels*, 2nd ed. (San Francisco: Berrett-Koehler Publishers, Inc., 1998).

Diagnosing Talent Retention

By diagnosing who is leaving and why, sales analytics can help leaders improve sales force retention.

Measuring Turnover Costs

Sales force turnover creates many costs, both direct and indirect. Sales analytics can measure these costs and help identify ways to reduce them.

Direct sales force turnover costs include:

• Termination and severance

• Recruiting

• On-boarding and training of new salespeople

Indirect sales force turnover costs include sales erosion due to:

• Departing salespeople "checking out"

• Territory vacancies

• Ramp-up time for new salespeople

Usually, the direct and indirect costs of losing a good salesperson are multiples of that person's annual compensation.

Measuring Turnover Dynamics

Sales analytics can measure different types of turnover.

Systemic Versus Controllable Turnover

Sales force turnover rates vary by industry, but a certain amount of *systemic* turnover is part of every industry's selling model. Even at the best companies, some employees will find better opportunities elsewhere or will experience life events that require them to switch jobs. Leaders can reduce *controllable* turnover that results from hiring errors or from salespeople feeling dissatisfied with the company, the people they work with, the job they do, the success they achieve, or the rewards they receive.

Sales analytics can track sales force turnover and compare it annually against the company's historical norms or industry averages. Insight about which portion of turnover is systemic comes from looking at turnover among the best companies in the industry (or in industries with similar selling models). External surveys for benchmarking sales force turnover data are available in many industries.

Desirable Versus Undesirable Turnover

Turnover statistics only become useful when they are linked to salespeople's current performance and future potential. It's desirable that low-performing salespeople with little potential for future success leave the company.

One company developed insights about turnover by looking at reasons for departure (obtained through exit interviews and surveys) and comparing reasons cited by the group of salespeople in the upper half of performance ratings with those for the group in the lower half. The analysis in Figure 6-12 shows that many performers in the lower half cited inadequate pay or recognition as the primary reason for their departure, suggesting that perhaps the current pay and recognition programs *were* having the desired effect. Leaders focused their attention on improving advancement opportunities and respectful treatment—the stated reasons for the departure of many performers in the upper half.

> *Turnover is undesirable only when strong or high-potential performers leave.*

Primary Reason for Departure	% of Sales Force	% of Salespeople in Upper Half of Ratings	% of Salespeople in Lower Half of Ratings
Respectful treatment	23	52	48
Recognition	21	26	74
Pay	20	27	73
Advancement opportunities	13	70	30
Interesting and challenging work	10	45	55
Quality of life	9	40	60
Other	4	50	50
Overall	100	42	58

Figure 6-12. Reasons for the departure of salespeople in one sales force

Future Potential of Departing Salespeople	**High**	**Enable success with:** • Training and development • Coaching • Information support • Warm leads that build confidence	**Motivate with:** • Autonomy • Appreciation • Recognition • Pay and incentives • Inclusion on a company task force
	Low	**Improve quality of talent by:** • Improving applicant pool • Enhancing candidate selection and attraction • Counseling poor performers into roles that allow them to succeed	**Manage carefully:** These salespeople may hit the ceiling soon
		Low	High

Current Performance of Departing Salespeople

Figure 6-13. Ways to address a sales force turnover problem

Insights about desirable and undesirable turnover can come from categorizing turnover statistics according to salespeople's current performance and future potential. Measures of current performance can include traditional results metrics (e.g., sales and goal attainment) and metrics derived using data analysis (e.g., performance frontier). Measures of salespeople's future potential can come from managers' assessments of salespeople through the performance management process. By segmenting salespeople who depart into four performance groups, companies can use the framework shown in Figure 6-13 to discover the best way to address a turnover problem.

Finding Ways to Reduce Undesirable Turnover

Diagnosis can reveal the underlying causes of undesirable sales force turnover and point to possible solutions. For example, an insurance company paid salespeople entirely on commission and allowed salespeople to keep their accounts permanently after making an initial sale. Over 60 percent of new salespeople left the company before completing their first year of employment. While the market was growing, leaders tolerated this high level of turnover as a cost of doing business. The company recruited thousands of new salespeople every year, knowing that those who discovered they were unsuited to the job would leave quickly. But as the insurance market became saturated, there was less opportunity to make a good living, and too many salespeople with long-term potential were leaving. The company was squandering its recruiting and training investments because too few employees stayed long enough to produce results.

To help understand and solve the problem, the sales analytics group produced the diagnostic analysis shown in Figure 6-14. Sales force retention was closely related to employees' first-year sales production. Salespeople who were successful early in their tenure tended to stay. Less than 30 percent of the salespeople who sold under $50,000 in their first 12 months were still with the company at the end of the year. Of the salespeople who sold more than $150,000 in the first year, 97 percent stayed with the company for a year, and 80 percent remained past three years.

This insight uncovered a path forward. The company launched a strategy to boost newly hired salespeople who had the potential to succeed. Sales managers were asked to give these salespeople a few existing customer accounts with good growth potential. The company also improved its training and coaching of new salespeople. These initiatives helped new salespeople get off to a faster start, thereby increasing retention and lowering the recruiting burden. In addition, the company developed a more targeted hiring profile for screening candidates during the recruiting process, thus

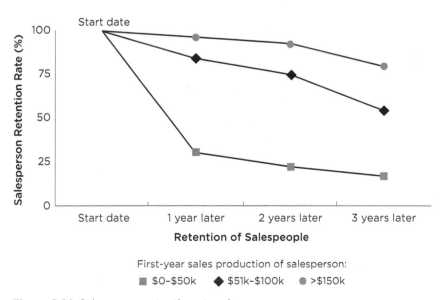

Figure 6-14. Salesperson retention at an insurance company

improving the quality of new recruits and reducing the number of low performers without potential who were hired in the first place.

Two years later, turnover had dropped to below the industry average. The original diagnostic analysis became part of a holistic quarterly human talent review conducted in partnership with HR. These continual health checks helped company leaders diagnose problems early so they could take timely action.

Conclusion

Most sales forces overlook the opportunity to use sales analytics to help shape sales force talent. In many organizations, HR focuses largely on *supporting* talent management. This leaves a big opportunity for sales analytics to add value by *diagnosing* the effectiveness of talent management and discovering insights for *designing* better processes, programs, and systems for acquiring, developing, and retaining sales talent.

By using analytics to guide the management of sales force talent, companies are increasing the retention of strong performers, energizing their sales teams, and ultimately driving positive financial results.

CHAPTER 7

Compensating the Sales Force and Paying for Performance

Analytics help companies diagnose sales compensation plan performance and design plans that lead to the best possible results despite an uncertain future.

Chad Albrecht

 **Chad Albrecht** is a principal in ZS Associates' Evanston, Illinois, office, where he leads the firm's B2B Sales Compensation practice. He is a Certified Sales Compensation Professional (CSCP) with more than 15 years of consulting experience. Chad has helped clients in the software, business services, medical devices, telecom, distribution, and manufacturing industries implement motivational incentive plans and set fair and challenging sales goals. He has an MBA from the University of Michigan and is a graduate of the University of Iowa.

The author thanks former ZS associates Jonathan Ezer and Steve Herz for their contributions to this chapter.

Sales Compensation: A Key Sales Force Effectiveness Driver

Few programs get as much scrutiny and blame when something goes awry in the sales force as the sales incentive compensation (IC) program.

- People are leaving? *Must not be paid enough.*
- Product launch failed? *Didn't incentivize it correctly.*
- Missing quota but paying a lot of incentives? *The plan is easily "gamed."*

No matter what ails the sales force, the IC plan is often on the short list for potential fixes. And the sales analytics function is often front and center when it comes to owning and fixing the sales compensation program.

In addition to helping the company attract and retain sales talent, the sales compensation plan is a key driver of sales force behavior. Often, the IC plan provides the clearest guidance to salespeople about what is important, how hard to work, and what to sell to whom.

> **Observations About Sales Incentive Compensation in the United States**
>
> • The average ratio of salary to incentive pay in sales forces has remained relatively constant at 60:40 since 2000.
>
> • In some industries (for example, high-tech, medical devices, financial services, and distribution) more than 50 percent of sales force pay is incentive compensation.
>
> • Many companies spend more on sales incentives than on advertising.

But if management chooses the wrong IC plan type or metric, or implements the plan poorly, an IC plan can lead to unintended—even disastrous—consequences.

Given the magnitude of the investment and the downside of getting it wrong, sales leaders must know how the IC plan is working (or not working) and whether it is really driving desired sales force behavior and performance. Although many companies spend more on their sales incentive plan than on advertising, those same companies sometimes give the effectiveness of their advertising far more scrutiny. Sales analytics can help bring a rigorous approach to managing a sales compensation program that accomplishes the four objectives shown in Figure 7-1. This leads to benefits that flow directly to the company's bottom line.

Without a rigorous analytic approach, the probability of creating an effective sales compensation program approaches zero.

An IC plan that accomplishes these objectives leads to the following benefits:

- **Happier salespeople**—a more motivated sales force with less turnover.

- **"Right" sales effort**—activity focused on the right products at the right price for the right customers.

- **Better results**—more likely achievement of the company's financial goals.

When it comes to sales compensation, the objectives are straightforward, the benefits are high, and the cost of not executing well is great. So why, then, do sales organizations consistently complain about the state of their

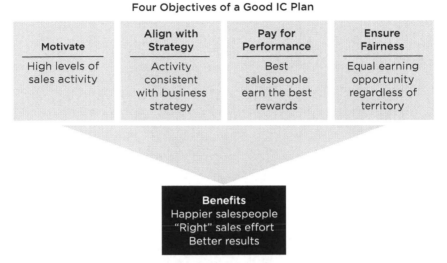

Figure 7-1. The four objectives of a good IC plan

IC programs? The answer, in short, is that the dynamics underlying sales compensation decisions are universally complex. Salespeople have diverse capabilities and motivations, and their behaviors are uncertain. And implementing an effective sales compensation program involves difficult technical and administrative requirements.

Analytics can bring excellence to the sales compensation program through support, diagnosis, and design, as shown in Figure 7-2.

Support	Diagnose	Design
• Timely, accurate IC payments • Actionable information for sales force and other stakeholders	• Tracking to ensure a plan achieves desired objectives • Early indicators of future issues	• Analytics for creating a good plan • Anticipate unintended consequences of a plan

Figure 7-2. The impact of sales analytics on sales incentive compensation

Providing Accurate and Timely IC Support

Too often, the quality of the systems and processes that support IC plans is highly variable. Good IC support ensures:

- Accurate and timely calculation of IC plan results
- No delay in getting payments to the sales force and information to key stakeholders
- Error-free and efficient administration, leading to reduced costs and increased sales force trust in the IC plan

Support provides key stakeholders with dashboards and reports that answer several questions, such as those listed in Figure 7-3.

Audience	Typical Questions
Field (salespeople and sales managers)	• What are my sales, goal attainment, and payout? • Exactly how were my results calculated? • What will happen if I continue along the current trend? • How does my performance compare to that of my peers?
Sales analytics and information technology leadership	• Are we getting payments and reports out on time? • How many mistakes are we making? What is the cause of errors? Where and how are we finding them? • How efficiently are we utilizing resources? Where can we improve?
Executive and senior sales leadership	• Are we on track to achieve our short-term financial goals? • How is performance trending over time, and should we make changes now for long-term success? • Is our pay level competitive, enabling us to retain good salespeople?
Finance and accounting	• How do the results affect the budget? Exactly where do variances arise? How can we mitigate fiscal risk? • How do payout results affect cash flow and accruals? • Is the sales force exploiting loopholes?

Figure 7-3. Sample questions that IC support can address

Supporting the Field (Salespeople and Sales Managers)

For a sales IC plan to be effective, the company must communicate certain information regularly to the field, including the metrics upon which salespeople are measured and the payouts associated with those metrics. Less obvious is the mistake of providing too much information to salespeople. Too often, an analytically focused team at headquarters overengineers dashboards in an attempt to provide additional insights to the field "just in case." The result is information overload for salespeople, leading to a lack of

> *The best dashboards provide the specific information salespeople need to make their decisions — and nothing more.*

focus on key metrics. The best dashboards enable salespeople to focus on the key metrics within their control that align with company goals.

Supporting Information Technology/ Sales Analytics Leadership

The right operational and administrative metrics not only help reduce the compensation cost of sales, but also provide a framework for improving the quality and efficiency of sales operations. Metrics for tracking operations include:

- **Process metrics:** cycle time (from data receipt to dashboard distribution), issue resolution time, timeliness of output distribution

- **Quality metrics:** number of errors, number of reruns

- **Resource utilization metrics:** head count, hours logged, administrative costs

---

The Danger of Internal Spreadsheets

Although most sales organizations administer their sales IC plans with spreadsheets, there are dangers in using spreadsheets to extract data, perform calculations, look up rates, and determine payout amounts. Those dangers include:

- Poor documentation of calculations and business rules, risking Sarbanes-Oxley (SOX) noncompliance (U.S.-based businesses)

- Higher likelihood of calculation errors (The technology research firm Gartner estimates 3 to 8 percent more errors.)

- Higher administrative costs due to inefficient operations

Although the up-front, out-of-pocket expenses are lowest with a spreadsheet-based solution, consider the long-term implications of these dangers. Often, a custom in-house, off-the-shelf, or outsourced solution is better. Only very small sales forces with simple needs should consider spreadsheet solutions.

The most sophisticated operational reporting systems are automated, comprehensive, and oriented toward uncovering the root cause of issues. Even a basic set of core metrics—such as cycle time, error rate, and hours logged—can provide information for improving IC administration.

Supporting Executive and Senior Sales Leadership

Sales analytics help leaders understand the health and impact of the IC plan. Although the plan is designed before the start of the fiscal year, with certain objectives in mind, actual results can deviate for any number of reasons: unachievable forecasts, unfair quotas, or salespeople finding ways to "game" the plan. By monitoring metrics regularly, leaders can track plan results, ensure the plan is not going awry, and, if needed, make mid-period corrections. Metrics for helping sales leaders monitor the IC plan include:

- Percentage of salespeople making quota
- Percentage of salespeople earning no incentive
- Percentage of salespeople earning 2X their target incentive
- Ratio of 90th percentile payout to median and target ("excellence ratio")
- Percentage of incentive paid by product or customer group
- National percentage of forecast achieved
- Individual payout trends over time

The diagnostic analyses described in the next section, when performed regularly, can also support leaders in monitoring ongoing IC plan health.

Supporting Finance and Accounting

In some companies, the finance and accounting functions have requirements separate from those of executive and sales leadership, creating the need for additional metrics. Metrics for helping finance and accounting monitor IC include:

- Accruals, restatements, and adjustments
- Compensation cost by product
- Percentage of national compensation budget spent

Diagnosing Performance to Keep the IC Plan on Track

Sales analytics can do more than simply provide outputs to support internal partners; analytics can also diagnose IC plan performance to reveal potential problems and opportunities. Diagnosis involves conducting tests regularly and monitoring performance on key metrics against defined target zones. Ongoing diagnosis of IC plan health is an unrealized opportunity for most sales forces. Tests using available data and easy-to-do analytics can have high impact on sales effectiveness.

Conducting Regular Diagnostic Tests

Tests for diagnosing IC plan performance can address four questions.

- Does the IC plan motivate?
- Does the IC plan pay for performance?
- Is the IC plan aligned with sales and corporate strategy?
- Is the IC plan fair?

Does the IC Plan Motivate?

IC plans should motivate salespeople to perform a difficult job, but a plan that merely gets salespeople in front of customers is not enough. A good IC plan motivates salespeople to sell the right products and services, to the right customers, at the right price, and it rewards those who follow the path to success. It delivers the most rewards to the salespeople who exert the most successful effort in support of sales objectives. A good plan keeps salespeople engaged, even if they fall short of their goals.

Usually, companies set objectives for the desired distribution of incentive pay—for example, how many salespeople should earn the target pay level, how many should earn twice the target level, and how many should earn no incentive pay. One way to tell whether an IC plan is motivational in the right ways is to compare the actual distribution of performance across salespeople to the distribution that sales leaders expected when they created the plan.

The top chart in Figure 7-4 shows the quota attainment distribution that sales leaders at one company expected going into the year. The bottom chart shows what actually happened. Fewer salespeople than expected

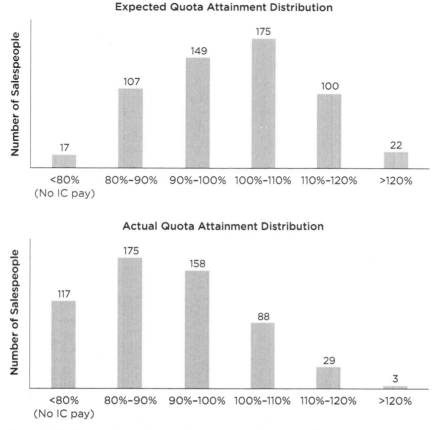

Figure 7-4. Comparison of expected and actual quota performance

achieved their quota, and more than expected were below the 80 percent threshold for earning incentives. This suggests that the national forecast may have been too high to motivate the sales force.

It's valuable to conduct this type of analysis partway into an incentive period. For example, at the end of the first quarter, it's possible to project a year-end distribution based on the current sales trend. Then leaders can proactively make adjustments if needed. For example, if the projected distribution looks like the bottom chart in Figure 7-4, leaders can adjust the payout threshold down. This allows the plan to continue to motivate despite an overly aggressive forecast and ensures that only a handful of the lowest performers are penalized with no incentive pay, as intended. Whether the plan should have been designed to be so aggressive in the first place is another issue entirely.

Sales analytics can monitor performance distributions and key metrics (for example, the percentage earning no incentive). Ongoing and timely feedback allows leaders to proactively implement plan adjustments throughout the year as needed to stay aligned with the goals of the organization and the reality of the business.

Does the IC Plan Pay for Performance?

The concept of pay for performance is straightforward in theory: find the right metric (for example, territory sales or profits), set challenging and fair objectives for salespeople's performance on that metric, and pay the most to salespeople who meet or exceed objectives by the widest margin, and pay the least to those who fall short the farthest. But the next question, "How much more (or less)?" is not easy to answer. The "excellence ratio" (incentives earned by the top 10 percent of performers compared to those earned by the median) is a metric to track and evaluate against best practice. The less direct impact salespeople have on sales results, the smaller the excellence ratio should be: companies shouldn't pay people for high sales that result from promotional efforts in other parts of the organization.

> See if the IC plan pays for performance by tracking the multiple of median IC pay earned by the top and bottom 10 percent of the sales force.

Similarly, the bottom 10 percent should earn substantially less incentive pay than median performers, and they should earn little or no incentive pay if a sizable portion of their pay comes from salary. Poor performers should receive a clear and consistent message—from their manager's feedback, from their performance review, and finally from their incentive payouts.

Is the IC Plan Aligned with Sales and Corporate Strategy?

The IC plan should motivate activities that enable achievement of strategic goals. For example, if the sales strategy calls for maintaining price discipline while increasing revenues by 3 percent, but instead the top line grows by 5 percent while average prices fall, the IC plan may be misaligned with strategy.

Typically, companies have multiple strategic goals. In addition to financial goals (for example, sales and profits), they may have goals for metrics such as new account acquisition, market share growth, optimal product line mix, and customer share of wallet. Evaluating IC plan alignment involves

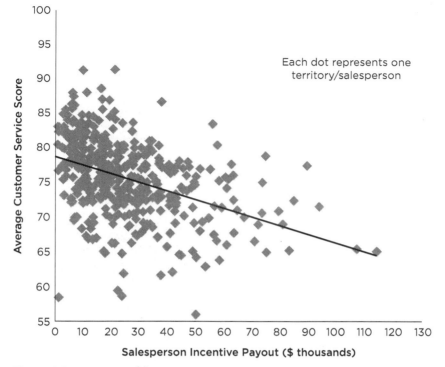

Figure 7-5. IC payout and customer satisfaction for retail salespeople

looking at correlations between incentive pay and the achievement of such objectives at the territory level.

The chart in Figure 7-5 shows one example of an analysis that looks at the correlation between IC payout and a strategic objective for a group of retail salespeople who aspire to improve customer service scores. The slightly negative correlation suggests that the plan in question is not well aligned with the objective. The company discovered that sales agents earned high incentives in the short term by aggressively selling customers extra (and sometimes unnecessary) features, leading to lower customer satisfaction in the long term.

The best analyses look across all strategic goals and consider the relative priority of each. Almost always, goals for short-term financial success, such as territory sales and gross margin, are among the most important sales IC program objectives.

Is the IC Plan Fair?

An IC plan is fair when no territory characteristic, other than the effort and ability of the salesperson assigned to that territory, influences incentive pay. For example, if salespeople in smaller territories systematically earn more than those in medium or large ones, then the plan is not fair. Although the perfect IC plan does not exist, some plans are certainly fairer than others.

The importance of fairness cannot be underestimated for salespeople. In practical terms, designing for fairness boils down to addressing two challenges: knowing which territory characteristics to test for bias; and then, if bias is observed, understanding how to adjust the plan to eliminate or reduce it. Several standard characteristics are used to test for bias, including territory size, territory sales growth, territory potential, and size of goal. Field sales managers can provide input about what fairness tests to run, increasing the odds of diagnosing fairness issues before faith in the plan is diminished.

> *Sales analytics can help ensure that the sales IC plan is fair to all, and leaders should communicate that fact clearly, concisely, and repeatedly to the sales organization.*

The chart in Figure 7-6 illustrates a fairness test that looks at the relationship between territory market potential (something that salespeople have no control over) and quota attainment. The analysis suggests that salespeople in territories with larger market potential have a moderate advantage over those in territories with less potential. Consequently, salespeople in high-potential territories are likely to have better quota performance regardless of their abilities and activities. Quotas would be fairer if market potential were incorporated into the quota-setting process, thus eliminating the bias and giving all salespeople a more equal chance of achieving quota. (See Chapter 8 for more information on setting quotas and goals.)

Monitoring Performance on Critical Metrics

At the beginning of the sales IC plan period, sales analytics leaders can work with sales leaders to determine which metrics to monitor. Ideally, measurement and reporting will occur at least monthly; however, resource-constrained sales forces can measure and report quarterly to identify and address IC problems before they grow to crisis levels.

Many companies define target "zones" for key metrics. These may come from externally sourced benchmarks, industry standards, historical company results, or financial standards that are important to the company.

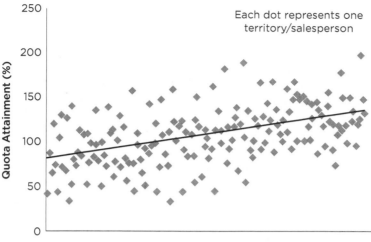

Figure 7-6. A quota fairness test for one sales force

Some typical target zones across industries and companies are shown in Figure 7-7. However, every sales organization will need to adjust these targets appropriately for its specific situation.

Designing a Better IC Plan to Drive Performance

Over 80 percent of companies annually assess the effectiveness of their current IC plan and make changes for the following year, although the change is rarely significant each and every year. Sales analytics can help detect triggers of plan design change, suggest alternative plan designs, and objectively test and compare alternative plans. Too often, companies implement IC plan changes without proper testing and analytic support, leading to poorly designed plans and undesired consequences. Good design ensures that an IC plan will continue to be effective despite an uncertain future.

The Drivers of IC Plan Change

The decision to change an IC plan is driven by many factors, including these common triggers:

- Diagnosis reveals problems or opportunities.
- Pressure for change comes from salespeople and field management.

Category	Recommended Metrics	Recommended Range	Rationale
Pay level	Base salary, total compensation (target and actual) vs. market	+/-10% of market pay target	Paying below market makes it hard to recruit qualified candidates; paying above market results in high costs.
Metrics	Number of metrics	≤3-4	Most salespeople can't focus on and affect more than 3-4 metrics.
	Weighting on each metric	≥15%	Salespeople will likely ignore metrics weighted less than 15%.
	Ratio of percentage weight on a metric vs. percentage of revenue or gross profit $	Growth products >2.0; mature products 0.5-1.5; declining products <0.5	Weights should reflect desired sales time devoted to products.
Payout formula ratios	Company 90th percentile/company median (excellence ratio)	2.0-3.0	Empirical (observed) benchmark data.
	Company 90th percentile/market 90th percentile	+/-10%	Top performers shouldn't be able to earn more elsewhere.
	Company 10th percentile/company median	≤0.3	Underperformers shouldn't be able to "coast."
	Company 10th percentile/market 10th percentile	+/-10%	Paying bottom performers more than market is wasted incentive.
Payout period	Target incentive pay per payout period	>3% of total annual pay	Less than 3% is too low to be meaningful and is not worth the administrative costs.
Other elements	Spiffs and contests as a percentage of actual incentive	3%-7%	More than 7% undermines motivational dynamics of main IC plan.
	Number of spiffs and contests	≤2 per year per role (most industries)	More than 2 per year undermines main IC plan.
	Recognition program participation	Top 5%-15%	Balances opportunity with exclusivity.

Figure 7-7. Typical target zones for key IC plan metrics

- External events require changes to the sales process.
- The company launches a new product or other corporate initiative.
- New company goals or target pay levels require IC plan recalibration.
- New leadership drives change.

Is It Really an IC Plan Problem?

The presence of any of these change drivers does not necessarily mean that the IC plan needs to change. Too often, organizations will change an IC plan in response to any perceived problem, even if that problem is actually rooted in other areas, such as territory design, goal setting, or hiring practices. When this happens, the underlying problem remains unresolved.

IC Plan Design Decisions

Designing an IC plan requires all of the decisions listed in Figure 7-8. Each decision is a lever that can bring the plan closer to, or push it farther from, achieving the organization's selling objectives.

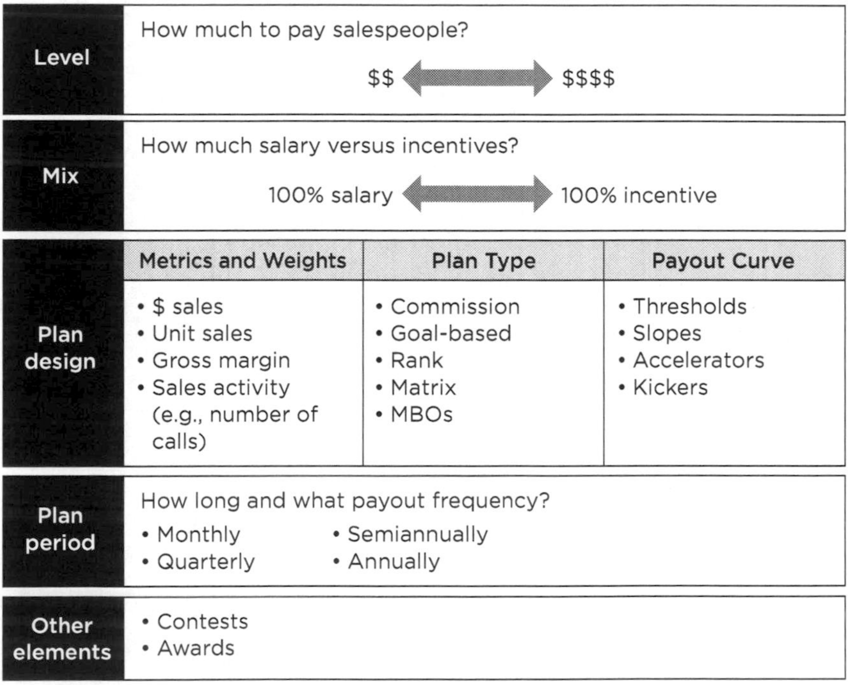

Level	How much to pay salespeople? $$ ⟷ $$$$		
Mix	How much salary versus incentives? 100% salary ⟷ 100% incentive		
Plan design	**Metrics and Weights**	**Plan Type**	**Payout Curve**
	• $ sales • Unit sales • Gross margin • Sales activity (e.g., number of calls)	• Commission • Goal-based • Rank • Matrix • MBOs	• Thresholds • Slopes • Accelerators • Kickers
Plan period	How long and what payout frequency? • Monthly • Semiannually • Quarterly • Annually		
Other elements	• Contests • Awards		

Figure 7-8. IC plan design decisions

Looking Beyond IC Plan Design

A medical services company redesigned its IC plan to address an excessive payout disparity among salespeople, some of whom had many accounts, while others had few. The complex new plan used widely divergent payout curves for different sets of salespeople. Using forward-looking modeling, the company projected a distribution of payouts with the new plan that indeed fit the mandate for payout equity across salespeople. But the different payout curves created confusion and a perception of unfairness in the field. Had the company addressed the true problem — territories with unequal potential and a flawed goal-setting methodology — it could have achieved the same distribution of payouts without creating confusion and the perception of unfairness.

The best design decisions depend on the desired outcomes, as well as on the circumstances of the selling environment. Figure 7-9 on page 138 shows the design options that typically work best for achieving different outcomes in different circumstances.

Testing the Financial Impact of a Proposed IC Plan Design

Company stakeholders will have questions about a new IC plan design.

- Finance may ask, "What will the new plan cost?"

- Executive leadership may ask, "What will the new plan accomplish?"

- Field management may ask, "How will the top salespeople be affected?"

The analyses discussed so far have all been backward-facing. They use historical data to evaluate the past performance of an existing plan. But answering these three questions requires projecting design choices into a mostly unknown future. A future-oriented model requires two inputs:

1. **Proposed plan design.** This includes the type of plan (bonus or commission), the metrics (gross profit or sales revenue), and key plan parameters. For example, the parameters for a commission plan include the commission rate and any accelerators, decelerators, or caps. A goal-based plan requires a payout curve — for example, at what level of goal attainment will accelerators or bonuses kick in?

2. **Performance distribution.** Usually, the best starting prediction of the future performance distribution across salespeople is the historical distribution. However, there are times when it's appropriate to assume that the distribution will change in the future (for example, if a group of outlier territories will be realigned).

Plan Element	Desired Outcome	Typical Circumstance	Best Compensation Option
Mix	More "hunting" than "farming"	• Transactional selling • Short selling cycles	Higher variable pay
	Customer service and account maintenance	• Long selling cycles • Well-penetrated market, limited growth potential	Higher base pay
Metrics	Awareness building; adoption	• Product launch	New contracts metric
	Aggressive growth	• Product growth phase	Total revenue or revenue growth
	Sales stability; profit maximization	• Product maturity	Profit or price discipline metric
Plan type	Establish position in a young market	• New product launch • Entry into new market	Commission
	Account retention and upselling	• Mature market • Blended hunter/farmer role	Goal/quota
	Focus on two strategic objectives that salespeople can trade off	• Need to defend share and grow opportunities • Individual and team selling	Matrix
	Nonstandard selling activities	• Unique selling situations requiring customized account management	MBO (management by objectives)
Payout curve	Increased selling effort to achieve challenging goals	• Extra effort required to exceed performance thresholds	Increase slope in payout curve
	Minimum performance before any incentives paid	• Some sales this period are due to previous period effort • Send strong pay-for-performance message	Payout threshold
	Budget risk mitigation	• Highly volatile revenues from period to period • Windfall opportunities	Payout cap or "decelerator," per-deal cap
Plan period	Create immediate results	• Product launch • Transactional sale	Monthly or quarterly
	Long-term relationship building	• Strategic accounts • Long selling cycles • Low percent variable pay	Annually

Figure 7-9. IC plan design decisions for different outcomes and circumstances

With these inputs, it's possible to project what the sales force *would have* earned had a new plan been in place, given the past distribution of performance. It's possible to evaluate alternative plans using the diagnostic analyses described earlier. (Does each plan motivate, pay for performance, align with strategy, and provide fair opportunity?) And it's also possible to evaluate alternative plans on important financial metrics, such as those shown in the sample analysis in Figure 7-10.

Monte Carlo simulations can help companies understand the range of costs under different performance scenarios. By varying plan parameters, it's possible to discover ways to achieve the desired performance on key metrics. And it's possible to compare alternative plans to discover which one is best for achieving the desired outcomes across a range of performance scenarios.

> *Comprehensive testing dramatically increases the odds that a proposed IC plan will accomplish the desired sales and financial objectives.*

Testing a proposed IC plan, given an uncertain future, is complex and difficult work. Sales analytics can add tremendous value to the IC plan testing process. For a more detailed discussion of the analytics required to support IC plan testing, read *The Complete Guide to Sales Force Incentive*

Metric	Projected Results—Plan A	Projected Results—Plan B	Industry Benchmark
Average percentage of target pay	112%	105%	100%–110%
90th percentile pay (percentage of median)	202%	286%	200%–300%
10th percentile pay (percentage of median)	41%	15%	10%–30%
Percentage engaged (earning enough to make the plan motivating)	75%	40%	60%–80%
Percentage earning no payout	3%	8%	0%–10%

Figure 7-10. Sample evaluation and benchmarking of IC plan metrics

Compensation by Andris A. Zoltners, Prabhakant Sinha, and Sally E. Lorimer (Amacom Books, 2006).

Conclusion

Sales analytics are a key element of a successful sales compensation program. The value that sales analytics add is significant across the full support-diagnose-design spectrum.

Most companies are aware of the importance of good support for administering a smoothly functioning program. In addition to providing efficient, timely, and accurate support, a big unrealized opportunity for companies comes from using analytics to enhance sales compensation plan diagnosis and design. Diagnosis, enabled by analytics, allows leaders to proactively track the performance of the sales compensation plan, anticipate problems and opportunities, and make timely course corrections. Design, backed by the right analytics, enables leaders to make sales compensation plan choices that lead to the best performance outcomes and avoid undesired consequences, despite an uncertain future.

World-class sales analytics are a key factor in creating and sustaining a sales compensation program that consistently drives sales results.

CHAPTER 8

Setting Motivating Sales Force Goals

Analytics allow companies to set sales goals that lead to better sales outcomes for the company and better payouts for the sales force.

Stephen Redden

Stephen Redden is a principal in ZS Associates' Evanston, Illinois, office and the leader of the firm's Sales Compensation practice. He has helped develop innovative compensation plan designs and goal-setting approaches that are in widespread use today. He has also led numerous managed services and capability-building engagements globally. Stephen has an MBA from the Rotman School of Management at the University of Toronto and also has engineering degrees from Cornell University and the University of Western Ontario.

Motivate and Direct Sales Activity with the Right Goals

Many sales forces tie incentive compensation (IC) to the achievement of sales or profit goals. A sales IC plan is only as good as the goals underlying it, yet companies struggle with setting motivating sales goals. Goal setting has been noted among the top three sales IC challenges in every release of our Incentive Practices Research (IPR) study since 2007.[1]

Forecasting uncertainties and diverse business conditions across local markets complicate the setting of sales goals.

It's natural for salespeople to tell their managers that their goals are too high. But some complaints that we hear from salespeople about goals do reveal legitimate concerns:

- "My goal is unreasonable. No one is on track to make goal this month. Company leaders' aspirations don't reflect market realities."

[1] The annual Incentive Practices Research (IPR) study conducted by ZS Associates is provided to participating companies in multiple industries worldwide.

- "My goal is unfair. I have all small accounts. A salesperson who manages several mega-accounts has the same goal. He'll make goal with minimal effort. I'll have to work 60-hour weeks just to make the first payout threshold."

- "I don't understand my goal. Headquarters sets it using outdated data and fancy math. My income rides on a black box."

The right goals benefit customers, salespeople, and the company in the following ways:

- **Customers.** The right goals encourage customer focus and discourage the selling of products or services that customers don't need.

- **Salespeople.** The right goals provide a tangible target for performance and create a sense of accomplishment in addition to incentive income.

- **The company.** The right goals align sales effort with business objectives, maximize sales force motivation, and increase sales.

Many companies—due to either lack of time or lack of expertise—do not apply the necessary rigor to setting territory goals and testing for their likely impact on sales and profits. An analytic approach to goal setting can lead to better motivation, improved sales force buy-in, and ultimately better financial results. Sales analytics can have impact at three levels, as shown in Figure 8-1. In this chapter, we share approaches for using sales analytics to diagnose, design, and support sales force goal setting.

Diagnose	Design	Support
Reveal improvement opportunities: • Company forecast accuracy • Fair goal allocation • Sales force commitment to goals	Design and implement a goal-setting approach: • Triggers for redesign • Goal design steps • Dealing with uncertainty	Support goal setting: • Oversee sales force goal refinement • Communicate goals • Provide goal-achievement feedback • Address questions and adjustment requests

Figure 8-1. The impact of sales analytics on goal setting

The Impact of Setting Accurate Goals

The right goals optimize sales force performance. Salespeople's goals affect how hard they work and where they direct their effort. If there are multiple goals (say for different products), goal levels affect how salespeople allocate their time. Goals affect territory sales, incentive pay, and ultimately financial

Higher goals can lead to higher sales, but impossible-to-achieve goals will lead to lower sales.

contribution. Figure 8-2 shows how territory goal levels, expected sales, and incentive pay are related.

- **A low, meaningless goal** (or any goal in the "overpay range") is too easily achieved. It leads to windfall IC payouts for salespeople who can exceed the goal by putting forth minimal effort. Sales come in at a reasonable level, but incentive pay is high, and overall financial contribution is

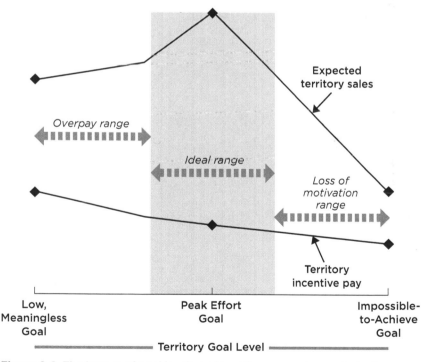

Figure 8-2. The impact of goal levels on incentive pay and expected sales

lower than it would have been with more challenging goals. Worse, the sales force may expect the company to continue to offer high pay levels for little work.

- **An impossible-to-achieve goal** (or any goal in the "loss of motivation range") destroys salespeople's enthusiasm for selling. Morale suffers, salespeople may leave the company, and sales fall off as salespeople give up or begin to hold sales over to the next period, when they expect goals will be more achievable. Financial contribution is lower than it would have been with more reasonable goals.

- **A peak effort goal** (or any goal in the "ideal range") motivates the highest performance. Salespeople view the goal as challenging yet achievable, so they'll work hard to make goal and earn a fair incentive, maximizing their financial contribution to the company.

Three Goal-Setting Challenges

There are three main goal-setting challenges:

- Getting the company sales forecast right
- Allocating the forecast fairly among salespeople
- Gaining sales force commitment

Getting the Company Sales Forecast Right

When 10 or 20 percent of salespeople miss their goal, there may be a problem with those salespeople. However, when the majority of salespeople miss their goal, the problem is most likely that the overall company forecast is too high. Company leaders must make forecasts in the face of uncertain market conditions. Occasionally, the company forecast is too low, making territory goals systematically too easy and resulting in overpayment of incentives to the sales force. More often, the company forecast is too high, making territory goals consistently too high and dampening sales force motivation. Paradoxically, companies that face this situation will actually sell more by lowering the company forecast to a realistic level.

Allocating the Forecast Fairly Among Salespeople

Companies frequently ask every salesperson to grow sales by the same percentage as the company's desired sales growth. This goal-setting approach is simple to implement and easy for salespeople to understand. Yet it neglects to acknowledge the likely reality that territories differ in their competitive environment, current penetration level, and other factors affecting growth *potential*. Even if the company forecast is accurate, the allocation of the forecast across salespeople will be unfair unless it recognizes differences in opportunity across territories.

Gaining Sales Force Commitment

Goals have impact only if salespeople are committed to them. Commitment starts with goals that the sales force views as achievable, and it is fostered when the sales force understands how the goals were set or when salespeople and managers were involved in the goal-setting process. Companies need to balance the analytic sophistication of an advanced goal-setting approach with the need for the sales force's understanding and buy-in. At the same time, sales force involvement in goal setting needs to be managed so that proper checks and balances ensure objectivity and prevent "sandbagging."

Diagnosing Goal Quality

Sales analytics can reveal early signs of trouble with goals, enabling adjustments to be made before performance veers too far off course. Diagnosis addresses the three goal-setting challenges.

Is the Company Sales Forecast Reasonable?

The reasonableness of a company sales forecast is tested by comparing a goal to sales trends, while accounting for expected changes in market conditions (such as market growth and competition) and company investment (such as in product quality and marketing support). Too often, company sales forecasts are based solely on top-down planning. They reflect the aspirations of ambitious leaders, rather than thoughtful analysis of trends and

> *The best performance is possible when goals are challenging yet viewed as achievable by salespeople.*

influences. The sales force may have little input into determining the company forecast and limited ability to change a forecast, even if analysis shows it is too aggressive.

The demotivating impact of an inaccurate company forecast can be limited with these goal-allocation strategies:

- Consider overallocating a company goal that is too low to "stretch" the sales force. This also provides a buffer for reducing goals in some territories due to unexpected local circumstances.

- Consider underallocating a company goal that is too high so salespeople will view their goals as attainable and therefore be more motivated.

Is the Goal Allocation Fair to All Salespeople?

Four diagnostic tests can reveal problems with goal allocation.

IC Pay Test

When an IC plan is goal-based, a fair goal allocation produces an expected pay distribution. For example, did the expected proportion of salespeople earn no IC pay? Did top performers earn the multiple of target pay that the company had planned? If not, poor goal setting is a possible cause. One company conducted the IC pay analysis shown in Figure 8-3. More salespeople than expected fell well short of goal and received no IC pay, while the top earners received more IC pay than planned. This revealed a bias in

---

Ensuring a Reasonable Top-Level Forecast

The company goal that a biotech company allocates to the field is the lesser of the actual product forecast or the trend of historic sales, accounting for the average growth rate of competitive products. This ensures that salespeople perceive goals as achievable. Making this a matter of policy provides direction and creates commitment from the sales force.

Metrics	Company Objective	Actual Outcome	Deviation
Forecast achievement	100%	97%	–3%
Payout to budget	100%	105%	5%
Proportion of no-pays	5%	11%	6%
Payout to 90th percentile (percentage of target incentive)	225%	250%	25%
Maximum payout (percentage of target incentive)	300%	310%	10%

Figure 8-3. The impact of goal misallocation at one company

When the Company Forecast Is Too High

If leaders discover midyear that the company forecast is too high, they should:

- Balance a desire to remain committed to the goal with the need to energize a demotivated sales force.

- Keep the original goal intact, but prevent further sales shortfalls and loss of salespeople by replacing lost income with contests, spiffs, and other add-on incentives.

- Limit midyear goal changes to major events outside the control of the sales force (for example, major economic changes, pricing changes, and acts of nature).

---

the goal allocation; the goal-setting formula did not adequately account for differences in territory potential. The goal misallocation had an additional undesired consequence: IC payouts exceeded the budget even though company goal achievement fell short.

Fairness Test

All salespeople should have a fair opportunity to achieve goal, despite differences in territory potential.

A high correlation between goal achievement and any factor outside a salesperson's control (that is, a factor other than the salesperson's effort and ability) suggests a bias in goal allocation. A fairness test, such as the analysis shown in Figure 8-4, correlates goal achievement with measures

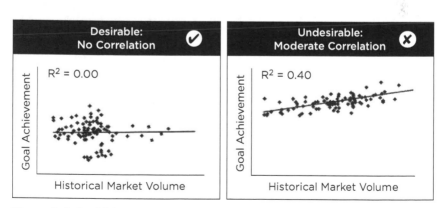

Figure 8-4. Goal fairness test

Measuring Territory Potential

Many sales forces do not have estimates of local market potential readily available, and developing them may require effort and creativity. For example, a company selling insurance and financing for motorcycles used customer demographics, competitors, proximity of local credit unions, and the onset of spring weather (which triggered motorcycle sales) to predict territory potential. By using estimates of potential (although imperfect ones) when allocating goals, the company helped to level the playing field for all its salespeople. Chapter 2 provides more information on approaches for developing local market potential estimates.

---

of potential. In the chart on the right, the undesirable strong correlation between historical market volume and goal achievement shows that potential was not sufficiently considered in the goal-setting process, giving salespeople in high-potential territories an advantage over those in low-potential territories.

Pay-for-Performance Test

Territory performance measures that salespeople can affect — such as revenue growth, profitability, and market share gain — should correlate with goal achievement at the territory level. The pay-for-performance analysis in Figure 8-5 shows an undesirable weak correlation between market share growth and goal achievement, suggesting that strong performers who were successful in increasing market share may have been penalized with goals that were overly challenging.

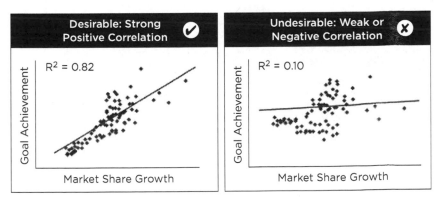

Figure 8-5. Pay-for-performance test

Performance Stability Test

Salespeople sometimes complain, "I had a great year last year, so the company rewards me with an even higher goal for this year that I'll never achieve!" Goal-allocation formulas based on past results, rather than on future potential, can penalize top performers, making it difficult for them to sustain strong performance. This "hero to zero" outcome can cause salespeople to defer sales to future periods when they believe their goals will be easier to achieve. This is not in the best interest of customers or the company, and it can damage sales force motivation and undermine sales force trust in the IC plan.

The analysis in Figure 8-6 checks for "ping-ponging" in territory goal attainment from one period to the next. Salespeople should generally have consistent goal achievement over time; there shouldn't be a negative correlation between goal achievement last period and this period.

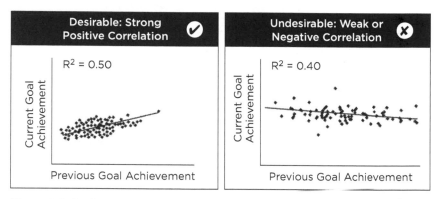

Figure 8-6. Performance stability test

Is the Sales Force Committed to Goals?

Input from the sales force can reveal the extent to which sales team members understand and are committed to their goals. By conducting field surveys, focus groups, and interviews with salespeople and sales managers, it's possible to uncover misperceptions about goals that can be addressed through improved field communication, as well as legitimate issues with the goal-setting process that can be addressed by modifying the goal-setting approach.

Designing an Effective Goal-Setting Approach

By regularly diagnosing goal quality and recognizing triggers for goal-setting change, sales analytics can help the sales organization determine when and how to redesign the goal-setting approach. It may be necessary to redesign a goal-setting approach if:

- Diagnosis reveals concerns with current goals.
- The selling environment changes (for example, customer needs and buying processes change, competition varies, market growth increases or declines).
- Company sales strategies change (for example, new products are launched, new selling processes are implemented, selling becomes more team-oriented).
- New data sources and analytic techniques become available.
- The company changes other sales force effectiveness drivers, such as sales force structures, sales compensation plans, or performance metrics.

Three Steps for Designing Effective Goals

The process of designing goals for a sales force requires three steps:

- Set the company sales forecast
- Allocate the forecast across the sales force
- Gain sales force commitment

Setting the Company Sales Forecast

Setting a company sales forecast usually involves integrating input from three sources:

- Company aspirations
- Product sales forecasts from marketing
- Input from the sales force

If the company sales forecast is too high or too low, it will be impossible to set good territory-level goals.

   The sales analytics function can help ensure that sales force input gets sufficient weight when setting a company sales forecast. By taking into account historical sales and market potential trends, along with objective bottom-up viewpoints collected from salespeople and managers, leaders can ensure more realistic company sales forecasts.

With strong analytic support, the sales team is better prepared for the likely negotiation required between sales, marketing, and top management that results in the final company forecast.

Allocating the Forecast Across the Sales Force

Figure 8-7 summarizes some of the many goal-setting methodologies that are available.[2]

Goal-Setting Technique	Description and Details
Straight growth	Apply a straight percentage or unit growth expectation for every territory. Simple, but does not provide equal earning opportunity unless all territories have equal growth potential.
Trending	Use time-series regression to project future territory sales based on the historical sales trend. Suitable when sales growth is stable and potential is reflected in historic growth trends.
Weighted index	Allocate goals to territories based on a weighted average of multiple factors (market growth, previous period sales, and customer demographics, for example). Suitable for most goal-setting circumstances.
Regression	Use statistics to evaluate the strength of the relationship between territory performance and independent territory factors. Suitable in data-rich environments with a sales force that can appreciate a complex goal-setting approach.
Frontier analysis	Establish goals that challenge all salespeople to perform as well as the best performers in the sales force who have territories with similar sales potential. Suitable in data-rich environments with a sales force that can appreciate a complex goal-setting approach.
Bottom-up forecasting	Allow salespeople to set their own goals with management guidance. Encourages commitment to goals, but needs to be managed so salespeople don't understate their opportunity. Suitable when salespeople have a better understanding of territory potential than the company does.

Figure 8-7. Common goal-setting methodologies

[2]For more detail on these and other goal-setting approaches, read *The Complete Guide to Sales Force Incentive Compensation* by Andris A. Zoltners, Prabhakant Sinha, and Sally E. Lorimer (Amacom Books, 2006).

By analyzing historical territory-level data, it's possible to gain insight into market dynamics and to identify the best measures of territory opportunity. This understanding forms the basis for evaluating alternative goal-setting methodologies and determining which is best. Factors that influence which method is best include:

- **Data availability.** In industries with high-quality territory-level sales and potential data, it is easier to use approaches that incorporate potential (for example, weighted index, regression, frontier analysis).

- **Buying patterns.** For products that follow seasonal buying patterns (for example, air conditioners during warm-weather months), the best approaches account for recent sales trends and seasonal effects.

- **Analytic sophistication.** An analytically complex goal-setting process creates little value if salespeople do not comprehend and embrace the resulting goals. It's important to balance the value of analytic sophistication with the value of goals that the sales force understands and accepts.

Gaining Sales Force Commitment

If a company uses an analytic goal-setting methodology without sufficient sales force input, the sales force is unlikely to embrace the goals. It's important to engage sales force members in shaping the methodology and criteria used for setting goals. It's also critical to allow sales managers and salespeople to review and adjust goals before implementation to account for local conditions and to build sales force acceptance (see Supporting the Ongoing Goal-Setting Process section).

Dealing with Uncertainty

Sometimes even the best data and forecasting techniques cannot overcome the uncertainty inherent in setting goals. Goal setting for a new product (especially one that is the first of its kind) is difficult because historical data do not exist. Several goal-setting strategies address the uncertainty in unpredictable selling environments:

- Set goals with short time frames. That way an unrealistic goal will affect the sales force only for a limited period of time.

- Set goals that reward a range of performance rather than goals that focus attention on a single number. For example, define a "success" range that begins at a lower percentage of goal attainment so that more salespeople feel successful, especially when the goal is likely to be unrealistically high.

Testing Goals Using Historical Data

As part of the goal-design process, it's important to test a proposed new goal-setting methodology before it is implemented. Testing requires two years of territory-level data, including sales and the other factors used in the goal-allocation formula (such as market potential estimates). The analysis works as follows:

1. Apply the proposed methodology using data from Year 1 to calculate territory goals for Year 2. Assume that the total company sales forecast for Year 2 is equal to actual sales in Year 2 (that is, company goal achievement in Year 2 is 100 percent).

2. Compare the calculated Year 2 goals to actual Year 2 sales for each territory, as shown in the example in Figure 8-8.

3. Use these data to conduct the four tests described earlier in the chapter (IC pay test, fairness test, pay-for-performance test, and performance stability test). A good goal-setting methodology passes all of these tests.

4. Look at gaps in goal achievement territory by territory to see if they are intuitive. Understanding who is helped and who is hurt by a goal-allocation approach helps to evaluate the soundness of the methodology.

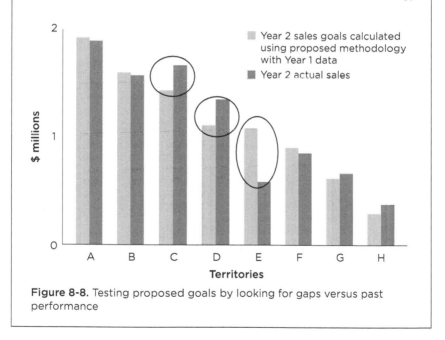

Figure 8-8. Testing proposed goals by looking for gaps versus past performance

- Design an IC plan that anticipates possible goal-setting inaccuracies. Design IC payout curves that adjust to keep motivation high when company goals are too high and to minimize undeserved IC payouts when company goals are too low. Earnings caps and decelerators are common plan features used to protect against excessive IC payouts.

- Consider a non-goal-based IC plan. For example, use a commission plan that pays from the first dollar sold, or a ranking plan that pays for performance relative to peers. Introduce goals only after market knowledge increases.

Supporting the Ongoing Goal-Setting Process

Companies need a process to support the setting of sales force goals. The process will be repeated each selling period. A good way to start is by standardizing the battery of diagnostic tests described in this chapter to evaluate the quality of past goals. By looking at standard, consistent diagnostic reports at the end of each selling period, sales leaders can understand a period-over-period comparison of results and can make adjustments to improve goal-setting formulas and methodologies for the next selling period.

The best goal-setting data, formulas, and analytic techniques lead to a preliminary set of territory goals for the next selling period. Standard tools

---

IC Payout Curves That Protect Against Goal-Setting Errors

One sales force facing a volatile market guarded against goal-setting errors by designing an IC plan that linked an individual's incentive payout not only to territory goal achievement, but also to company goal achievement. The payout curve philosophy is illustrated in Figure 8-9. The plan helped manage sales force motivation and IC costs in an unpredictable environment.

		Individual's Territory Goal Achievement		
		Under 100%	Exactly 100%	Over 100%
Company Goal Achievement	Under 100%			Pay more than target
	Exactly 100%		Pay target amount	
	Over 100%	Pay less than target		

Figure 8-9. The payout curve philosophy for a volatile market

> **An Ongoing Process for Setting Goals and Improving Quality**
>
> A manufacturer of kitchen cabinets evaluates goals prospectively before the start of each quarter and retrospectively at the end of each quarter. The analyses are supported with standard reports produced automatically by the goal-setting system. The manufacturer analyzes results each quarter and implements improvements to the goal-setting methodologies for the future.

(for example, spreadsheets or third-party software) and defined processes enable easy and consistent goal setting across products, sales teams, and time, with minimal operational investment.

A sales analytics function plays a key role in gaining the sales force's commitment to goals. Four key elements of gaining this commitment are discussed here:

- Overseeing the goal-refinement process
- Communicating goals
- Providing goal-achievement feedback and tools
- Addressing questions and adjustment requests

Overseeing the Goal-Refinement Process

Sales organizations enhance commitment to goals by engaging sales managers and salespeople in developing and refining their goals. An efficient and effective goal-refinement process for the field can allow sales managers to make zero-sum adjustments to the preliminary sales goals calculated by headquarters. With the right information and online tools, sales managers and salespeople can review and adjust goals easily, submit changes to headquarters for review and approval, and document and accurately communicate goal adjustments.

Communicating Goals

In addition to communicating to the sales force what the sales goals are, it's important to communicate how the goals were set. Standard goal communication is best delivered through efficient, consistent vehicles, such as email or the web. If goal-setting approaches have changed or are complex, higher-touch approaches such as meetings or webinars are more effective options. Communication makes goals transparent and enhances sales force motivation.

> *Goals have the most impact when salespeople understand and are committed to them.*

The "Yo-yo" Sales Force Goal Refinement Process

A sales force with multiple management levels — regions, districts, and territories — uses a down and up "yo-yo" approach to allocate sales goals. The approach involves the following steps:

1. Set regional goals.
   a. Allocate the national goal to the territory level based on a prescribed, data-based formula. Sum the territory goals to the regional level to produce preliminary regional goals.
   b. Get input from regional directors about regional goals. Allow the directors to negotiate if they feel the formula has overlooked important regional factors. Changes to regional goals are subject to approval by headquarters. Headquarters must ensure that after adjustments, the regional goals still sum to the national goal.

2. Set district goals.
   a. Allocate each region's adjusted goal to the territories in the region using the prescribed formula. Sum the territory goals to the district level to produce preliminary district goals.
   b. Get input from district managers about their goals. Allow managers to negotiate if they feel the formula has overlooked important district factors. Changes to district goals are subject to approval by regional directors. Regional directors must ensure that after adjustments, the district goals still sum to the regional goal.

3. Set territory goals.
   a. Allocate each district's adjusted goal to the territories in the district.
   b. Allow district managers to make adjustments to territory goals if they feel the formula has overlooked important territory factors. District managers must ensure that after adjustments, the territory goals still sum to the district goal.

The company facilitates this adjustment and review process using web-based software that provides quick turnaround, ensures accuracy of adjustments, and provides an audit trail of all changes.

This back-and-forth approach provides the benefits of using a formula to set goals and, at the same time, captures the local knowledge of regional directors and district managers. Sales directors and managers better understand how goals are set and can more knowledgeably communicate them to salespeople, which increases the sales force's commitment to the goals.

Providing Goal-Achievement Feedback and Tools

Salespeople can benefit from territory reports that show goals broken down by product, channel, or customer, along with the period-to-date performance against each goal. This helps salespeople understand areas in which they are over- or underperforming and helps them focus attention on those accounts or products that will allow them to reach or exceed their goals.

Facilitating Field Involvement in Territory Goal Setting

At a large pharmaceutical company, field sales managers are involved in two stages of the goal-setting process. First, field managers provide input on the company's contract status with local managed care plans, a key piece of data affecting the territory potential used as one input to the goal-allocation process. Second, headquarters creates preliminary territory goals (developed analytically using agreed-upon data and formulas) and sums them to the regional level for senior sales leaders to review. These leaders can shift goals for their direct reports from one region to another based on market knowledge. Then each subsequent level of sales management makes similar adjustments to goals for their direct reports in a cascading manner. The process is supported with online tools to ease the administrative burden while allowing the field to incorporate local market knowledge. This enhances the quality of the results and creates strong sales force commitment to goals.

Some sales forces provide payout calculators that motivate by allowing salespeople to enter "what if" scenarios that demonstrate potential earnings for various levels of goal attainment.

Addressing Questions and Adjustment Requests

A sales analytics function plays a key role in addressing ongoing field inquiries regarding goals. Despite thorough up-front communication about how goals are set, many salespeople will request additional detail. Some may feel that goals were set with incorrect assumptions about local circumstances

---

Allowing Mid-period Changes to Individual Territory Goals

If leaders choose to allow mid-period changes to individual territory goals, they should:

- Create and communicate a policy about individual goal adjustments that aligns with the company's philosophy about changing the top-level forecast (see "Is the Company Sales Forecast Reasonable?" earlier in this chapter).

- Have a defined approval process. Consider requiring requests for goal adjustment to go through the sales management ranks, so that sales analytics personnel are not bombarded by direct calls from salespeople.

- Place restrictions on goal changes to protect the integrity of goals and to minimize the number of trivial requests. (For example, a closed account must comprise at least 5 percent of a territory's business to warrant goal adjustment.)

- Strive to set the most realistic, fact-based territory goals from the start, while considering midyear corrections in exceptional circumstances.

---

that have changed, potentially warranting goal adjustments. It's important to establish the ground rules for making mid-period goal adjustments and to provide mechanisms for ensuring that adjustments are systematic and objective.

Conclusion

Sales analytics can add value to the support, diagnosis, and design of sales force goal setting. Design is a particular area of emphasis, as the best companies will redesign goal-setting approaches frequently in response to changes in the selling environment, market growth, company strategies, data sources, and analytic techniques. Sales analytics contribute to goal setting by:

- **Encouraging more accurate goals and strong field ownership.** Use of analytics ensures that goals are challenging, objective, and achievable, while sales force participation in goal setting ensures strong field commitment.

- **Providing better measures of territory potential.** Measures of territory potential enhance many of the analytic approaches described in this chapter (and also in other chapters). It's critical to identify good sources of data for measuring territory potential and to get the input of sales managers with local knowledge for evaluating and improving these data.

- **Ensuring more effective and efficient use of sales force time.** Sales analytics support the goal-setting process and provide appropriate tools so that the sales force can participate in setting goals without requiring excessive field energy that detracts from selling.

- **Communicating goals to motivate.** Communication about goals and how they are set, using language that resonates with salespeople, can motivate goal achievement.

CHAPTER 9

Managing Sales Force Performance

Analytics enable a performance management process that gets the right information to the right people at the right time using the right medium.

Mahmood Majeed, Kelly Tousi, Josh Rosen, and Pranav Srivastava

Mahmood Majeed is a principal in ZS Associates' Evanston, Illinois, office and leads the firm's Mobility practice. His expertise includes commercial technology transformation, with a specialized focus on enterprise mobility, sales and marketing analytics, and business technology capability development and outsourcing. Mahmood has a Master of Information Systems degree from DePaul University and an executive MBA certificate from Northwestern University's Kellogg School of Management and is a graduate of the University of Oklahoma.

Kelly Tousi is a principal in ZS Associates' Evanston, Illinois, office and is a leader in the firm's Medical Products and Services practice. With over 25 years of experience in healthcare and life sciences, Kelly has developed deep expertise in helping companies transform their sales organization. She was named one of *Consulting Magazine*'s top female leaders in consulting for 2013. Kelly has an MBA from the University of Michigan and a BS with a focus in molecular biology from Purdue University.

Josh Rosen is an associate principal in ZS Associates' Chicago office, where he advises B2B organizations on how to improve their marketing and sales effectiveness by developing and executing integrated programs. He has consulted with clients in the energy, chemicals, distribution, high-tech, packaging, and healthcare industries. Josh has an MBA from Duke University's Fuqua School of Business and is a graduate of the University of Michigan.

Pranav Srivastava is a business consulting manager in ZS Associates' Chicago office. His focus is on market research, market coverage optimization, business intelligence reporting, and analytics for pharmaceutical clients. Pranav has an MBA from the Booth School of Business at the University of Chicago and an MS in electrical engineering from the University of Pennsylvania.

Enhancing Performance Management with Analytics

The old management adage "You can't manage what you don't measure" is certainly true in sales forces. Salespeople and sales managers need feedback to keep performance on course and to continually improve sales force capabilities, activities, and results. Many sales forces use a performance management process similar to the six-step process shown in Figure 9-1.

These six performance management steps are more effective when enabled by sales analytics and decision frameworks:

1. When salespeople work with their managers to *set goals and expectations*, they need sound analytics and market information.

2. When salespeople and managers *develop plans* for how to achieve their goals, they need accurate and timely customer information.

3. When salespeople *take action* to carry out the plans, the right data and tools make them more effective.

4. When companies *measure* results, timely and accurate measurement allows the sales force to respond quickly to potential problems and opportunities.

5. When salespeople work with their managers to *evaluate* results, analytics enable richer discussions and improvement strategies.

6. When companies *implement consequences*, analytics and decision frameworks ensure that the right people get rewarded and that those with weaknesses get appropriate help. This leads to new goals and expectations, as the performance management cycle begins anew.

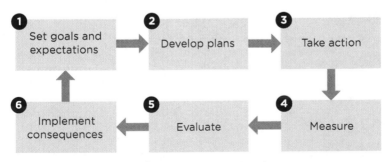

Figure 9-1. A six-step performance management process

Good performance management keeps sales force activity aligned with company goals. There are additional benefits:

- Discovering unique behaviors that drive the success of *star performers* and sharing this learning across the sales force to boost performance
- Helping *middle performers* improve by providing them with the right coaching, support, information, and tools
- Discovering quickly whether *poor performers* have the success characteristics to improve, and encouraging those who do not to seek other job opportunities

The simple sales trend shown in Figure 9-2 may point to a problem, but without analytics that can shed light on why the problem exists, it's difficult to know what to do to solve it.

Analytics and decision frameworks can help reveal possible causes:

- **Motivation.** Does the salesperson have the will to succeed?
- **Ability.** Does the salesperson have the knowledge and skill to succeed?
- **Role clarity.** Does the salesperson understand the job expectations?
- **Activity.** Is the salesperson engaged in the right behaviors—for example, focusing on the right customers, products, and selling activities?
- **Situational factors.** Is the problem with the salesperson or with the territory (for example, tough competition or declining market opportunity)?

The right analytics and decision frameworks help salespeople and their managers figure out what actions to take to keep performance aligned with

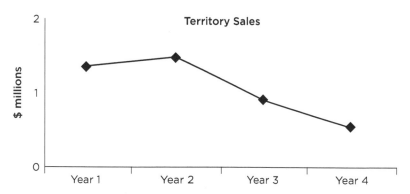

Figure 9-2. Sales analytics can not only show a decline in sales but can also help an organization figure out the "why" behind the decrease

Support	Diagnose	Design
• Fair and realistic goals and expectations • Sales plans and actions supported by real-time information • Metrics that enable evaluation and consequences	• Insights through integrated data • Information that highlights concerns and opportunities • Qualitative capability assessment to guide action	• Frameworks for consistent evaluation across the sales force

Figure 9-3. The impact of sales analytics on performance management

company goals, reverse unfavorable trends, capitalize on opportunities, and otherwise improve performance.

This chapter lays out a framework for managing sales force performance and driving continual improvement. It shows how analytics can enhance performance management by meeting sales force support, diagnosis, and design needs, as shown in Figure 9-3.

A Performance Management Framework

The framework in Figure 9-4 illustrates how performance management focuses on improving both *what* results are achieved (outcomes) and *how* those results are achieved (inputs), while taking into account situational factors that are beyond an individual's control in the short run.

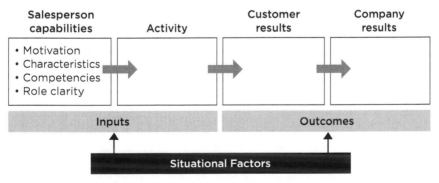

Figure 9-4. A performance management framework

Inputs, Outcomes, and Situational Factors

Performance management requires understanding inputs, outcomes, and situational factors:

- **Inputs.** A salesperson needs *motivation*, as well as the right *characteristics* (for example, empathy) and *competencies* (for example, customer knowledge). There should be sufficient *role clarity* around what the company wants the salesperson to do to enable high-impact *activity* (for example, quality call plans, many high-impact customer calls). Focusing performance management attention on inputs — for example, by setting goals for specific competency improvements or sales activities — may not lead to immediate results but often has long-term impact.

- **Outcomes.** The right inputs lead to positive outcomes for *customer results* (for example, high customer satisfaction and repeat sales) and *company results* (for example, sales and profits). Focusing performance management attention on outcomes — for example, by pressuring a salesperson to make goal this quarter — can affect results in the short term.

- **Situational factors.** The environment can constrain or facilitate sales force inputs and outcomes. Outcomes will suffer if a salesperson doesn't have enough time, lacks resources, or doesn't have sufficient opportunity in his or her territory. It's critical to take situational factors into account when managing performance. For example, if salespeople have territories with unequal potential and they are evaluated based on territory sales volume without controlling for differences in potential, the wrong salespeople may appear to be "star" performers.

> *It's critical to take situational factors into account so that performance management consequences align with true performance.*

The Role of Sales Managers

First-line managers (FLMs) are key participants in the performance management process.[1] Through regular discussions with and observation of their direct reports, FLMs seek to understand each individual's strengths and weaknesses and to tailor their feedback, coaching, and guidance to each individual's needs.

---

[1]For more information about the role of FLMs in the sales force performance management process, see Andris A. Zoltners, Prabhakant Sinha, and Sally E. Lorimer, *Building a Winning Sales Management Team: The Force Behind the Sales Force* (ZS Associates, 2012).

Increasingly, sales forces are leveraging mobile technology, real-time data, and social performance tools on company intranets that make ongoing feedback, coaching, and guidance from FLMs easier and more powerful. As a result in many sales forces, the importance of this continuous part of performance management is increasing relative to the importance of more formal quarterly or annual performance reviews. Aided by mobile technology and real-time data, FLMs can

> *"In any sales force, you can get along without the vice president of sales, the regional sales directors, or the training manager, but you cannot get along without the first line manager."* (Andy Anderson, former vice president of sales and president of US Pharmaceuticals, Searle U.S.)

provide coaching and guidance when it is needed to keep the performance management process alive and continuous, rather than limiting feedback mostly to review time. Social performance tools enable managers and peers to easily share with others within the company timely recognition of individuals for their accomplishments, thus increasing employee engagement.

Sales analytics can help FLMs overcome three roadblocks to effective performance management:

- **Performance management takes courage.** Giving people honest feedback is tough. Real-time information, well-designed scorecards, and performance management frameworks help salespeople see for themselves how they are performing and help FLMs engage in fact-based and objective discussions with salespeople.

- **Performance management takes judgment.** Salespeople have diverse needs, and it's not easy for FLMs to understand what to do to improve the performance of their people. Salespeople frequently become FLMs because of their sales skills, not their management skills, and many FLMs struggle with giving feedback. Analytics and frameworks help FLMs discover the best course of action to take with each salesperson.

- **Performance management takes time.** FLMs are pulled in many directions. They often use the excuse of having urgent work to avoid the hard work of performance management. Sales analytics can provide FLMs with easy access to the information and with technologies for sharing information and collaborating with their people. Sales analytics can also help by customizing competency models and coaching tools so they are relevant to and aligned with specific sales force needs. This makes it easier to provide more frequent coaching and gives FLMs more time to focus on critical performance management tasks.

Supporting the Performance Management Process

Analytics can support each step of the performance management process by getting the *right information* to the *right people* at the *right time* using the *right medium*. In this section we provide several examples of how sales analytics can support performance management.

Supporting Goals and Expectations with Analytics

Sales analytics can help ensure that goals and expectations for salespeople are realistic, fair, and well understood. This can include setting goals for capability development (for example, improve consultative selling skills), sales activity (for example, make at least six calls per day), customer results (for example, achieve high customer satisfaction scores), or company results (for example, exceed territory sales goals). See Chapter 8 for more information on how sales analytics can support goal setting.

Supporting Plans and Actions with Real-Time Information

Tools and data help salespeople gain customer knowledge so they can better understand the marketplace, prioritize opportunities, solve customer problems, and use their time effectively and efficiently. The sales force's information needs depend on the sales environment and vary with the complexity of the sales and customer buying processes.

Good support for territory planning focuses on key questions that salespeople must address during various sales process stages. One company organized sales force information needs around the three stages of call planning shown in Figure 9-5 — presales strategy and planning, execution, and

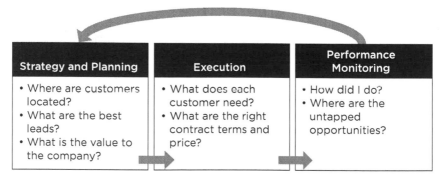

Figure 9-5. Information support for sales force plans and actions

post-fact performance monitoring—to identify improvement opportunities and to guide future planning.

Many companies arm their sales forces with mobile technologies and tools so that sales force members can access real-time information to support sales planning and action. These tools can be powerful enablers, but unless they provide salespeople with the information they need in a format that is simple to use, the investment is wasted. The following examples show some of the benefits of implementing mobile sales force technology.

Better Account Planning. Salespeople in the field can easily revisit what they discussed with a customer on the last visit, what they promised for the next visit, and developments since the last contact. They can also efficiently coordinate across multiple company touch points that serve the same customer (for example, an account manager, product specialists, and inside customer support people). This leads to better use of salespeople's time and a more coordinated effort for the customer.

Figure 9-6 shows an example of the account planning information that a medical supply company provides to its salespeople through mobile technology. Salespeople can access anytime and anywhere the latest information about each customer and prospect in their territory, including up-to-date sales performance data, recent order activity, notes from past visits, and suggestions for products that customers may be interested in, based on their profile and past purchasing patterns.

Less Volume But More Relevant Information. Instead of sifting through dozens of reports to find the information a customer needs, salespeople can see just the five or six key points most relevant to the situation.

Higher-Impact Calls. Using a mobile device, salespeople can facilitate a discussion with a customer. They can enhance their sales calls by accessing customized information on the fly that addresses specific customer questions or concerns. This can include, for example, a product demonstration, a video proving value, or a customized modular product catalog and price list.

More Efficient and Flexible Routing. Salespeople can plan their route at the start of the day using GPS tools and can reroute in the field if a meeting gets canceled. Salespeople not only see which customers are close by and can be seen without an appointment; they also see the value of those customers, so they can reroute to the customer most likely to help them achieve their goals.

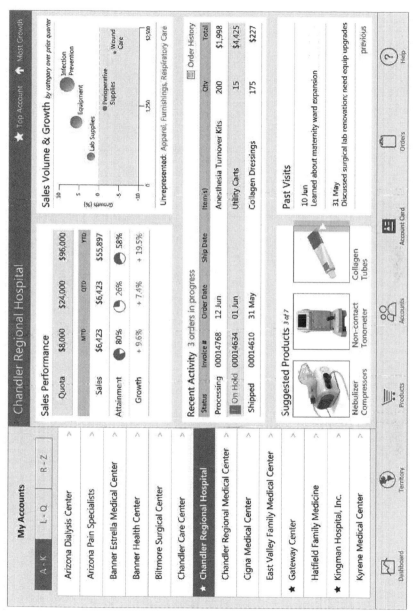

Figure 9-6. Account planning support for a medical device sales force

167

Tools on Mobile Devices Help Both Salespeople and Customers

An after-market truck parts distributor gave its sales force tools on mobile devices that made data more relevant and actionable, both for salespeople and for customers. Benefits included:

- **Better leads for salespeople.** A mobile app gave the distributor's salespeople recommendations about opportunities to sell specific products to specific customers, based on historical buying patterns and likely bundles. It suggested prioritized "leads" and a recommended purchase price and volume offer. Salespeople could capture feedback from their customers and score the leads; this information was used to improve the model.

- **Improved inventory management for customers.** The distributor's salespeople could scan a customer's parts inventory. By comparing inventory to historical usage and by looking at pricing trends and availability at nearby distribution centers, the tool recommended a reorder point and suggested purchase volume. This allowed the distributor to better manage its upstream inventory, prevent stock-outs, and deliver to customers quickly when needed. Customers tied up fewer assets in shelf inventory and reduced the footprint of their stockrooms.

Ultimately, the use of these mobile tools led to stickier customer relationships, higher customer satisfaction, and higher margins for the distributor.

Best Practice Sharing. When salespeople learn something from a customer (for example, new competitive intelligence), they can instantly communicate that information to peers using information-sharing tools on a company intranet.

Better Coaching. The right tools and data can also help sales managers be better coaches and more effectively guide the plans and actions of sales team members. Chapter 6 provides more information about the opportunity for analytics to improve sales manager coaching.

Increasingly, companies are leveraging the power of social performance tools and real-time data to enhance coaching and performance management processes. Some sales forces have systems or modules within sales force automation (SFA) systems that keep all data relevant to the performance management process organized in one place, including coaching forms, goals and objectives, and real-time metrics for measuring the achievement of goals and objectives. These systems can result in:

- Improved FLM efficiency in preparing for performance management, coaching, and mentoring sessions

- Improved effectiveness during these sessions, as FLMs have easier access to the right data for responding to key issues as they arise

- More feedback and comment from FLMs following sessions (for example, an FLM can easily provide encouraging comments and support on issues discussed on a field visit)

These improvements allow salespeople to make more timely course corrections to improve performance. And they help engage the sales force in the performance management process and culture.

Supporting Measurement, Evaluation, and Consequences with Metrics

Sales analytics can support the sales force by tracking and making available the latest metrics across categories of performance inputs and outcomes. Sample metrics for each category are shown in Figure 9-7.

Supporting the evaluation and consequences steps of performance management requires providing the sales force with up-to-date dashboards that include key metrics for each category. Because the best dashboards include diagnostic information, we will cover this topic in detail in the next section of this chapter.

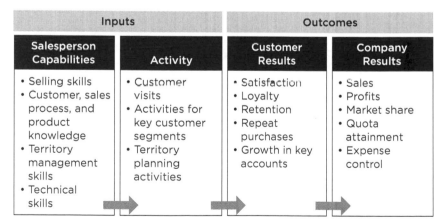

Figure 9-7. Performance management metrics

Three Rules for Providing a Sales Force with Excellent Support

- **Context is critical.** The most valuable information comes from juxtaposing just a few critical pieces of data to address a particular issue. For example, showing territory sales and potential data side by side helps a salesperson see if a sales decline is due to dominant competition or a shrinking market.

- **Less is more.** With too much information, sales force members either ignore the data or spend too much time trying to find what they are looking for, diverting time away from customers.

- **Information, *now*.** A practical solution that provides most of the data that the sales force needs now is better than an elegant solution that provides all of the data too late.

Diagnosing Performance Through Analytics

The diagnosis of performance is enhanced by integrating data from multiple sources, directing sales force attention to key issues without overloading the sales force with data, and providing frameworks for performing a qualitative diagnosis of sales force capabilities.

Integrating Data Across Multiple Sources

Analytics and dashboards are more insightful and actionable when they integrate data on results, potential, and effort to address the three questions shown in Figure 9-8.

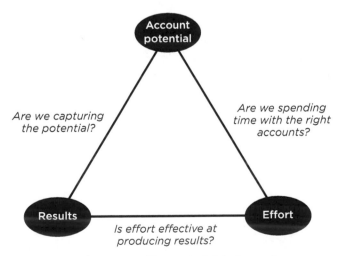

Figure 9-8. The power of integrated data for performance management

Sales Coverage Tool Increases Coaching Impact

"Coaching effectiveness improved when we began providing managers with a new sales coverage tool that integrated data on sales results with data on account potential," says John Barb, a former vice president of sales at xpedx, a distribution division within International Paper. "The tool allowed managers to compare performance of their salespeople on key results metrics, such as territory sales and gross profit, and to drill down to look at results by account, product, or industry for each salesperson. A huge value of the tool for coaching came from giving managers account potential data, calculated based on factors such as industry, account size, and past sales. With an understanding of account potential, managers could have a more balanced discussion with people about the best tactical territory plans and goals. They could point salespeople toward the best prospects and coach them on how to focus their time and energy against the best opportunities. And because the sales coverage tool presented information in a concise and visually friendly format, it was a powerful vehicle for helping managers communicate with their people and take action to improve performance."

Directing Sales Force Attention to Key Issues

Sales dashboards can turn data into actionable information. Mobile technologies can deliver the information to the sales force in real time, so it is available where and when it is needed.

The dashboard shown in Figure 9-9 on page 172, available on a mobile device, allows salespeople at a medical supply company to see an up-to-date

Tips for Effective Dashboards

Over time, dashboards can proliferate until the number of dashboards becomes overwhelming. Providing too much information is no better than providing too little information. Four strategies can help companies avoid information overload in sales dashboards:

- **Pare down.** Eliminate reports that are rarely used, and don't agree to every new request without thoroughly evaluating its potential usefulness.

- **Pinpoint the most important metrics.** On each report, include just a few key metrics that align directly with sales goals and strategies. Show comparisons that make metrics meaningful and indicators that highlight exceptions.

- **Prioritize.** Give quick access to the most important information that everyone needs (for example, implement a "favorites" option). Allow analytically savvy users to dig deeper to get more detail when they need it.

- **Provide an analytic concierge service.** Assign a person or team to respond to individual requests for analyses that address specific questions or concerns. Some companies have offshored this responsibility for high impact at low cost.

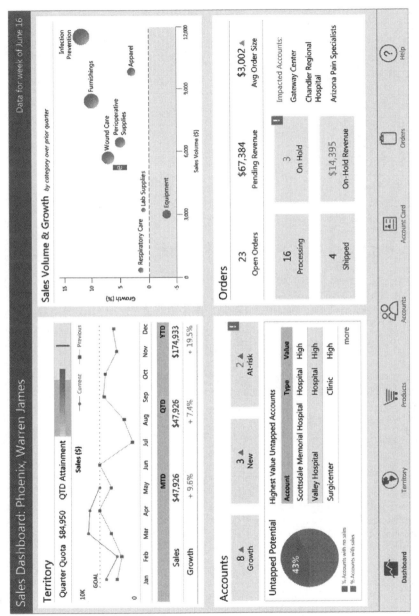

Figure 9-9. A dashboard to help salespeople focus their time

snapshot of territory sales volume, growth, and quota attainment, as well as a summary of open orders. Salespeople can drill down to see which accounts are growing, new, or "at risk," and can look at a list of high-value accounts with untapped potential. The information is presented in a visual and accessible format, making it easier for salespeople to determine the best way to spend their time.

Sales managers at the same company can get information on their mobile devices to help them coach each salesperson who reports to them. As shown in Figure 9-10, a manager can see a summary of a salesperson's sales, growth, and quota performance. The manager can also track sales activity compared to goals; can see which accounts are growing, new, or at-risk; and can see a list of high-value accounts with untapped potential. Managers can also organize notes from their coaching sessions. With easy access to current data, managers can coach with higher impact and can take more timely action to improve performance.

At another company, the dashboard shown in Figure 9-11 helps a sales leader monitor performance of key leading and lagging indicators relative to plan. From this page, the leader can drill-down into key dimensions (geography, product, customer, seller, and pipeline) to understand outliers or unexpected results and therefore prioritize areas for focus.

Three Principles for Providing a Sales Force with Excellent Diagnostics

- **Business speaks a different language.** Crunch the numbers and deliver the results, not the methodology. The most effective delivery uses "sales speak"—fewer numbers and more visuals.

- **Less is more.** Even when the diagnostic analysis is very complex, focus on just the key aspects to make the information usable and easy to digest.

- **Provide flexibility.** Many sales force questions are not from a standard playbook. Adapt the data to address the question at hand. Standard formats are helpful but not always sufficient to provide insight. An analytic concierge service can be a good way to enhance flexibility.

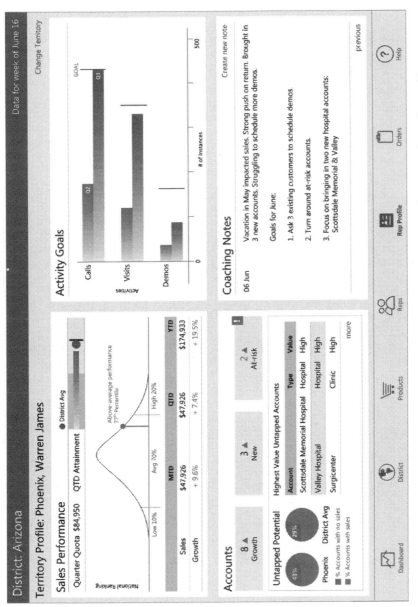

Figure 9-10. A dashboard to help sales managers improve salesperson performance through coaching

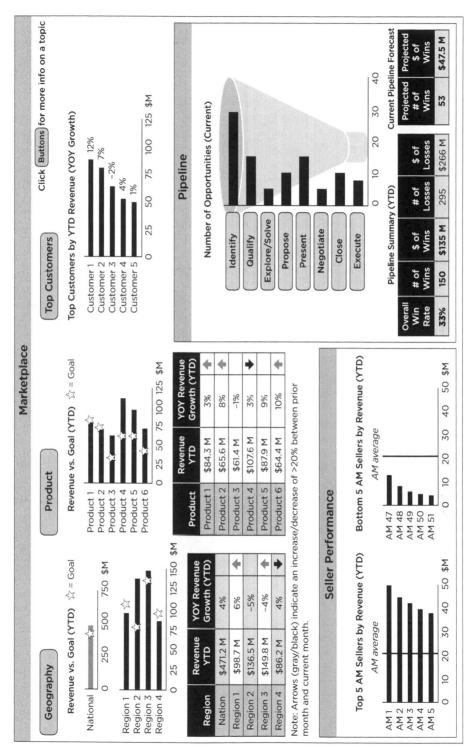

Figure 9-11. A dashboard to help a sales leader monitor performance of key leading and lagging indicators relative to plan

Providing Frameworks for Qualitative Diagnosis of Capabilities

Frameworks can help FLMs discover the right strategies for helping salespeople improve performance. For example, the qualitative framework shown in Figure 9-12 compares salespeople's capability and motivation levels to give FLMs insights about what actions are most appropriate for ensuring sustained success across their sales team.

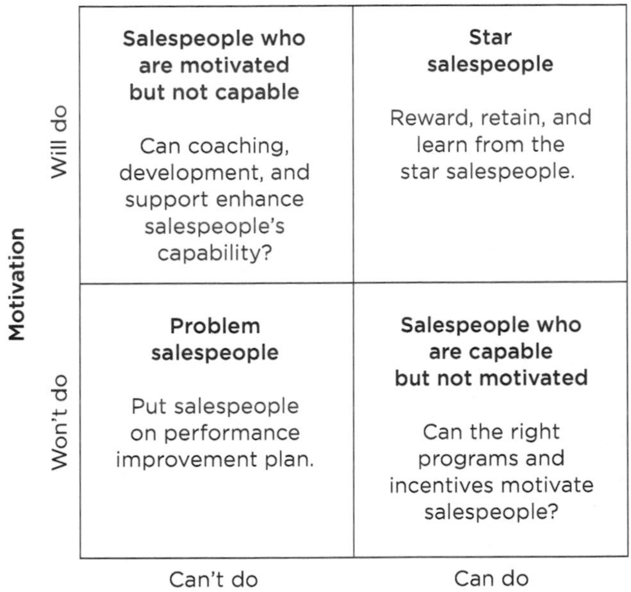

	Can't do	Can do
Will do	Salespeople who are motivated but not capable — Can coaching, development, and support enhance salespeople's capability?	Star salespeople — Reward, retain, and learn from the star salespeople.
Won't do	Problem salespeople — Put salespeople on performance improvement plan.	Salespeople who are capable but not motivated — Can the right programs and incentives motivate salespeople?

(Motivation is shown as the vertical axis.)

Figure 9-12. A qualitative framework to help FLMs manage their salespeople

Designing Performance Management Frameworks

Sales analytics can contribute to the design of frameworks that encourage the consistency of metrics and evaluation across the sales force and over time. Figure 9-13 shows some popular frameworks that can help companies manage different dimensions of sales force performance.

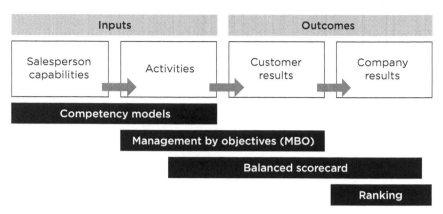

Figure 9-13. Frameworks for managing sales force performance

Competency Models

Salesperson capability and activity are perhaps the most difficult performance categories to measure objectively. Salespeople can self-report their activities, or managers can assess activity as well as capability through observation and judgment. Many sales organizations use competency models that define the level of skill and knowledge needed for success in a sales role. Competency models provide a blueprint for performance management and also guide sales force selection, learning and development, and other support programs. The sales analytics function usually plays a limited role in competency model development; typically, Human Resources (HR) and sales leaders jointly take responsibility for developing competency models. However, sales analytics functions sometimes work with HR to establish and administer the evaluation systems and processes for

> *Competency models should focus on skills, knowledge, and behaviors, not characteristics (personal qualities).*

assessing competencies over time. Chapter 6 provides more information about how to define the competencies and characteristics needed for success in a sales job.

Management by Objectives

Management by objectives (MBO) is a process through which managers work with their subordinates to jointly identify common goals, to define responsibilities and expected results, and to evaluate activities and results relative to goals as a basis for assessing each subordinate's performance. MBOs often focus on three to five "critical few" metrics that reflect sales force activities and customer results. Two examples:

- **Activity MBO.** Visit each key account at least once a month.

- **Customer results MBO.** Acquire three or more new customers each quarter.

Sales leaders and HR jointly take responsibility for guiding sales managers and salespeople through the sales force MBO process, with the sales analytics function providing input and data for tracking MBO achievement.

A best practice: If financial results are objectively measurable, tie all or almost all incentives to company results metrics. If a portion of incentives is tied to MBO achievement, keep that portion to less than 20 percent. Focus on MBO achievement during the performance evaluation process, and use it as one input for determining salary increases and career progression.

Balanced Scorecard

A balanced scorecard organizes metrics across multiple categories to provide a consistent framework for evaluating performance. Scorecards can include metrics from all of the performance categories (inputs and outcomes), but if outcomes are controllable by the salesperson and are measurable, it's best to emphasize outcome metrics.

By combining financial measures of past performance with the determinants of future performance, a balanced scorecard focuses sales force

---

A Balanced Scorecard for First-Line Sales Managers (FLMs)

"At Boston Scientific, a balanced scorecard guides the quarterly performance discussions that FLMs have with their bosses," says Chris Hartman, vice president, Central Zone, for Boston Scientific's Cardiology, Rhythm, and Vascular Group. "We have four quadrants of scorecard criteria for evaluating FLMs:

Financial metrics (for example, sales growth; percent to plan)

Customer metrics (for example, number of new customers; customer retention)

People metrics (for example, voluntary turnover; retention)

Compliance metrics that ensure adherence with FDA guidelines

We also use the scorecard as input for an annual performance appraisal and succession planning discussion."

attention on tangible and objective metrics that align with strategy and are used consistently across the sales team. The sales analytics function can play a role in working with sales leaders and HR to design balanced scorecards and will likely take the lead in providing data that track achievement on many scorecard metrics.

Ranking

Most companies rank salespeople on results metrics, such as sales and quota achievement. Companies use several arguments to explain their use of rankings:

- **Motivation.** "Salespeople like competition. They will work harder to move up in the rankings."

- **Differentiation.** "Ranking distinguishes excellent from average from poor performance. It tells us who makes President's Club."

- **Communication.** "Ranking lets people know where they stand. We don't have to deliver bad news. Salespeople at the bottom get a clear message."

Forced ranking has value for most sales forces, but it's not clear what the best strategy is for communicating rankings to individuals. Some leaders like to make all sales force rankings public, but this can have negative consequences:

- **Internally focused competition.** For one person to move up in rank, another has to move down. Salespeople focus on beating peers instead of winning against competitors, serving customers, and helping others.

- **Many visible "losers."** Most salespeople will feel unsuccessful if they are not ranked at or near the top, so ranking risks alienating the "middle" performers (75th to 25th percentile)—a large group important to the company's success.

- **Undermining a supportive culture.** Particularly if published rankings are used as a substitute for ongoing performance feedback from managers, rankings can make salespeople feel undervalued and fearful of taking risks.

- **Demotivation.** If there are only small performance differences across many salespeople, the perceived difference between a very high and a very low ranking can exaggerate the actual performance difference.

- **Diminished importance of managers.** Weak managers can allow the rankings to deliver bad news to underperformers, instead of summoning the courage to have honest discussions to help salespeople improve.

Three strategies help manage the downsides of published forced ranking:

- **Publish only the list of top performers.** These individuals become role models for the rest of the sales team. Managers can meet privately with others to share individual rankings and discuss improvement strategies.

- **Keep the time period short.** This allows salespeople to recover quickly from a low ranking.

- **Rank on multiple criteria.** This gives salespeople many ways to win. A ranking on *total sales* favors a large sales territory, *sales growth* favors a small sales territory, and *market share* rewards the best performance relative to the competition.

Forced ranking should always be based on clearly articulated objective criteria that are accurate and fair to all. For example, a ranking based on goal attainment will only reflect true performance differences if the goal-setting process is

A forced ranking based on unfair or inaccurate measures can make a satisfactory employee appear to be underperforming or can make an average performer appear excellent.

sufficiently robust. A ranking based on territory sales will only be fair if territory potential is distributed equally. Unfair or inaccurate rankings are demotivating.

Conclusion

In today's data- and technology-enabled world, sales analytics can provide sales forces with real-time information for supporting, diagnosing, and designing the sales force performance management process. Analytics add value across a spectrum of needs but are particularly valuable for helping sales forces diagnose performance issues and take timely action to keep performance on track and to capitalize on new opportunities.

The right sales analytics improve *what* results the sales force achieves (outcomes) by providing sales force members with insights that help them determine *how* results are best achieved (inputs). By getting the right information to the right people at the right time using the right medium, analytics are a key contributor to the process of managing sales force performance.

Building the Capability to Make Sales Analytics Work

Section 2 shows companies how to overcome some key implementation challenges to making analytics work. The first chapter in this section provides an overview of how to identify and build the capabilities for using analytics to improve sales force decision making. Subsequent chapters discuss specific challenges and opportunities that can affect implementation success.

■ **Chapter 10** Implementing Sales Analytics Capabilities
Complete a worksheet-based exercise to identify the capabilities, including the people and competencies, processes, and data and tools, required to deliver sales force analytic needs. Learn the steps for creating and strengthening capabilities, and find out what solutions work best for addressing common challenges.

■ **Chapter 11** Delivering Sales Analytics Through Outsourcing and Offshoring
Discover how a strategically designed network model that combines company and outsourced resources in multiple global locations can help a company identify expertise and reduce long-term costs when delivering sales analytics capabilities.

■ **Chapter 12** Aligning Sales and Information Technology
Understand the role that a sales analytics group can play in facilitating a healthy collaborative relationship between the sales force and the information technology (IT) group, and learn some strategies that work for achieving strong sales, sales analytics, and IT alignment.

■ **Chapter 13** Implementing Sales Analytics When Launching a New Sales Force

Learn about the critical role that sales analytics can play in the design of and early diagnosis for new sales organizations, and how a strong partnership between the sales force and a sales analytics function contributes to a new sales organization's success.

CHAPTER 10

Implementing Sales Analytics Capabilities

Delivering high-impact, cost-effective sales analytics requires capability development in people, processes, and tools.

Scott Shimamoto, Doug Oettinger, and Jude Konzelmann

Scott Shimamoto is the office managing principal of ZS Associates' Evanston, Illinois, office and the leader of its Business Operations Capability group. With expertise in both sales force strategy and sales operations, Scott has helped clients achieve excellence in their sales performance for more than 16 years. He also has extensive experience in sales incentive plan design and goal setting and program management. Scott has an MBA from Stanford University and a BS in electrical engineering from Vanderbilt University.

Doug Oettinger is a managing principal in ZS Associates' Evanston, Illinois, office and oversees the firm's operations in Latin America. For more than 25 years, Doug has helped leading pharmaceutical, healthcare, and industrial products companies address a broad range of sales and marketing issues, including sales force design, deployment, and compensation; customer valuation and targeting; and commercial information systems design and operation. Doug has an MBA from the Booth School of Business at the University of Chicago and is a graduate of Harvard University.

Jude Konzelmann is the office managing principal of ZS Associates' New York office and the leader of the firm's Sales Force Design practice. He has helped clients address an array of sales issues, including sales force sizing and resource allocation, customer targeting, and sales incentives design and operations. He has worked with dozens of organizations to develop and implement advanced analytics and decision support and has directed many analytics engagements offshore. Jude has a BA in economics from the University of Pennsylvania.

The authors thank former ZS associates David Vinca and Eric Seelig, and ZS principals Jeff Gold and Murali Venkatesan for their contributions to this chapter.

Sales Analytics Capability for Meeting Diverse Needs

A sales analytics team is called on to deliver many different types of work. One minute team members are racing to identify the cause of a detailed technical data problem that could delay the distribution of incentive reports and paychecks. The next minute, they are called on to participate in a senior-level meeting to share ideas on redesigning the company's sales process to better align with evolving customer needs.

Delivering on this wide-ranging set of expectations is no easy task. It requires three categories of capabilities:

- **People and competencies** to provide a range of expertise, starting with strong leadership and enabled by a culture that breeds success

- **Processes** for accomplishing work efficiently and effectively

- **Data and tools** that enable the processes and create insights

There are several challenges inherent in building these capabilities:

- Delivering high value effectively by providing expertise and service at the right time to meet sales force needs

- Delivering efficiently and reliably as corporate belts tighten and cost pressures increase

- Meeting diverse needs for support, diagnosis, and design across many sales force effectiveness (SFE) drivers and over time

Many capabilities are SFE driver–specific. For example, meeting sales force territory design needs requires *people* who are knowledgeable of and skilled in territory design issues, *processes* for working with field sales managers to execute territory changes and keep internal systems up-to-date, and specialized *data and tools* that support territory design decision making. Other SFE drivers require their own specialized expertise, processes, and data and tools.

> *Making sales analytics work requires building an array of capabilities for delivering value through support, diagnosis, and design.*

Each of the three categories (support, diagnosis, design) requires unique capabilities. Consider the representative list in Figure 10-1 of the capabilities often required for success in each category. Building and managing the diversity of these capabilities is a challenging task.

Capability	Support	Diagnose	Design
People and competencies	• Detail and process orientation • Operational mind-set	• Understanding of sales force issues • Analytic skills • Communication ability	• Wisdom about sales force issues • Project management skills • Collaboration ability
Processes	• Efficient, repeatable, automated processes	• Flexible processes and problem-solving approaches	• Problem-solving and design approaches • Change management processes
Data and tools	• Accurate, up-to-date, and consistent data • Data management and delivery tools	• Data integrated from multiple sources • Tools that support ad hoc analytics	• New data, perhaps requiring primary market research • Analysis and modeling tools

Figure 10-1. Capabilities needed for sales analytics success

This chapter shows how to build these capabilities. It is organized into three main sections:

- "Determining the Analytic Capabilities Required to Deliver on Sales Force Needs" contains a worksheet-based exercise to help companies identify the specific capabilities they will need.

- "Implementing the Capabilities" shares practical guidance and steps for creating or strengthening capabilities within an organization.

- "Addressing the Challenge of Diverse Work and Capability" describes some common difficulties that sales analytics leaders face and some solutions that can work.

Determining the Analytic Capabilities Required to Deliver on Sales Force Needs

Figure 10-2 summarizes the two steps required for identifying the capabilities needed for sales analytics to deliver on the promise of supporting, diagnosing, and designing critical SFE drivers.

Step 1: Assess Analytic Needs	Step 2: Identify Capability Gaps
Key questions for each SFE driver • What support, diagnose, and design services do we currently provide? • Do the usage and value of the services justify the cost? • What additional services could we provide?	**Key questions for each SFE driver** • How good is our current capability for delivering on sales force needs? • Where are the capability gaps?

Figure 10-2. Two steps for determining needed sales analytics capabilities

This chapter will provide guidance and sample templates that take readers through these two steps. Figure 10-3 provides a conceptual overview of the activities and worksheet tools to use; more detailed versions of the worksheets and instructions for completing them follow Figure 10-3.

Step 1: Assessing Sales Force Analytic Needs

Determining the necessary sales analytics capabilities starts with understanding what the sales force needs to be successful. Here's how to do it:

• First, list the support, diagnose, and design services that the sales analytics organization delivers today across the various SFE drivers. Look at the use of these services and their value to the sales force, and eliminate any that are not used consistently or no longer add enough value to justify their cost.

• Next, identify what else the sales analytics organization can do to better meet current and future sales force needs. The chapters in Section 1 of this book describe ways sales analytics can add value.

Use the Sales Force Needs Assessment worksheet in Figure 10-4 on page 188 as a guide for an assessment.

Step 2: Identifying Gaps in Analytic Capabilities

A self-assessment helps identify gaps in critical capabilities, including the people and competencies, processes, and data and tools required to meet sales force needs. Use the Analytic Capabilities Report Card template in Figure 10-5 on pages 190–91 as a guide for assessing readiness to deliver on the support, diagnosis, and design requirements identified in the Sales Force Needs Assessment. The questions at the top of the template can

Step 1: Assess Analytic Needs

Complete a Sales Force Needs Assessment (see Figure 10-4)

Decision Area	Current Support-Diagnose-Design Services	New Support-Diagnose-Design Services
Customer potential estimation and targeting		
Sales process		
Sales force size and structure		
Sales territory design		
Hiring and training		
Incentive compensation		
Goal setting		
Performance management		
Other SFE decision areas		

Step 2: Identify Capability Gaps

Complete an Analytic Capabilities Report Card (see Figure 10-5)

Capability	Support Rating	Diagnose Rating	Design Rating
People and competencies	1 2 3	1 2 3	1 2 3
Processes	1 2 3	1 2 3	1 2 3
Data and tools	1 2 3	1 2 3	1 2 3

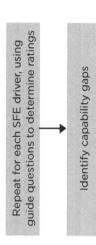

Repeat for each SFE driver, using guide questions to determine ratings →

Identify capability gaps

Figure 10-3. Activities and tools for determining needed sales analytics capabilities

SFE Driver	What support-diagnose-design services do we provide currently? (Eliminate those that don't add value to justify cost.)	What else could we do to provide value to the sales force?
Customer potential estimation and targeting		
Sales process		
Sales force size and structure		
Sales territory design		
Hiring and training		
Incentive compensation		
Goal setting		
Performance management		
Other SFE decision areas		

Example for One SFE Driver*

SFE Driver	What support-diagnose-design services do we provide?	What else could we do to provide value to the sales force?
Goal setting	**Support:** Set quarterly territory sales goals, provide tools and data to sales force for refining goals, oversee refinement process, address questions and goal-adjustment requests, track and report on goal achievement throughout the quarter.	**Diagnose:** Test company sales forecast for reasonableness, test goal allocation for fairness, and assess salespeople's commitment to goals. **Design:** If diagnosis reveals unfairness or other problems, revisit the goal-allocation approach.

*See Chapters 2 through 9 for more ideas on how sales analytics can add value through support, diagnosis, and design across the full range of SFE drivers.

Figure 10-4. Sales Force Needs Assessment worksheet

help determine the correct rating. Answer these questions independently to assess support, diagnosis, and design for each SFE driver. Figure 10-1 provides insight about the ways that capability needs may vary across the support-diagnose-design spectrum. It is useful to get input from company leaders outside sales analytics and from external experts when determining ratings.

Identify capability gaps to fill, especially those with a "1" rating on the report card.

Use the guide questions, worksheet, and example to rate capability to deliver on the support, diagnosis, and design needs for each SFE driver.

Implementing the Capabilities

With the gaps in capabilities well understood, attention turns to what to do to fill the gaps. Implementing new capabilities often requires investment in people, processes, and data and tools. This section describes some thoughtful approaches to implementing needed capabilities. These include developing a vision and strategy and creating an implementation road map, while working closely with sales leaders to ensure high sales force impact and strong commitment.

Developing a Vision and Strategy

The simplest solution to capability gaps is to throw resources at them, for example, by licensing new tools or by hiring high-level experts. But resources are expensive, and at a time when sales analytics groups face more cost pressure than ever before, it is critical to develop a vision and strategy that achieve both effectiveness and cost-efficiency.

Two activities help with developing the right vision and strategy for providing sales analytics capabilities:

- Prioritize sales force needs and focus on investments that are both effective and cost-efficient.

- Consider whether it's best to use internal resources to do the work or to leverage external partners that can bring more value for the cost.

Capability	Questions for Rating Capability to Deliver
People and competencies	• Do competency models guide performance management, development, and recruiting? • Do career paths motivate and develop people to excel? • Do team members possess needed knowledge and skills? • Does the culture support quality work and customer focus?
Processes	• Is the work streamlined and completed routinely on time without requiring rework or last-minute heroics? • Are processes well documented, automated, and effective at producing quality results? • Is there sufficient ability to respond to ad hoc requests?
Data and tools	• Does the data management capability produce high-quality, timely information? • Are applications and tools available that enable consistent quality delivery of sales force needs?

How to Rate Capability on the Analytics Capability Report Card
1 = lack basic capability to deliver (answer is "no" to all/most questions)
2 = have basic capability to deliver (answer is "sometimes" to all/most questions, or answer is "yes" to some and "no" to some questions)
3 = have advanced capability to deliver (answer is "yes" to all/most questions)
NA = the need is not a current priority for sales analytics

Potential Estimation and Targeting	Support	Diagnose	Design
People and competencies	NA 1 2 3	NA 1 2 3	NA 1 2 3
Processes	NA 1 2 3	NA 1 2 3	NA 1 2 3
Data and tools	NA 1 2 3	NA 1 2 3	NA 1 2 3

Sales Process	Support	Diagnose	Design
People and competencies	NA 1 2 3	NA 1 2 3	NA 1 2 3
Processes	NA 1 2 3	NA 1 2 3	NA 1 2 3
Data and tools	NA 1 2 3	NA 1 2 3	NA 1 2 3

Sales Force Size and Structure	Support	Diagnose	Design
People and competencies	NA 1 2 3	NA 1 2 3	NA 1 2 3
Processes	NA 1 2 3	NA 1 2 3	NA 1 2 3
Data and tools	NA 1 2 3	NA 1 2 3	NA 1 2 3

Figure 10-5. Analytic Capabilities Report Card template

Sales Territory Design	Support	Diagnose	Design
People and competencies	NA 1 2 3	NA 1 2 3	NA 1 2 3
Processes	NA 1 2 3	NA 1 2 3	NA 1 2 3
Data and tools	NA 1 2 3	NA 1 2 3	NA 1 2 3

Hiring and Training	Support	Diagnose	Design
People and competencies	NA 1 2 3	NA 1 2 3	NA 1 2 3
Processes	NA 1 2 3	NA 1 2 3	NA 1 2 3
Data and tools	NA 1 2 3	NA 1 2 3	NA 1 2 3

Incentive Compensation	Support	Diagnose	Design
People and competencies	NA 1 2 3	NA 1 2 3	NA 1 2 3
Processes	NA 1 2 3	NA 1 2 3	NA 1 2 3
Data and tools	NA 1 2 3	NA 1 2 3	NA 1 2 3

Goal Setting	Support	Diagnose	Design
People and competencies	NA 1 2 3	NA 1 2 3	NA 1 2 3
Processes	NA 1 2 3	NA 1 2 3	NA 1 2 3
Data and tools	NA 1 2 3	NA 1 2 3	NA 1 2 3

Performance Management	Support	Diagnose	Design
People and competencies	NA 1 2 3	NA 1 2 3	NA 1 2 3
Processes	NA 1 2 3	NA 1 2 3	NA 1 2 3
Data and tools	NA 1 2 3	NA 1 2 3	NA 1 2 3

Other SFE Decision Areas	Support	Diagnose	Design
People and competencies	NA 1 2 3	NA 1 2 3	NA 1 2 3
Processes	NA 1 2 3	NA 1 2 3	NA 1 2 3
Data and tools	NA 1 2 3	NA 1 2 3	NA 1 2 3

EXAMPLE

Goal Setting	Support	Diagnose	Design
People and competencies	NA 1 2 ③	NA ① 2 3	NA ① 2 3
Processes	NA 1 2 ③	NA 1 ② 3	NA 1 ② 3
Data and tools	NA 1 2 ③	NA 1 ② 3	NA 1 ② 3

Figure 10-5 (continued)   Capability gaps

Determining the Most Important Sales Force Needs

The cost of sales analytics is generally a small fraction of the total sales force budget; yet most sales analytics groups are ultimately evaluated based on cost-effectiveness. Delivering cost-effective sales analytics requires prioritizing sales force needs and focusing on those that create the most value for the investment. It also requires regularly assessing sales analytics services and eliminating those that no longer add enough value. Too often sales forces experience "analytics creep." Sales force and customer needs change, and new dashboards, tools, or other programs and services are launched to support the new needs. At the same time, too few old services get eliminated, even though some are no longer used regularly. Soon, the sales force becomes overwhelmed by the volume of analytics, and the cost of providing all of the services spirals out of control. Avoiding this situation requires discipline to regularly eliminate old services as new ones are added. By tracking the use of current services or by conducting periodic surveys of salespeople and customers, analytics groups can ascertain the use and ongoing value of their services, making it easier to determine which services to eliminate to remain cost-effective as new needs emerge.

> *Sales forces experience "analytics creep" when they launch new dashboards, tools, or other services without eliminating old services that are no longer used regularly.*

Deciding Who Will Do the Work

Sales analytics vision and strategy include a plan for who will perform the work: an internal group, external partners, or a combination. Here, we touch briefly on this issue. Readers who want more detail can read Chapter 11 about creating a network model for optimized delivery of sales analytics work that draws on company and outsourced resources in multiple geographic locations.

There are several advantages to doing sales analytics work internally. An internal group allows companies to:

- **Build and retain institutional knowledge** that becomes a source of competitive advantage. This can require providing career paths that encourage retention of talented sales analysts.

- **Maintain control of the work** and avoid dependence on outside consultants. Doing work internally helps ensure that the company's intellectual property is protected.

The company introduced in the example in Figure 10-5 was considering seven possible investments to improve goal-setting diagnosis and design capabilities. Three of the investments involved people and competencies, two focused on process improvement, and two involved data and tools upgrades. The company faced resource constraints and needed to prioritize and invest in a small number of the most important projects first. The scorecard shown in Figure 10-6 helped the company set priorities based on strategic impact and ease of implementation.

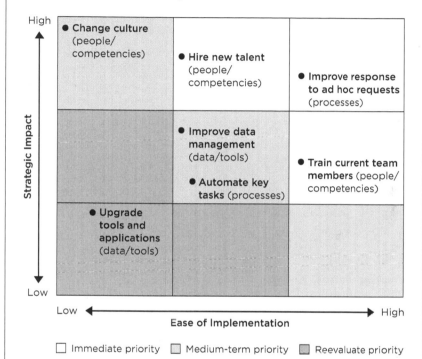

Figure 10-6. Scorecard for prioritizing goal-setting improvement projects

Strategic impact scores measure the extent to which each project would improve goal-setting diagnosis and design. These scores were derived based on management judgment and input from outside experts. Ease of implementation scores reflect the time and cost of each project and the extent of sales force disruption involved. These estimates were prepared by sales analytics team members and external partners.

The scorecard provides a snapshot of the current situation that is useful for setting priorities. The highest priority opportunities are those for which both ease of implementation and strategic impact are high. In deciding which projects to tackle first, leaders also took into account the timing of the impact on sales force performance. Some projects will produce results quickly (for example, training current team members); others will take longer to impact results (for example, changing the culture). By conducting assessments like this on a regular basis, companies can make smart sales analytics investments and drive continuous sales force improvement.

- **Avoid transaction costs** associated with coordinating work among multiple outside partners. As the number of partners grows, it becomes increasingly difficult to control partner management costs and achieve watertight coordination and accountability.

There are also advantages to outsourcing. Many companies find that outsourcing at least some of their sales analytics work allows them to:

- **Achieve cost savings**, especially by moving work to offshore partners.

- **Access best-of-breed expertise**, especially when work requires specialized experience or skills. Talented internal staff can then develop broader skills that can allow them to advance beyond an analytics role, making them more likely to stay with the company.

- **Manage peaks and valleys in workload**, especially when sales analytics are needed for special projects (such as a sales process transformation) that could stretch an internal team beyond its limits. Experienced partners can contribute strategically to the design of special projects. Or outside partners can "keep the lights on" by supporting standard processes and giving internal staff time to focus on design. It's easier to "downsize" an outside partner than it is to cut internal staff when a special project finishes.

Companies may outsource work for some SFE drivers while using internal staff to perform work for others. They may also split the work for any SFE driver between internal staff and external partners. For example, they may use internal staff to *support* basic sales force needs for incentive compensation (IC) plan administration and tracking and to *diagnose* how well the IC plan is working. But they may choose to tap into outside expertise when it comes time to *design* a new IC plan.

Creating a Road Map

With a vision in place, sales analytics leaders must figure out how to get from point A to point B. A road map includes a concrete list of steps for moving the organization from what it is today to what it should become. Consider the case of one sales analytics group that sought to improve the territory design service it provided. Its road map consisted of specific steps for closing capability gaps. Figure 10-7 shows how those steps went beyond a simple restatement of the challenges.

Although road maps are important for guiding implementation, they must be flexible, especially in situations with evolving needs and uncertainty

Restatement of the Challenge	Specific Plan for Closing the Capability Gap
Improve leadership in territory design	• Hire a new manager for the territory design team. • Seek candidates with territory design expertise and strong project management skills.
Improve territory design business processes	• Create and maintain standard operating procedures for making territory changes. • Include milestones, data requirements, key roles, and ownership for each step in the process. • Hold decision makers accountable for time line delays.
Provide analysts with easy access to data across functions	• Work with a third party to develop a robust data infrastructure that provides analysts with access to the data they need. • Internalize operation of the data warehouse within 18 months.

Figure 10-7. A road map for closing territory design capability gaps

about requirements. A flexible road map allows leaders to adapt and change plans as they learn.

Working with Sales Leaders and Other Stakeholders

Implementing high-impact sales analytics capabilities requires sales analytics team members to work closely with the sales force and other internal stakeholders. Changes, even those that involve saving money in the long term, often require an immediate investment. This can include hiring new personnel or eliminating some roles, redirecting internal resources, or outsourcing some work to a third party. Shared expectations and agreement about priorities ensure that:

• Analytics meet sales force needs, focus on critical issues, and continually deliver value to the sales force and customers.

• There is a commitment to invest in the resources required to deliver the analytics.

• The amount of the investment is appropriate and produces tangible improvements and measurable success.

• A plan is in place for managing any disruption created by changes in analytics capabilities and services.

Addressing the Challenge of Diverse Work and Capability

Many sales analytics organizations find it difficult to overcome the fundamental challenge of delivering the diverse capabilities required to meet the wide range of sales force analytic needs. Whether the capabilities come in the form of people, processes, or data and tools, one size does not fit all, and requirements vary substantially with the role that sales analytics play. Building and managing a world-class sales analytics organization requires managing the three sources of diversity illustrated in Figure 10-8. This section describes useful approaches for addressing these challenges.

- **Diverse people and competencies.** The competencies required for *supporting* the sales organization are quite different from those required for *diagnosis* and *design*. Sales analytics leaders must hire, develop, and manage at least two different profiles of individuals to accomplish the required heterogeneous work. Diverse profiles lead to nonhierarchical career paths within sales analytics, as well as between sales analytics and other company departments. Managing this requires creativity in bringing individuals in and out of the function to encourage their continued growth.

- **Different work styles.** Sales analytics support work is ongoing, requiring a process-oriented work style. Diagnosis and design work is episodic, requiring a project-oriented work style. Sales analytics leaders must effectively manage both types of work simultaneously.

- **Variety of data and tools.** Support work requires accurate data and tools that enable efficient and reliable delivery. Diagnosis and design usually

	Support	Diagnose	Design
1 People and competencies	Process/detail expert	Analysis/design expert	
2 Processes	Process	Project	
3 Data and tools	Accurate, timely data Efficient tools	Integrated data Flexible tools	

Figure 10-8. The challenges of managing diverse work and capabilities

require additional data, often integrated from multiple sources, and decision support tools that enable flexible, creative, and timely analysis.

Managing Diverse People and Competencies

It is challenging to manage the roles and career paths of sales analytics team members who have diverse competencies and career aspirations.

Structuring Roles for Diverse People and Competencies

A sales analytics function needs a wide range of support, diagnosis, and design competencies to meet sales force needs. Consider what is required for just one SFE driver: incentive compensation. A team responsible for supporting IC must include individuals with competencies for executing an efficient, error-free, on-time process for calculating and paying incentives. In contrast, a team charged with diagnosing IC problems or with redesigning an IC plan needs individuals with an understanding of human behavior, insight into how certain IC features affect salespeople's behavior, and financial acumen for projecting the costs and benefits of different IC plans. This requires conceptual abilities and knowledge of IC plan design principles. It might also require leading discussions with a vice president–level audience.

An individual who is good at IC support is unlikely to possess the competencies needed for IC diagnosis and design. At the same time, an individual who is good at diagnosis and design is unlikely to find support work sufficiently analytic to be gratifying and probably lacks the process discipline required to be good at it. Yet both the support and the diagnosis/design participants are contributors and are on the same team.

People with at least two different profiles are required for delivering analytics that span sales force support, diagnosis, and design needs.

Accomplishing heterogeneous work starts with defining the roles and the specific competencies required of each. Roles vary based on the size and scope of the sales analytics organization, but at least two different profiles are required for spanning the support-diagnose-design spectrum.

- **Process/detail expert:** Someone who, in addition to being process-driven and detail-oriented, is passionate about quality control and efficiency, technically sound, and prefers structured work, even if it's repetitive.

- **Analysis/design expert:** Someone who likes less structure and more variety in work, is a problem-solver, and likes developing creative solutions, diagnosing issues, and creating new systems and processes.

Asking a "detail whiz" to do the work of a "designer" (or vice versa) is a recipe for disaster.

There are also challenges inherent in managing the two individuals. A manager with an analysis/design profile is unlikely to be good at teaching or overseeing someone who has a process/detail profile; the reverse is true as well. Individuals with these different profiles need different managers, or at least different coaches or mentors to help them learn and grow and do a good job.

Companies such as General Electric have had success using internal consultants to oversee sales analytics teams and projects. These individuals receive training in quality management and process improvement methods (such as the Six Sigma techniques and tools developed by Motorola in the mid-1980s and made famous by GE in the mid-1990s), giving them analysis and design expertise, along with a strong appreciation for processes and details. Internal consultants can structure problems, delegate work, and help process/detail-oriented people see the big picture so that team members work cohesively together toward a common goal.

Managing Nonhierarchical Career Paths

It's hard enough to design a sales analytics organization that allows people in diverse roles to work well together at a static point in time. Further complicating matters, the organization has to evolve and sustain itself over time, creating a new set of challenges related to career paths.

Individuals at the bottom of the sales analytics organization chart often have diverse and specialized expertise. A sales analytics manager likely manages people who have a range of skills and knowledge and who do fundamentally different jobs. Some may have technical expertise in a specialized sales decision area, such as compensation, territory design, or performance management. Some may be process/detail experts, others analysis/design experts. Most likely, at least some of the individuals have skills and knowledge that the manager doesn't possess. And it's likely that the career aspirations of many of the individuals involve something other than becoming a sales analytics manager. Looking up the organization chart, individuals find that some of their superiors, whom they admire, are on an altogether different career path, and they become unsure of where their career is headed.

Sales analytics organizations must find ways to manage through this difficulty. Often, the best way to manage nonhierarchical career paths is through job rotations that look outside the immediate group to other company departments where common skills are needed and developed.

Rotations between the sales force and the sales analytics function allow salespeople or managers to build on their experience in the field while broadening their skill set. Former sales force members bring a deep understanding of sales force and customer needs to sales analytics. The right individual possesses technical and analytic knowledge and interest in addition to sales experience. Selecting the wrong person from the sales force just to fill a position is unlikely to work well for the individual or for the sales analytics function. But as sales forces become increasingly tech-savvy, more and more salespeople are likely to emerge as candidates for sales analytics positions.

Successful rotations can also occur between sales analytics and other headquarters functions. Good candidates often flourish in roles in finance, for example, where a passion for details and analysis, coupled with a strong understanding of business information and metrics, is critical to success. Rotations back and forth with marketing or marketing research can work well too. These departments have many people who possess a process/detail or an analysis/design profile. And some brand team members can excel in analysis/design sales analytics roles as well.

Aligning the Work Style to the Type of Work

The best approach for managing sales analytics work varies across the support-diagnose-design spectrum. Managing an efficient, error-free, and on-time monthly process for calculating and paying incentives, for example, requires a different approach than managing a one-time project to diagnose or redesign the IC plan. Sales analytics leaders must recognize that different work requires different work styles. They must remain flexible in managing heterogeneous work appropriately to deliver on sales force needs. There are at least two different work style approaches.

- A **process-oriented** approach and mind-set help ensure the efficiency and quality of structured, repetitive work, such as ongoing support tasks or regularly performed diagnoses. Such work is best guided by a process map that details the steps, participants, and milestones required.

- A **project-oriented** approach and mind-set provide structure for tasks that require problem solving and creativity, such as a one-time diagnosis of an issue or the design of a new sales force system or program. Such work is best guided by a project plan that organizes the work required and keeps activity on track, while allowing for sufficient flexibility to meet sales force needs.

Improving the management of ongoing process-focused work is a huge opportunity for sales analytics. Productivity gains are achieved in three primary ways:

> *Productivity gains of 15 percent or more have been achieved through initiatives aimed at making ongoing processes more efficient.*

- Improving internal sales analytics processes to increase speed and quality, especially by automating error-prone steps or documenting steps that rely too heavily on the heroic efforts of star performers

- Improving the boundaries and handoffs with other functions (for example, streamlining the sharing of data with marketing or human resources)

- Focusing relentlessly on continuous process improvement

Managing Data and Tools to Meet Heterogeneous Needs

The tools and data required to deliver sales analytics work vary across the support-diagnose-design spectrum. Providing support requires data that are accurate and timely and tools that enable the efficient and reliable delivery of information, often via mobile technology. Diagnosis and design usually involve more extensive data integrated from multiple sources, as well as decision support tools that enable flexible and quick response, creative analysis, modeling, and the creation of compelling outputs.

Figure 10-9 shows an example of the data and tools that one organization needed to support, diagnose, and design its incentive compensation plan.

Cutting Administration Costs by Simplifying the Incentive Plan

The sales analytics group for a large multinational company with over 3,000 salespeople and over a dozen sales roles faced the challenge of administering a complex incentive compensation plan. Sales managers frequently requested case-by-case adjustments to territory sales goals in the middle of an incentive period in response to changes in local market conditions. Handling all these adjustments made the IC plan administration process inefficient, prone to errors, and therefore very costly. The company simplified the plan and allowed mid-period goal adjustments only in response to significant unanticipated market events. This reduced the complexity of IC plan administration, drastically reduced the number of errors, and cut plan administration costs from $6 to $2 million a year. The improvements in timeliness and accuracy led to increased field engagement and motivation.

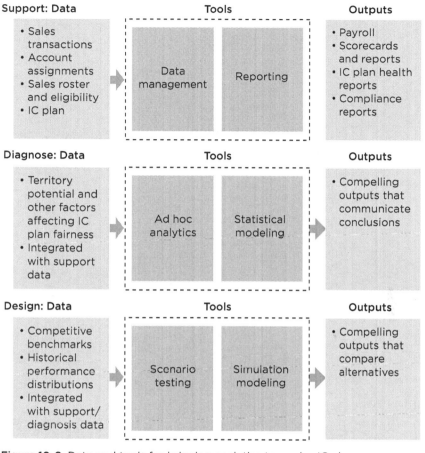

Figure 10-9. Data and tools for bringing analytics to a sales IC plan

Conclusion

A structured approach, such as the one described in this chapter, can help companies determine and build the sales analytics capabilities needed to meet sales force needs. In addition to the general implementation challenges described in this chapter, many companies face situation-specific challenges and can benefit from the advice provided in the next three chapters:

- Chapter 11: Delivering Sales Analytics Through Outsourcing and Offshoring
- Chapter 12: Aligning Sales and Information Technology
- Chapter 13: Implementing Sales Analytics When Launching a New Sales Force

Delivering Sales Analytics Through Outsourcing and Offshoring

Companies can strategically outsource and offshore many sales analytics capabilities to source expertise while reducing long-term costs.

Dharmendra Sahay and Ram Moorthy

Dharmendra Sahay is a managing principal on ZS Associates' executive team and is based in the firm's New York office. For more than 25 years, he has worked with pharmaceutical clients to outsource and offshore sales and marketing support functions. Dharmendra has an MBA from Northwestern University's Kellogg School of Management, an MS in computer science from Northwestern University, and a degree in electrical engineering from the Indian Institute of Technology, New Delhi.

Ram Moorthy is a principal in ZS Associates' Los Angeles office. He has over 15 years of experience addressing strategic sales and marketing issues in the pharmaceutical, biotechnology, and medical supply industries. His areas of expertise include sales force design and structural reorganization, performance improvement and tracking, incentive compensation, and management of cost-effective outsourced engagements using a mix of local and offshore resources. Ram has an MBA from the University of Chicago and a PhD from Tufts University.

The authors thank former ZS associate Anand D'Souza for his contributions to this chapter.

Outsourcing and Offshoring: A Network Model of Optimized Delivery

The practice of outsourcing (using vendors, consultants, or other outside partners) and offshoring (using globally distributed resources) is not new in sales analytics. For years, many sales organizations have outsourced portions of their analytics work, including both *process-based* analytics (for example, sales reporting, incentive compensation administration) and *knowledge-based* analytics (incentive compensation design, sales force sizing and structuring). Beginning in the 1990s, some companies sought cost savings by moving portions of their process-based analytics work offshore. Today, advances in technology and the reduction of cultural barriers create opportunities to move knowledge-based analytics work offshore as well.

When done correctly, outsourcing and offshoring can provide a range of high-value, cost-effective sales analytics services. However, companies that have tried outsourcing and offshoring have experienced mixed results. Working with outside partners in dispersed locations creates challenges for coordinating work, creating accountability, and protecting intellectual property. Companies that overcome these challenges can capture the huge opportunity that outsourcing and offshoring bring to sales analytics.

Companies at the frontier of using outsourcing and offshoring are moving toward what we call a *network model of optimized delivery*. This model creates a virtual organization that meets sales force analytic needs through a combination of company and outsourced resources in multiple global locations. Figure 11-1 shows how outsourced, onshore, and offshore resources

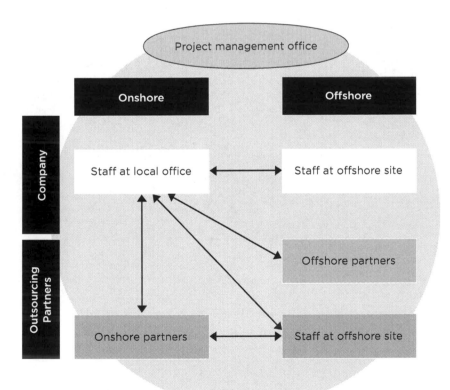

Figure 11-1. The network model of optimized delivery for sales analytics

Employing the Network Model at a Pharmaceutical Company
A pharmaceutical company uses a globally distributed network of company resources and external partners to meet sales analytic and operational needs. The company outsources most sales analytics to its two partners. One partner focuses on analytics-driven needs, such as sales force resource and territory planning; the other focuses on more routine work, such as sales reporting and sales automation system administration. Both perform much of their work in their offshore operations. The company's internal sales analytics staff focuses mostly on program management and partner coordination. It acts as a consulting interface with the sales organization and other internal users and departments. It also governs service-level agreements for each partner. All participants—internal or external, onshore or offshore—are viewed as part of one organization.

come together in a network model, guided and coordinated by a company's cross-functional project management office (PMO).

This holistic approach optimizes the opportunity to:

- *Source expertise* by tapping into a network of specialized capabilities in the multiple locations of the company and its outsourcing partners
- *Reduce long-term costs* by using the most cost-effective resources for different types of work

Companies hope to achieve a variety of objectives through an outsourcing/offshoring sales analytics solution, but there are also arguments for keeping those capabilities in-house.

Objectives for Outsourcing/Offshoring Capabilities:

- Optimize cost.
- Manage peaks and valleys in workload.
- Access best-of-breed expertise.

Arguments for Keeping Capabilities In-House:

- Retain institutional knowledge and create competitive advantage.
- Maintain control of work.
- Reduce coordination requirements.

The best model for delivering sales analytic capabilities depends on the importance of these objectives in a given situation. Figure 11-2 summarizes the major strengths and weaknesses of three possible models relative to each objective.

Objective	In-House in a Single Location	In-House with a Captive Offshore Center	Network of Multiple Partners and Locations
Optimize cost		✓	✓✓
Manage peaks and valleys in workload			✓✓
Access best-of-breed expertise			✓✓
Retain institutional knowledge	✓✓	✓	
Maintain control of work	✓✓	✓	
Reduce coordination requirements	✓✓	✓	

✓ = supports the objective ✓✓ = strongly supports the objective

Figure 11-2. Objectives achieved by three capability delivery models

A network model is often the best choice for large sales organizations that face pressure to cut costs and need flexibility to adapt to rapidly changing business needs.

Steps for Setting Up a Network Model

Companies transitioning to a network model can follow a structured five-step approach that addresses the key issues, as shown in Figure 11-3.

Define a Vision and Goals for the Network Model

Because the best design for a network model depends on business goals, it's important to start with a clear vision of those goals. A goal of reducing costs likely suggests the use of offshore resources. A goal of maintaining control of work likely suggests the use of in-house resources. The priority and importance of the objectives listed in Figure 11-2 have direct impact on network model design.

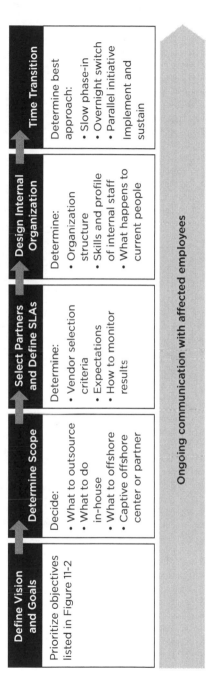

Define Vision and Goals	Determine Scope	Select Partners and Define SLAs	Design Internal Organization	Time Transition
Prioritize objectives listed in Figure 11-2	Decide: • What to outsource • What to do in-house • What to offshore • Captive offshore center or partner	Determine: • Vendor selection criteria • Expectations • How to monitor results	Determine: • Organization structure • Skills and profile of internal staff • What happens to current people	Determine best approach: • Slow phase-in • Overnight switch • Parallel initiative Implement and sustain

Ongoing communication with affected employees

Figure 11-3. Steps for building a network model

Type of Company	Situation	Sales Analytics Goals
Large insurance company	• Sales analytics deliver quarterly sales reports to a network of thousands of agents and their managers. • A head count shortage for managing quarter-end workload creates significant quality issues. • The focus is on the *support* of operational sales force needs.	• High-quality output • Manage peaks and valleys in workload
Midsize technology company	• The company strategy is to grow through acquisition. • Sales analytics struggle to keep up with the ongoing integration of newly acquired companies. • With each acquisition, the focus is on *design* across sales force decision areas, while meeting growing *support* needs.	• Integration expertise • Rapid implementation
Large custom equipment manufacturer	• The company seeks to reduce the high cost of delivering sales analytics in-house. • The focus is on providing standard *support* services, while also performing *diagnosis* in response to ad hoc sales force requests.	• Reduced cost of operation • Agility to address quickly changing business needs

Figure 11-4. Sales analytics goals in three situations

Goals also depend on the type of sales analytics work. Often, a network model must deliver on a broad range of support, diagnosis, and design needs across many sales force decision areas. Figure 11-4 shows some examples.

A network model requires a strong partnership between the internal sales analytics team, the sales organization, and other company functions—and the partnership must extend to onshore and offshore external partners. A clear vision of sales analytics needs is a critical first step in establishing this partnership.

Determine the Scope of the Network Model

Determining scope involves defining the tasks to outsource and offshore.

What to Outsource?

Technology has reduced the coordination effort associated with outsourcing work today. As a result, companies find it cost-effective to outsource a broad scope of sales analytics work, including support, diagnosis, and design. For process-based support work, outsourcing partners can easily create a high level of transparency by monitoring and reporting on metrics such as run times, error rates, and process improvements. The characteristics of business processes influence the outsourcing decision, as do company culture and philosophy.

Outsourcing is often the best option when these conditions exist:

- **There are peaks and valleys in the workload.** Partners can redeploy resources efficiently, minimizing costs associated with tasks linked to planning cycles, such as call planning and quota setting. They can also provide temporary resources for one-time, event-driven projects, such as a sales force resizing.

- **A partner offers economies of scale.** For some ongoing services (for example, IC plan administration), partners with considerable experience are well positioned to deliver high-quality work efficiently. When outsourcing new systems development (for example, a customer relationship management system), it's usually cheaper to buy rather than build because a partner can spread development costs across many clients.

- **An outside company offers unique expertise.** It's hard to develop in-house expertise on issues that occur infrequently, such as transforming a sales process or combining two sales organizations in a merger.

Some functions are clear candidates for outsourcing on many dimensions. However, any one dimension can provide a sufficient reason to outsource.

Outsourcing may not be a good option when a function is highly strategic. For example, one company declined to outsource the management of customer targeting data because, even though the capability appeared to be a good outsourcing candidate otherwise, leaders viewed the company's targeting approach as a source of competitive advantage.

What to Offshore: Process-Based or Knowledge-Based Work?

The first offshoring operations in the 1990s focused on process-based work, such as standard report production. This work had predictable content and required little interaction with users. Recent trends make it possible to expand the scope of the sales analytics work that can be offshored:

- Reduced time, distance, and language barriers due to technology
- Fewer cultural barriers as offshore partners use on-site rotations and accent neutralization training to promote a global business culture
- More offshore partners that have business issue expertise

As a result of these trends, many offshore partners now perform knowledge-based work, such as ad hoc analysis, qualitative sales research, and IC plan design. This work requires more frequent interaction with users and quicker response to changing business conditions. Often, the work performed offshore is supplemented with on-site support.

The degree of structure in the work and the amount of user interaction required determine whether work is more suitable for process-based or knowledge-based offshoring. One company used the framework in Figure 11-5 to determine which type of offshoring partner it should seek for

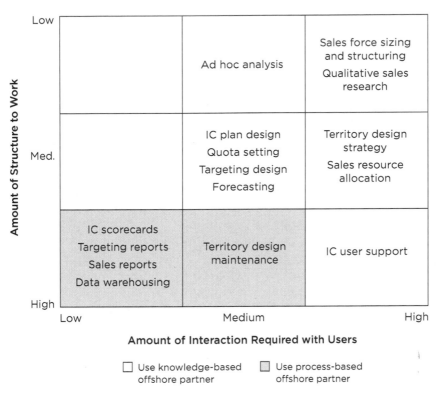

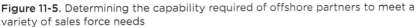

Figure 11-5. Determining the capability required of offshore partners to meet a variety of sales force needs

different pieces of the work it planned to offshore. It selected two off-shore partners: (1) a process-based partner that had functional, technical, and process expertise and emphasized both cost savings and quality and (2) a knowledge-based partner that had business and consulting expertise, could handle unscheduled, frequent contact with quick response, and put primary emphasis on quality with secondary emphasis on cost savings. In some cases, it's possible to find a single offshore partner that offers both process-based and knowledge-based expertise.

Select Partners and Define Service-Level Agreements

A successful network model requires selecting the right partners and then setting expectations and monitoring performance relative to expectations through a robust service-level agreement (SLA).

How to Select Partners?

A partner evaluation scorecard, such as the one shown in Figure 11-6, facilitates the evaluation and comparison of potential partners.

In the example shown in Figure 11-6, Partner 1 may be better at providing a wide spectrum of outsourced business functions that require both process-based and knowledge-based capabilities, due to its high score on sales and marketing expertise. But Partner 2 is a better choice if the engagement includes only routine and process-based offshoring functions. This company might consider a two-partner model that gives Partner 1 the more knowledge-based functions and Partner 2 the more process-based functions. Using two partners provides the benefits of "best of breed" for each function, but it also creates added costs to coordinate with two partners.

Partner evaluation goes beyond a facile inspection. There must be a good cultural match between the outsourcing partner and the client company, including similar values and responsiveness. Because these dimensions are intangible and difficult to assess, it's useful to work with a partner for a trial period before making a long-term commitment. As part of the trial, making a typical change to the scope of the work required can test how well the partner responds.

> *The most common error when selecting outsourcing partners is to overemphasize the importance of cost while underemphasizing the importance of expertise and cultural fit.*

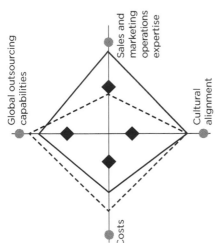

		Weight*	Score** Partner 1	Score** Partner 2
Global outsourcing capabilities	Has successfully served other clients of similar size and scope	3	4	4
	Has the offshoring capabilities for routine as well as onshore, knowledge-based processes	3	3	5
	Has the program-management capabilities, tools, and processes for large-scale engagements	3	5	4
Sales and marketing operations expertise	Has breadth of expertise in different sales and marketing operations functions	3	4	2
	Has demonstrated innovation in addressing unique sales and marketing issues	3	5	2
	Has the assets in relevant areas for quick setup	2	4	2
Cultural alignment	Exhibits similar core values, capabilities, and professionalism	2	4	4
	Has worked with the organization successfully in the past	2	3	3
	Will have the resources and the mind-set to stretch if unexpected needs arise	2	4	4
Costs	Long-term and short-term costs	2	2	4
	How much effort will your team need to spend when the engagement is under way?	2	4	4
	Are there any exit costs?	2	4	4

*1 = low; 2 = medium; 3 = high   **1 = poor > 5 = excellent

Figure 11-6. A partner evaluation scorecard

> **Recognizing the Consequences of a Cultural Mismatch**
>
> In one large outsourcing engagement, a partner's structured bureaucratic culture of working within the contractual domain of service-level agreements was incompatible with the client company's culture of reacting quickly to business needs. Although the partner met the terms of the agreement with the client, the partner's lack of empathy for the client's sense of urgency undermined the service.

Set Expectations and Monitor Performance

A good relationship between a company and an outsourcing partner requires clear expectations up front, as well as the ongoing monitoring of performance against those expectations. Some best practices for setting expectations and monitoring performance include:

- Set practical and enforceable objectives in the SLA.
- Develop and track performance metrics that are consistent with the objectives.
- Seek full transparency and use technology to track metrics.
- Require cost deflation and ongoing process improvements on long-term projects.
- Define in the SLA the ownership of responsibilities, the triaging of issues, and any multipartner coordination required.
- Specify in the SLA any incentives and penalties tied to performance.

Figure 11-7 shows the dimensions and metrics that one company used to track the performance of an outsourcing partner and includes an example of the actions tied to the partner's performance.

Design the Internal Organization

With responsibilities moving to outside partners, two major changes are likely to affect the internal sales analytics organization:

- **Downsizing.** Often star performers and senior team members stay on, but many positions are eliminated; leaders can help employees find positions elsewhere within the company.
- **New competencies.** The internal group takes on a new role focusing on coordination and partner management. Current personnel are often ill-suited to take on these new responsibilities.

Dimension	Metric	Performance	Weight	Overall Performance	Action
Quality	Number of accurate data items	92%	60%		No penalty but partner has to submit a plan to address quality issues
	Total data items **!** *8 errors in deliverables*				
Timeliness	−5% for each delay +5% reward for each early delivery	105%	20%	96%	
Flexibility	−5% for each scheduled change not implemented +5% for each unscheduled change implemented	98%	20%		

Figure 11-7. Tracking partner performance, incentives, and penalties

Sometimes leaders are so focused on head-count reductions and cost savings that they overlook the resources required to manage and coordinate partners in the network. Without these resources, the network cannot respond quickly and appropriately to changes. Although moving to a network model usually creates cost savings, a greater proportion of costs must be dedicated to network coordination and management, as illustrated in Figure 11-8.

The internal organization supporting a network model includes a project management office, which is a cross-functional team charged with enabling effective relationships with outside partners by:

- Providing a strategic view of long-term needs

- Selecting best-of-breed partners

- Facilitating multipartner coordination

- Establishing common denominators and managing performance

The internal organization needs individuals who perform different tasks than those of traditional sales analytics personnel. These tasks include:

- Working with sales and marketing leaders in a consultative role to understand their needs and to translate those needs into an action plan

- Working collaboratively with internal and external partners

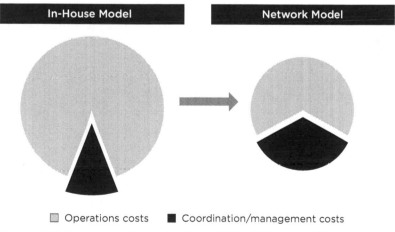

Figure 11-8. Cost comparison of sales analytics delivery models

- Getting others to do it right rather than doing it yourself (quality management)

- Estimating effort by month for partners and internal staff, planning for uncertainties, identifying interdependencies, and ensuring adherence to time lines

- Enforcing discipline to minimize custom requests and last-minute changes

Accomplishing these tasks requires new skills and knowledge. In addition to content knowledge, members of the internal sales analytics team need:

- Business insights and synthesis skills

- Consultative skills for working with sales and marketing leaders

- Change management proficiency

- Project and process management skills and capabilities

- Partner management expertise

- Finance and business skills

Sales analytics personnel in most traditional departments are analytic and task- and customer-service-oriented, rather than process-oriented. They often find the new roles required in a network model to be difficult and stressful. Worse, any lack of process discipline can result in increased costs and poor-quality or untimely deliverables.

Building the right internal sales analytics team for a network model requires selecting people with the right characteristics. It's important to rigorously screen and select team members based on characteristics such as organizational savvy, business insight, ability to synthesize and consult, process orientation, and strategic thinking—traits that are difficult to train and take long periods of time to develop. If some critical characteristics are missing in internal candidates, it's best to hire externally. With the right individuals on the team, training and other development programs can cultivate specific job skills and knowledge.

It's often possible for current team members with outstanding analytic skills to play a useful role on the internal team. In many cases, a small group of expert analysts is needed at headquarters to perform key analyses and generate insights. If the more process-oriented work is outsourced, talented analysts can take on elevated and higher-value roles. They can also become part of a "quality team" that oversees the partner's work and ensures the quality of the analytics. Some organizations create new job titles for these employees commensurate with their greater responsibility. With appropriate planning and preparation for personnel transitions, it's possible to achieve positive outcomes for both the organization and the sales analytics employees.

Time the Transition

When timing the transition to a network model, current sales force operations should proceed without interruption. Figure 11-9 shows how a transition can be deliberate and phased in slowly, accomplished overnight, or initiated in parallel with the current system for a period of time. The choice depends on the type of capability being transitioned to the network model, the scope of impact, and the risk tolerance of the company.

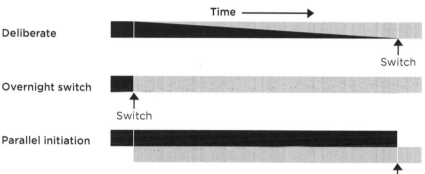

Transition	When It's Appropriate
Deliberate	• Limited resources and willing to accept moderate risk • Looking for a compromise between the high-risk overnight approach and the high-cost parallel approach
Overnight	• Small organization with limited resources • Implementing noncomplex or noncritical capabilities — for example, a nice-to-have but nonessential sales report • Rolling out a system or process for the first time
Parallel	• Large organization with many resources • Implementing complex or critical capabilities — for example, a system for placing customer orders

Figure 11-9. Alternatives for timing the transition to a network model

Implementing and Sustaining a Network Model

The successful implementation of a network model requires a well-planned, carefully executed, and clearly communicated change management approach. The engagement of internal stakeholders — including executive and senior sales leadership, salespeople and sales managers, and participants in other internal functions — is critical for preparing the organization to function in new and better ways.

Engaging Executive and Senior Sales Leadership

It is essential to gain the understanding and commitment of executive and senior sales leaders with regard to the objectives that the company hopes to achieve through a network model. Up-front agreement about the objectives and their priority reduces confusion later about whether the project is succeeding.

There are always internal winners and losers when moving to a network model. The buy-in of senior management helps address resistance from those who stand to lose through the initiative and helps resolve intergroup issues and bottlenecks quickly. Senior management's endorsement also creates greater enthusiasm and support for the project throughout the company.

Implementing a Network Model at a Transportation Company

When a large transportation company transitioned to a network model for delivering sales analytic needs, leaders placed a high priority on communication with internal stakeholders as part of the change management effort. Communication throughout the transition included the following:

- **For current sales analytics personnel:** After announcing the transition, the company shared job descriptions of new positions available in sales analytics as well as positions available in other areas of the company.

- **For executive management and sales management:** Periodic meetings were held to give an update on the transition, to talk about the next steps, and to reinforce the impact of the transition on the company.

- **For salespeople and sales managers:** A company intranet was used to communicate information and encourage dialogue about the transition, the expected changes, and how those changes would affect the day-to-day activities of the field.

This communication strategy helped create a seamless transition and increase employee satisfaction following the change.

Gaining Top Leadership's Commitment at a Financial Firm

Sales leaders at a midsize financial firm had three primary objectives when they offshored their sales analytics. In priority order, their objectives were to:

1. Increase customer satisfaction by giving salespeople up-to-date information during customer visits, including customer profile data, sales history, current opportunities, and recent support requests and their resolution

2. Accelerate development time for the sales information platform by putting more resources on the project

3. Generate modest cost savings initially, with greater cost savings expected in future years

Unfortunately, the priority of these objectives was not communicated effectively to senior management and the board of directors. Six months into the project, although achievement on all three objectives was beyond expectations, senior leaders dwelled on the fact that cost savings were only modest. One board member said, "I've read that offshoring typically results in 20 to 30 percent cost savings. Why are we seeing so little?" Better up-front understanding and agreement on project objectives by the senior leadership team could perhaps have prevented project leaders from having to take a defensive stance in their explanations, despite the project's success.

Engaging Salespeople and Sales Managers

Salespeople and sales managers in the field—the "users" of sales analytics—must understand, in advance, the implications of the new model, including any trade-offs. For example, a network model may provide less flexibility to customize analytics to meet individual needs, but in return, it could provide higher-quality and timelier reports to the field. Communication to gain up-front buy-in for these trade-offs can prevent user disappointment that weakens project success.

Engaging Other Functions

The successful implementation of a network model requires organizational agreement across all affected functions (besides the sales force), including marketing, human resources, and information technology. A detailed project charter makes priorities, scope, and responsibilities clear to all who are affected as the project progresses. The charter includes detailed specifications (for example, the number and type of data sources and reports, the

---

Communicating Up Front About Trade-offs

A firm outsourced its sales reporting function with the goal of improving efficiency. While scoping out the project, leaders observed that of the 100-plus different reports posted routinely, the sales force accessed only a few regularly. Leaders asked the outsourcing partner to provide just a dozen of the most-used reports that included the most important key performance indicators. A few weeks after implementing the new slimmed-down report set, a small number of sales managers began calling in-house analysts to request the old reports. Producing these reports drained the time the analysts had to work on strategic analysis. The analysts sometimes routed the requests to the outsourcing partner, but this created higher outsourcing costs and missed deadlines for the production of standard reports.

After some time, senior management stepped in to help sales managers see the benefits of focusing on the dozen reports that provided all the critical information. Eventually the sales managers embraced the new model, but it took months for the initial unhappiness of a few managers to abate. In hindsight, project leaders realized that better up-front communication with sales managers could have improved buy-in and reduced the initial tensions.

---

frequency of data refreshes) and ownership and accountability across internal stakeholders and external partners.

A charter is useful for getting agreement on and enforcing consistency. This includes a common set of business rules and approaches, consistent key performance indicators (KPIs), metrics, and report types and appropriate conformity across all aspects of sales analytics. Without this discipline, expected cost savings and efficiencies may never materialize, and worse, the business may (continue to) experience confusion and delays in decision making.

A Long-Term Challenge to Sustaining a Network Model

Usually, sales organizations start their outsourcing and offshoring endeavors with a few well-defined analytic capabilities that require limited interaction with users, such as data warehousing and sales reporting. Then, as their experience grows, these organizations expand their outsourcing and offshoring footprint to include more capabilities, eventually outsourcing or offshoring even highly knowledge-based capabilities that require extensive user interaction—for example, a customized analysis to help sales managers coach their salespeople or a market coverage analysis to help sales leaders diagnose the impact of the current sales force size and structure.

One challenge to long-term success as a network model expands is balancing a desire to outsource and offshore with the need to keep a core amount of capability in-house and on-site to effectively manage the work

Encouraging Organizational Alignment at an IT Firm

An IT firm launched a year-long effort to develop a system called Sapphire, which would improve capabilities for managing and analyzing sales, customer, and sales force data. The IT and sales analytics teams worked jointly to develop the project charter. In addition to specifying project scope and costs, the charter stated that if other departments changed systems that shared data with Sapphire, the PMO would review the implications and decide on an appropriate course of action. Funding for changes would come from IT and the appropriate department.

The charter proved useful when, about three months into the Sapphire project, HR announced a planned upgrade of its systems. The upgrade would launch several months after Sapphire and would affect key Sapphire inputs and outputs. The PMO considered the impact of the upgrade and worked with IT, HR, and the Sapphire project team to develop a transition strategy. Guided by the charter, the PMO decided that Sapphire would launch as planned and that a follow-on initiative funded jointly by HR and IT would make Sapphire compatible with the new HR system. The charter facilitated quick decision making without confusion about who would make the decisions and who would pay for the needed changes to Sapphire.

of outsourced or offshore partners. The best candidates for overseeing and managing the quality of a partner's work not only have the requisite management skills; they also have experience doing the work themselves. Over time, as more and more work moves to outside partners, there will be fewer internal, on-site candidates who have the skills and experience required to ensure quality work and ongoing innovation. As sales analytics leaders expand a network model, they must also ensure that enough work stays in-house to maintain expertise for successfully sustaining the model.

Generally, it takes companies about two years to complete the transition to a network model and to reach a state of equilibrium. Yet, as in any relationship, there will always be ongoing challenges. Continued evaluation and discussion about which capabilities to outsource and which ones to keep in-house are common. Special challenges arise when company strategy or organization structure changes or when a partner changes its strategy or organization structure. By discussing issues openly (while protecting confidentiality), working through problems together, and adapting constantly to changing needs, companies and their outsourcing partners can develop a high level of trust in one another that enables a successful ongoing relationship.

Ongoing communication is critical to sustaining a network model.

Conclusion

Although many companies have tried piecemeal outsourcing and offshoring, there is an increasing trend toward a strategically designed network model to optimize the opportunity to source expertise while reducing long-term costs. Setting up a network model is an involved process, requiring five steps to maximize the impact of the transition: defining the vision, determining the scope, selecting partners, designing the internal organization, and timing the transition. Continued communication and commitment to change management throughout the process help ensure effective implementation.

Once set up, a network model needs continued attention to operate on a day-to-day basis. Sales analytics leaders can learn from the collective experiences of others who have made the transition to a network model in order to avoid pitfalls and maximize the positive impact of a network model on company results.

CHAPTER 12

Aligning Sales and Information Technology

The right sales analytics culture, people, and processes will narrow the mind-set gap between sales and information technology.

Dharmendra Sahay and Faisal Zaidi

Dharmendra Sahay is a managing principal on ZS Associates' executive team and is based in the firm's New York office. For more than 25 years, he has worked with pharmaceutical clients to outsource and offshore sales and marketing support functions. Dharmendra has an MBA from Northwestern University's Kellogg School of Management, an MS in computer science from Northwestern University, and a degree in electrical engineering from the Indian Institute of Technology, New Delhi.

Faisal Zaidi is a principal in ZS's Princeton, New Jersey, office and leads the firm's Business Technology Solutions practice. He has more than 15 years of experience helping clients implement technology solutions that enable better sales and marketing decision making. His expertise includes data warehouses, business-intelligence-driven performance reporting, Master Data Management solutions, and data mining. Faisal has an MS in management of information systems and a BS in finance and decision sciences from the University of Illinois at Chicago.

The Need for Sales Analytics and Information Technology to Collaborate

Data and technology play a key role in delivering sales analytics. *Supporting* the sales force and *diagnosing* issues require data and tools for creating customer insight and enabling decision making. Analytics for *designing* sales force effectiveness (SFE) drivers—such as a sales process, a sales force size and structure, or a sales compensation plan—typically require building a database to support the analysis. And implementing changes to SFE drivers often requires making adjustments to sales systems.

The sales analytics team often does not have all of the expertise required to perform these tasks from beginning to end, so it relies on the company's information technology (IT) group for technical capability. Reliance on IT

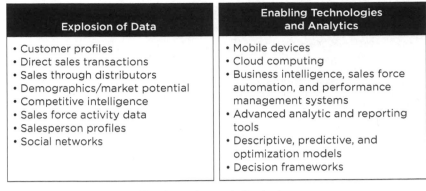

Explosion of Data	Enabling Technologies and Analytics
• Customer profiles • Direct sales transactions • Sales through distributors • Demographics/market potential • Competitive intelligence • Sales force activity data • Salesperson profiles • Social networks	• Mobile devices • Cloud computing • Business intelligence, sales force automation, and performance management systems • Advanced analytic and reporting tools • Descriptive, predictive, and optimization models • Decision frameworks

Figure 12-1. Innovations affecting sales analytics today

becomes increasingly critical as an explosion of data and enabling technologies and analytics affect the sales force. Some examples are listed in Figure 12-1.

In a ZS survey of attendees at a senior sales executive conference on sales operations, sales analytics leaders reported that working with IT is one of their biggest challenges. The feelings on the IT side are similar. Yet a strong partnership between the sales analytics and IT functions is essential for continually providing the sales force with timely insights and decision support. A good working relationship between sales analytics and IT is also critical for the successful implementation of transformational sales force change.

In this chapter, we address these questions:

- What does a healthy collaborative relationship between sales analytics and IT look like?

- Why is it so challenging to get sales and IT to work together, and what role can the sales analytics group play in making the relationship work?

- What are some strategies for overcoming the challenges to aligning sales and IT?

A Healthy Sales Analytics and IT Partnership

The sales and sales analytics groups are among IT's many users. Figure 12-2 suggests that the sales analytics group often acts as an intermediary between the sales team and IT to help meet sales force needs for data and technology. In this role, sales analytics team members must understand the sales team's objectives and requirements. Then they must partner with IT to meet those objectives and requirements.

Figure 12-2. The role of sales analytics in the sales-IT collaboration

A typical sales analytics–IT collaboration involves three main phases:

1. Set a vision, strategy, and priorities.
2. Design and build the systems and processes.
3. Implement and support the ongoing operations.

In a partnership, sales analytics and IT work together during each phase, with clear responsibilities and accountabilities that ultimately lead to a successful implementation. With ineffective collaboration, it's unlikely that even basic sales force support requirements will be met.

Figure 12-3 describes two contrasting scenarios of what could happen when a sales force seeks to implement a major change initiative — in this

Phase	A Successful Sales Analytics–IT Partnership	An Unsuccessful Sales Analytics–IT Partnership
Set vision, strategy, and priorities	• Share ideas and build commitment. • Develop integrated sales analytics–IT project plan. • Commit jointly to making initiative a success.	• Convey project urgency. • Create separate project plans. • Express doubt that project can be done on time.
Design and build	• Work collaboratively. • Rationally discuss how to address issues. • Have empathy for the other team's "way of working."	• Work independently. • Blame the other party as deadlines slip. • Fail to speak each other's language.
Implement and support	• Implement a working system that meets all key business needs by deadline. • Roll out new selling process on time. • Enhance careers of members from both teams.	• Implement a system that, although technically sound, does not meet all key business needs. • Roll out new selling process without key system capabilities. Scramble to provide stopgap measures for meeting some needs. • Create unplanned costs.

Figure 12-3. Possible outcomes for a sales process transformation

case, a sales process transformation. The outcome of the initiative depends on how effectively sales analytics and IT work together. Regrettably, the "unsuccessful partnership" scenario is all too common.

Figure 12-4 outlines a division of responsibilities between the sales analytics and IT functions through the major phases of an initiative such as a sales process transformation. The responsibilities listed are representative; specific sales analytics, IT, and joint activities will depend on the type and scope of each initiative. The sales analytics team takes primary responsibility for the sales- and customer-oriented activities during each phase and for communicating that perspective to IT. The IT team takes primary responsibility for the technology-focused activities during each stage and for communicating that perspective to the sales analytics team. The activities in the intersection of the two circles require joint decision making and cooperation between the sales analytics and IT teams. These activities require the two teams to work together in a synchronized effort.

	Sales Analytics Team	Information flow		IT Team
	Sales Analytics Activities	**Joint Activities**		**IT Activities**
Set vision, strategy, and priorities	• Understand sales force needs. • Develop business vision, strategy, priorities.	• Manage project. • Develop joint vision, strategy, priorities.		• Determine technical feasibility. • Develop technical vision, strategy, priorities.
Design and build	• Define business processes and requirements.	• Manage project. • Design system. • Conduct user-acceptance training.		• Select IT vendors, if needed. • Design and build technology. • Test system.
Implement and support	• Train users. • Support ongoing business needs.	• Manage project. • Steward the data and reports. • Govern the process.		• Support ongoing technology needs.

Information flow

Figure 12-4. The division of responsibilities between sales analytics and IT

Sales Analytics: Bridging the Sales-IT Mind-set Gap

A significant challenge for a sales analytics group is enabling an effective working relationship between the sales force and IT. People in sales and people in IT often express frustration about working with one another. For example, some people in sales say:

- "IT people don't understand our requirements and don't listen to us."
- "IT is too quick to push back."
- "IT is inflexible about adapting the approach to meet the varied needs of salespeople and customers."

Some people in IT say:

- "We don't get the engagement we need from the sales force."
- "Salespeople are always changing their minds about requirements."
- "Ideas proposed by the sales team are ambiguous, so we have to manage expectations to avoid overpromising."

These frustrations stem from the fact that people in sales and people in IT come from separate thought-worlds. Differences in departmental objectives and in people's backgrounds and skills create a "mind-set gap." Figure 12-5 shows how sales analytics can play an intermediary role between the sales force and IT, helping to manage the mind-set gap.

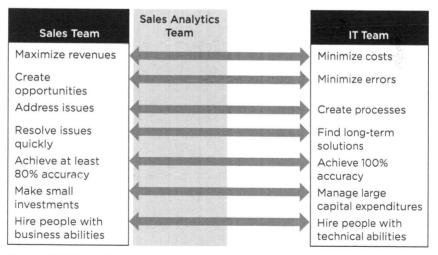

Sales Team	Sales Analytics Team	IT Team
Maximize revenues		Minimize costs
Create opportunities		Minimize errors
Address issues		Create processes
Resolve issues quickly		Find long-term solutions
Achieve at least 80% accuracy		Achieve 100% accuracy
Make small investments		Manage large capital expenditures
Hire people with business abilities		Hire people with technical abilities

Figure 12-5. The role of sales analytics in managing the sales-IT mind-set gap

Joint sales-IT projects often start out in the right spirit. But soon the mind-set gap leads to a mutual distrust and misperceptions between the two groups. Sales team members don't appreciate the discipline required for good systems design, so they articulate loosely defined needs and ask for too many noncritical features. IT team members lack the business wisdom for determining which needs are most important, so they push back on including features that are difficult to implement. Sales team members become frustrated with IT; they lose interest and stop contributing regularly. IT team members become frustrated with sales; with too little sales force engagement, they make design errors and include less than half of critical functionality. Many requirements are obsolete by the time the project finishes. The impact of the technology investment on the sales force is underwhelming, to say the least.

A sales analytics group can work in an intermediary role to close the mind-set gap. It can help the sales and IT teams plan and rationalize together in an atmosphere of mutual trust and respect. Sales team members brainstorm ideas for how data and technology can create opportunities to enhance value for customers. IT team members bring technical perspective and create a road map for meeting sales team needs through sustainable processes that minimize cost and risk. Sales and IT agree on the business goals, as well as on the expected time line and budget. The resulting solution is successful from both an IT perspective and a sales force perspective.

Overcoming Hurdles to Create Sales-IT Alignment

Vision and culture, people and roles, and processes can all help to facilitate sales-IT alignment. When used effectively, these facilitators help create an environment in which sales and IT understand each other's perspective and use their complementary approaches as a source of strength, not conflict. Figure 12-6 summarizes the goals and some representative solutions in the three categories of facilitators. The sales analytics group often plays a key role in implementing these solutions.

All three categories of facilitators are important for achieving lasting sales-IT alignment. Too often, we see companies relying heavily on process solutions. Although these solutions can work temporarily, they have lasting impact only when they are supported by people with the right skills and empathy and when they are enabled by a cooperative culture.

Some companies have implemented process solutions that involve contractual agreements between sales and IT, analogous to service-level

	Vision and Culture	People and Roles	Processes
Goals	• Sales force and customer focus • Trust and teamwork • Transparency and mutual understanding of goals	• People with the right skills and capabilities • Clearly defined roles and accountabilities	• Processes that facilitate alignment
Representative Solutions	• Align the vision around the customer. • Build a collaborative culture.	• Select people with dual capabilities. • Develop people's skills, knowledge, and empathy. • Create liaison roles. • Make focused project assignments.	• Use an agile development approach and rapid prototyping. • Agree on project objectives and specifications. • Agree on project budget and time line.

Figure 12-6. Facilitators of sales-IT alignment

agreements (SLAs) with outsourcing partners. These solutions rarely work well and frequently do more damage than good by thwarting efforts to create a team-oriented culture.

Companies have the most success making the sales-IT relationship work when they focus first on developing the right culture and the right people and roles for enabling that culture. Then process solutions can reinforce the culture and enable people's success.

Vision and Culture Solutions

Sales-IT alignment is encouraged when the sales, sales analytics, and IT teams share a vision of value for the company's customers, while promoting a collaborative organizational culture.

Aligning the Vision Around the Customer

Sales analytics can help mobilize and align the sales and IT teams around a common goal of creating value for customers.

Building a Collaborative Culture

Organizational culture plays a powerful role in getting the sales, sales analytics, and IT functions to align to accomplish business objectives. In a

Sales Analytics–IT Collaboration to Meet Sales Force and Customer Needs at a Pharmaceutical Company

The increasing diversity in the needs of pharmaceutical companies' customers (including physicians, hospitals, and managed care companies) has created the need for more flexible sales models. One company set out to replace its current one-size-fits-all sales approach with a more dynamic model that tailored sales resources and approaches to local opportunities, thus improving efficiency while at the same time driving top-line growth.

Creating a sales model that was flexible enough to meet the needs of diverse customers would require more dynamic and adaptable sales teams, deployed to accommodate market fluidity and specific local needs. Achieving this flexibility would have a huge impact on many IT systems. Without strong collaboration between the sales and IT teams, the effort would surely fail. The company's sales analytics group played a key role in facilitating collaboration between sales and IT to enable the project's success.

To start, the sales analytics group worked closely with sales leaders and with customers to establish a business case for the initiative. This included a vision of what customers needed and valued, the design of a flexible sales model that could deliver on that vision, and a plan for the capabilities required to enable the sales model. The plan was comprised of eight core capabilities, including a territory alignment tool and an incentive compensation system that provided flexibility to adapt to local needs. The business case also articulated the value to customers and provided an estimate of the revenue and cost impact for the company.

With the business case in place, the sales analytics group involved IT in the planning process. The sales analytics and IT teams worked together to create a detailed plan for delivering the needed capabilities within an aggressive but reasonable time line. The teams agreed that the internal IT team was best positioned to take responsibility for three of eight critical capabilities. For the other five capabilities, outsourcing partners, jointly selected by the IT and sales analytics teams, would provide the necessary expertise and capacity.

To manage the project, the company assigned a sales analytics lead and an IT lead to each capability area. These individuals were charged with collaborating to ensure that goals were achieved. Collaboration occurred at all levels — from analyst to senior leadership. The sales analytics–IT pairs had weekly formal check-in meetings. In addition, further discussion and collaboration occurred at monthly meetings with a broader sponsorship group, including representatives from sales, sales analytics, IT, and the external partners.

collaborative culture, professionals from all three functions routinely embrace values and choices that involve sharing, adapting, and appreciating the diversity of expertise that individuals from each function bring to the table. Strong leaders foster consensus around a collaborative culture; they demonstrate their commitment by:

- Creating transparency and encouraging a mutual understanding of each department's goals

- Communicating stories at every opportunity to the sales, sales analytics, and IT groups that reflect collaborative culture choices that lead to success

- Rewarding individuals with appreciation and recognition when they demonstrate cooperative behaviors

- Celebrating the heroes who consistently make collaborative culture choices

- "Walking the talk" by ensuring that their own actions and words are compatible

- Discouraging organizational politics

People and Role Solutions

Sales-IT alignment is enhanced when the sales analytics team comprises the right people and when those people continually develop their skills and knowledge to enable effective collaboration.

Selecting People with Dual Capabilities

Having individuals on the sales analytics team who can see the world from the lens of both sales and IT strengthens alignment. Individuals who understand both cultures and mind-sets can earn the trust and respect of people in both groups. Good candidates for this role include:

- People who started their careers in IT who have experience with and passion for understanding and working with the sales team and customers

- People who started their careers in sales who have experience with and passion for understanding and working with data and technology

- People who have worked in similar roles in other settings, such as with an outsourcing partner

Developing People's Skills, Knowledge, and Empathy

Sales analytics professionals can benefit by participating on projects or through formal job rotations that allow them to spend time in both the sales and IT functions. Companies have brought sales analytics and IT professionals together through joint training, orientation, or team-building sessions. In addition, sometimes simply having the two groups sit close to each other in the office can help people from both sides build relationships, understanding, and empathy that help to bridge the sales-IT gap.

Creating Liaison Roles

Alignment-enhancing assignments for individuals from both sales analytics and IT can encourage effective collaboration. These assignments can include responsibility for managing the communication flows and the collaborative activities (those in the overlapping section of the diagram in Figure 12-4). Typical responsibilities can include joint project management, data stewardship, governance, and systems education.

> *Encourage sales-IT alignment by selecting the right people, developing the right competencies, and defining the right roles for the sales analytics team.*

Making Focused Project Assignments

Often, alignment is stronger when IT personnel are dedicated to specific areas within sales analytics (for example, incentive compensation administration or sales reporting). Generally, members of a joint team who are at least 75 percent dedicated to a specific project build stronger team bonds and work more effectively together to get the job done, as team members identify more with the joint team than with their separate affiliation with either IT or sales analytics.

Process Solutions

Process solutions that enable sales analytics and IT to collaborate more effectively include:

- An agile development approach and rapid prototyping
- Agreement on project objectives and specifications
- Agreement on the project budget and time line

To have lasting impact, process solutions require a cooperative culture and people with the right skills and empathy.

Using an Agile Development Approach and Rapid Prototyping

Too often, traditional IT systems development relies on an unambiguous and comprehensive definition of functional needs. Design, development, and testing of systems occur only after all functional requirements are finalized. This approach works well in stable and well-defined environments (such as purchasing or manufacturing), but it often fails in a sales force setting, where needs evolve quickly as salespeople react to market conditions. Because customer and sales force needs are fuzzy in nature, can change frequently, and vary across customer segments, sales systems must be flexible to work well for individual salespeople and customers.

The traditional IT development approach sets up unreasonable expectations for the sales analytics team to define precise requirements that will endure over an extended time horizon; this is quite often virtually impossible to do. The volatility inherent in the sales environment often necessitates changes in the needed functionality after the requirement definition deadline has expired. The system development process gets drawn out as the sales force repeatedly submits change orders. Often, the system is obsolete by the time it is finished.

Companies have more success creating sales systems when they use an agile approach to systems development that includes:

- **Smaller, self-contained work streams.** Divide a large project into multiple mini-projects organized around the needs of different users.

- **Rapid and iterative tool development.** Break up the development cycle from requirement definition to final deliverable into smaller segments to minimize the cost of redos as requirements change.

- **Rapid prototyping.** Develop prototypes that allow users to experience a system hands-on rather than signing off on a paper design. This works especially well with systems such as sales dashboards on mobile devices. Salespeople can try out a prototype and experience the system's "look and feel." Then they can provide better feedback at a point where the design can be changed at less cost.

Agreement on Project Objectives and Specifications

An agile systems development approach does not eliminate the need for a plan to guide joint sales analytics and IT projects. The effective management and implementation of projects starts with documenting project scope, objectives, participants, business requirements, time lines, and success criteria. The best project plans are flexible and define the process of working together as a series of steps, each with specific goals, responsibilities, deadlines, and measurable performance standards. Up-front definition and agreement around a project plan creates:

- Shared expectation about performance, timing, and accountability
- A guide for working together efficiently and effectively to achieve business goals
- Understanding of how the actions of each individual affect other functions
- A platform for dialogue between individuals about trade-offs and shared expectations, allowing more objective cross-functional discussions

As a result, there is less tension between groups, including sales, sales analytics, IT, and other participating functions.

With internal groups, it's generally best to use a project plan to guide a project, rather than using a formal contract analogous to SLAs for outside partners. Although contractual agreements work quite naturally with outsourcing partners, they can run counter to a collaborative culture when used internally. In rare circumstances, a contract between internal groups can work if the handoff between groups is clear and dimensions such as time line, response time, accuracy, and change control can be tracked with simple, unambiguous, and easily developed metrics. But even in these circumstances, it's wise to revisit the need for the contract regularly and to eliminate it if the internal teams are working collaboratively.

Contractual solutions are best reserved for projects that involve outside partners. They can destroy a collaborative working relationship between internal groups.

Agreement on the Project Budget and Time Line

Two big challenges to an effective working relationship between sales analytics and IT center on the issues of budgeting and time line.

The IT and sales analytics groups manage their budgets differently. The dissimilarities shown in Figure 12-7 can make it challenging for the two teams to agree on how to pay for projects.

Projects can get delayed or scrapped, or can get outsourced even though an internal solution is better, simply because sales analytics and IT can't agree on how to pay for the project. By recognizing up front the differences in budgeting perspectives and then figuring out creative approaches for sharing project funding, companies can ensure that projects that create value for customers and the sales force get implemented.

Too often, project time lines become a major point of contention between sales and IT. Excitement about the potential benefits of a new sales

Dimension	IT	Sales Analytics
Scope of support	Prioritize among all business functions	Prioritize among sales force projects only
Expenditure type	Capital expenditures (capex)	Operating expenses (opex)
Timeframe	Multiyear; no incentive to accelerate expenditure	One year; "use it or lose it"
Certainty of specifications	Precision allows stability	Imprecision and change require flexibility

Figure 12-7. Differences in how IT and sales analytics manage budgets

force IT project creates pressure to set an aggressive time line for completion. A time line is established that assumes the IT team will dedicate 100 percent of its time to completing the project. Yet IT teams almost always have many projects on their plates. Other IT priorities get in the way, and the aggressive time line quickly becomes infeasible. By recognizing up front all IT responsibilities, and figuring out creative ways to get needed focus on high-priority sales force projects, sales analytics and IT teams can work together to set and adhere to realistic deadlines.

Emerging Trends Affecting Sales Analytics and IT

Three trends will have an impact on sales analytics and IT and therefore will shape the future relationship of these two functions:

- The blurring of functional lines
- Software as a service (SaaS) and cloud computing
- The outsourcing and offshoring of services

The Blurring of Functional Lines

Increasingly, the traditional lines between the IT and sales analytics functions are disappearing. Professionals from both disciplines are broadening their skill sets, leading to more collaborative working relationships and stronger implementations of sales force data and technology solutions. IT professionals are becoming more business savvy; instead of coming from a pure programming background, many have business skills, and an increasing number have earned MBA degrees. At the same time, many sales analytics professionals (especially career ones) are gaining experience with IT capabilities, giving them greater empathy for technology challenges. The broader skill sets on both sides encourage stronger alignment between sales and IT.

Software as a Service (SaaS) and Cloud Computing

With technologies such as software as a service (SaaS) and cloud computing, more companies are using pay-as-you-go services to support sales force needs such as sales performance reporting, customer relationship management (CRM), and incentive compensation support. A SaaS and cloud computing model brings three key benefits. First, it avoids the high fixed cost of developing new systems. Second, it can provide faster access to capabilities that are aligned with evolving market needs. Third, it allows companies to tap into the expertise of SaaS and cloud computing providers, who continually innovate and improve their systems to provide a higher-quality product with less risk. SaaS and cloud computing have shifted the sales automation mind-set away from designing and building customized solutions and toward subscribing to existing solutions that already meet 80 percent of sales force needs.

The trend is fundamentally changing the role of the IT group. A SaaS or cloud computing model moves many less rewarding and high-risk responsibilities (such as hardware and software acquisition, upgrading, management, and maintenance) to outside partners. The IT group is left to focus on selecting and managing vendors and consulting with the sales analytics team and with the sales force to determine the best way to configure and design systems that address needs.

A SaaS or cloud computing model has several implications for the relationship between IT and the sales analytics group:

- IT takes on a greater role as a consultative partner with the sales analytics team in finding approaches for meeting sales force needs.

- A pay-as-you-go model eliminates the need for original system design and the need for a large up-front investment. This makes it easier to implement an agile development approach and removes the incompatibilities in the time lines and budgets of the IT and sales analytics teams.

- Contractual agreements such as SLAs take on increased importance in managing the relationship with outsourcing partners.

- Vendor selection becomes more important.

The Outsourcing and Offshoring of Services

The trend toward using external partners (including offshore outsourced resources) to support analytic sales force needs affects both sales analytics and IT. Increasingly, both groups are turning to external partners as a means of providing greater flexibility to respond to changing sales force needs quickly, controlling costs, tapping into expertise, and managing peaks and valleys in workload. Chapter 11 discusses how companies at the frontier of this movement use a network model to optimize the use of outside partners to meet sales force needs.

Because of this trend, sales analytics and IT professionals are spending less time developing and maintaining systems and more time managing outside partners. This requires new skills and abilities from both sides. With multiple outside partners in the mix, strong collaboration between sales analytics and IT becomes even more critical, as all parties from inside and outside the company must work together to meet sales force needs. Without a collaborative working relationship, the sales analytics and IT teams may select vendors on their own and adopt a territorial mind-set; this further increases the sales-IT divide. Quite often, however, the need to work with outside partners strengthens the alignment between sales analytics and IT, as the two teams come together to ensure that outside partners deliver on what the sales force needs.

Conclusion

By establishing the right vision and culture, people and roles, and processes, the sales analytics group can play a key role in facilitating a healthy relationship between the sales force and IT. When the sales analytics and IT teams have to collaborate with one or more outsourcing partners, the importance of strong alignment between the two teams becomes increasingly vital for creating the best sales force solutions. One might conjecture that as companies outsource more sales analytics work, the need for separate sales analytics and IT teams will diminish and the two will blend into a single team.

CHAPTER 13

Implementing Sales Analytics When Launching a New Sales Force

By using analytics to design new sales forces and diagnose issues in the earliest launch stages, companies increase the odds of realizing the full potential of new market opportunities.

Jeff Gold

Jeff Gold is a principal in ZS Associates' San Mateo, California, office and is the leader of the firm's Business Intelligence practice. Over the past 15 years, he has helped nearly 100 companies increase their sales and marketing effectiveness through business intelligence, data management, analytics, incentive compensation design and administration, and sales and marketing operations. Jeff has an MBA from the Wharton School of the University of Pennsylvania and a BA in economics from the University of Pennsylvania.

The author thanks former ZS associate Caroline Hartford for her contributions to this chapter.

The Impact of Analytics in a New Sales Force

Setting up a new sales force is challenging. Critical activities include:

- Developing a sales and go-to-market strategy
- Designing the sales organization
- Hiring and training the sales force
- Setting up a compensation plan and other enablers of sales activity, such as metrics for measuring performance and gaining customer insight

Despite these challenges, establishing a new sales force creates a unique opportunity for making decisions with a clean slate. By learning from the legacy mistakes of others, companies can ensure that sales and sales analytics capabilities are handled correctly from the beginning.

Too often, companies setting up new sales forces rush to hire salespeople without devoting sufficient time to the frameworks and analytics that can enhance their decisions. As a result, the new sales force has less impact than planned, and businesses fall short of their full market potential.

Sales Analytics Help a Biopharmaceutical Company with Its First Product Launch

A biopharmaceutical company prepared to launch its first product—a prescription cardiovascular medication. The company had historically been led by scientists, and it needed to transition from a research and development (R&D) company into a commercial organization. Leaders had to make many decisions about how to sell the product:

- How can we identify potential customers?
- What is the market potential by geography and customer segment?
- What size sales force do we need, and where do we locate salespeople?
- Which salespeople and managers should we hire?
- How should we compensate salespeople?
- How should we track and manage sales performance?
- What tools and data does the sales force need to enable good sales and marketing decisions?

Leaders viewed sales analytics as a core competency that could help answer these questions and drive commercial success. At the same time, they had limited information about the size and certainty of the business opportunity, so they were concerned about investing too heavily and creating financial risk.

The company created an initial sales analytics group comprised of a handful of permanent employees. It supplemented the core group's capabilities by teaming up with external partners who provided expertise and capacity. By keeping the internal group small, the company had the flexibility to adapt as the size of the opportunity and the needs of the selling environment became more certain.

The internal sales analytics group worked with external partners and with the company's CFO, CIO, and other leaders to prioritize a list of "must-have" and "nice-to-have" sales analytics capabilities and developed a road map to guide the implementation of those capabilities. The company created an initial sales force design and piloted that design, making adjustments as necessary as it learned more about market needs. Then it launched several data management and analytic tools to help the sales force, including a data warehouse with a data mart tailored to the sales force's need for a customer master file and dashboards for salespeople, managers, and executives. At the time of the national product launch, all "must-have" sales force support capabilities were in place, including forecasts, customer target lists, promotional tactics, basic metrics and reporting capabilities, and a sales incentive plan. Throughout the launch and post-launch periods, the internal sales analytics group and its external partners collaborated with company leaders, as well as with IT. The goal was to support the sales force with the most essential capabilities, while at the same time maintaining flexibility to adapt those capabilities as market and sales force needs became more certain.

Although the initial launch encountered some speed bumps, ultimately, thanks in large part to sales and marketing analytic capabilities, the product launch was successful. About three years after the launch, a large biopharmaceutical firm acquired the company for over $1 billion.

Sales analytics can help a company *design* a new sales force and bring excellence to all of the sales force effectiveness (SFE) drivers. As salespeople begin to interact with customers, sales analytics can help the company *diagnose* how initiatives are performing and suggest adjustments as new learning occurs. Throughout the sales force launch and beyond, sales analytics can provide critical *support* for the sales force to enable smoother sales operations and better decision making.

A core set of sales analytics capabilities adds value in a new sales force even before the first salesperson is hired.

This chapter emphasizes the role that sales analytics can play in design and early diagnosis for new sales organizations. By relying on the sales analytics function as a strategic partner that can contribute to design and diagnosis in the earliest stages of a sales force launch, in addition to viewing it as a support function, companies can enhance their launch success.

Using Analytics to Address a Hierarchy of New Sales Force Decisions

Like the biopharmaceutical company, many companies that are starting up sales forces have a large business opportunity but also face uncertainty. They may operate with limited resources and a short time line for making complex decisions and developing critical sales capabilities.

New sales forces must address sales decision making and capability development in a logical sequence, as shown in Figure 13-1. Usually, these activities need to be accomplished in a short time, so leaders must act early and quickly.

Sales analytics can add value across the full range of SFE driver decisions. The chapters in Section 1 of this book (referenced in Figure 13-1) provide many insights relevant for addressing each decision. The first three categories of decisions are "must-haves." A sales force cannot operate without a strategy, organization, and a team of people. The final category of decisions — activity enablers — includes some must-have features (such as a sales compensation plan) but also includes many nice-to-have but nonessential analytic features. It's critical to choose the enablers that are most important and to optimize investments to the right ones.

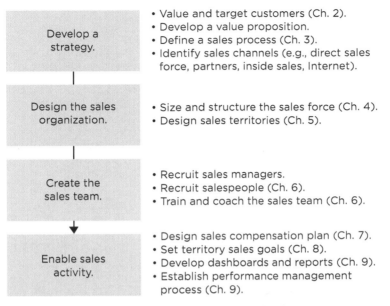

Develop a strategy.
- Value and target customers (Ch. 2).
- Develop a value proposition.
- Define a sales process (Ch. 3).
- Identify sales channels (e.g., direct sales force, partners, inside sales, Internet).

Design the sales organization.
- Size and structure the sales force (Ch. 4).
- Design sales territories (Ch. 5).

Create the sales team.
- Recruit sales managers.
- Recruit salespeople (Ch. 6).
- Train and coach the sales team (Ch. 6).

Enable sales activity.
- Design sales compensation plan (Ch. 7).
- Set territory sales goals (Ch. 8).
- Develop dashboards and reports (Ch. 9).
- Establish performance management process (Ch. 9).

Figure 13-1. Capability development for a new sales force

This chapter focuses on prioritizing investments in sales analytics for enabling sales activity in a new sales force. Investing in the needed capabilities requires addressing three key questions:

- **How much and how quickly to invest?** The amount and timing of the investment in sales and sales analytics capabilities depend on the size of the opportunity and the certainty of the business model that can drive success.

- **What capabilities to invest in?** By determining the most important sales analytics capabilities based on impact and ease and cost of implementation, a new sales force will be better enabled to provide early success and make the best use of limited resources.

- **What talent to bring to sales analytics?** Companies can hire an internal team, partner with external experts who provide expertise and flexible capacity, or both.

The rest of this chapter explores each of these three questions.

How Much and How Quickly to Invest?

New sales forces increase their chances of success when they match their investment in sales and sales analytics to the size of the business opportunity and the certainty of the business model that can drive success. Three possible strategies are shown in Figure 13-2.

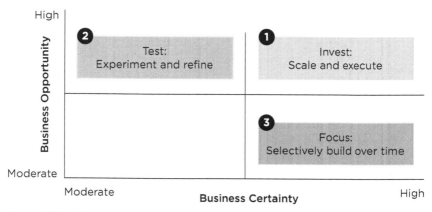

Figure 13-2. Three sales force investment strategies for a new sales force

Three Situations Demanding Different Strategies

The best sales analytics capability investment strategy depends on each situation.

Situation 1: Invest

Large opportunities with high certainty—for example, new products that have substantial competitive advantages in large, established markets—suggest large-scale investments. They are best supported by significant sales effort and a comprehensive sales analytics solution that is implemented before product launch, allowing the firm to hit the market in full force and be ready to capitalize on the opportunity.

Situation 2: Test

Large opportunities with less certainty about what business model will be successful require a flexible "test" approach. Especially when a new sales force enters a market without established competitors, leaders must determine the best customer offering, strategy to gain new customers, sales organization design, and sales force hiring approach, as well as a range of other

---

Situation 1: Invest Example — A Japanese Company Invests in a U.S. Sales Force

Leaders at a Japanese pharmaceutical company viewed their entry into the U.S. market as a large and relatively low-risk opportunity. They had already partnered with several U.S. companies to learn about the market. They were confident of the demand for their product based on success in Japan and feedback from key U.S. opinion leaders. With imminent U.S Food and Drug Administration (FDA) approval of their product, they wanted to act quickly to establish a large sales force, but they lacked the internal team and the expertise needed to design key SFE drivers. They considered using a single external partner who could help them with all of these priorities but ultimately decided instead to turn to several specialized external partners. One partner helped with formulating sales and go-to-market strategy and with determining the best sales force size, territory design, targeting plan, and incentive compensation structure. Another outside partner assisted with hiring and training salespeople and managers. A third partner developed data management platforms, sales performance dashboards, and other analytic and reporting capabilities. The heavy up-front investment ensured that the company's sales infrastructure fully supported sales efforts and maximized the success of an on-time product launch.

Situation 2: Test Example — eBay Invests in Flexible Analytics

Analytics helped leaders at online auction and retail space eBay develop an early business strategy. Because leaders were unsure about what business areas would capture the most market opportunity, they established a broad, flexible data collection and analytic capability to help them identify opportunities, even some they had not anticipated initially. "eBay's Data Warehouse provided the tools, reporting, and analytical capabilities needed to determine which existing business areas to focus on as well as new business opportunities," said Bob Sanguedolce, former Vice President and Chief Information Officer at eBay. This type of analytic flexibility can help with formulating and adapting sales strategies while a sales force moves up the learning curve.

---

decisions for driving sales force activity and results. An initial sales model for a test situation will likely undergo many changes and may evolve into a completely different model over time. Therefore, companies in this situation need to deploy capabilities that can change as the market evolves.

New sales forces facing a "test" situation are best served by a flexible and light sales and sales analytics investment that allows them to adapt their business, selling, and analytic support models quickly as they learn. A phased approach works well — for example, the company might start by developing 50 to 75 percent of sales analytics capabilities for launch, and then refine, enhance, and scale up capability as the selling model becomes more certain.

This strategy provides fewer resources and applications for supporting early decision making, but it also avoids excessive disruption and financial risk due to unnecessary or inappropriate implementation costs.

Situation 3: Focus

A "focus" strategy is best when a moderate-size, high-certainty opportunity suggests an appropriately sized investment in sales and sales analytics. This involves developing best-in-breed capabilities for the most critical sales analytics capabilities first, then selectively building over time. Each specific situation will lead to a variety of prioritized capabilities.

The Cost of Errors in Investment Strategy

Figure 13-3 shows what can happen in a new sales force when the investment in sales analytics capabilities doesn't match the size and certainty of the opportunity. The resulting missed opportunity or inflexibility is often costly.

Missed Opportunity in Scaling Too Slowly

A new sales force that scales up analytics capability too slowly provides insufficient support to the sales force, creating inefficiency and inconsistency and leading to lost revenues and profits.

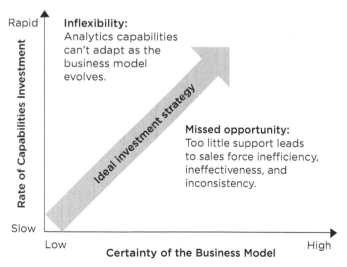

Figure 13-3. Investment scale-up strategy for a new sales force

> ### Situation 3: Focus Example — A Software Firm Focuses on Building a Customer Database
>
> A software firm was first to market with a moderate-size opportunity. Because limited customer data were available, leaders decided to make a heavy investment in applications that would enable the sales force to capture information about the needs and potential of prospective customers. This would allow salespeople to use analytics for customer targeting so they could focus on the right customers and give the firm an early competitive advantage. The sales analytics investment focused fully on developing these applications ahead of other projects (such as dashboards and precise territory design). This focused strategy created more value for the company than would have been realized had the investment been spread across multiple capabilities.

Risks from Defining Inflexible Capabilities

Scaling too quickly can lead to poor decisions that are difficult to reverse, leaving a sales force stuck with ineffective and inflexible support systems that don't meet business needs. Short-term mistakes that are especially difficult to undo include using the wrong channel strategy, increasing sales force size too quickly, hiring salespeople in the wrong locations, relying on an inappropriate sales hiring profile, and following a misguided sales compensation plan.

> ### Missed Opportunity Example — An IT Provider Underinvests in Sales Analytics Capability
>
> At an IT products and services provider, leaders were initially skeptical about whether sales analytics could deliver value. Despite high certainty that their business model would succeed, they did not develop a centralized analytics capability. As the company grew, two problems emerged. First, many salespeople and managers "bought" their own administrative and sales support assistants to free up time to sell. This created duplication of effort across the sales force, as expensive salespeople had to independently hire and train support people. Second, the lack of a centralized territory design or sizing led to large differences in territory potential. The first 20 salespeople to join the company covered large territories with high sales volumes. These salespeople did little selling; they waited for their phones to ring and received huge commissions for little effort. New salespeople had territories with too few profitable customers. They worked hard but made little money; more than 50 percent left the job within their first six weeks.
>
> As the sales force grew to more than 500 salespeople, the lack of centralized sales analytics support began to severely limit the sales force's ability to evolve and meet changing business needs. It wasn't until the firm had grown to 2,500 salespeople that leaders decided that change was urgently needed and implemented a centralized sales analytics function.

Inflexibility Example — A Medical Device Firm Learns a Lesson

Leaders at a medical device firm learned the following lesson: think about tomorrow when setting today's pay levels. The firm developed a revolutionary new cardiac medical device in the early 1990s and defined a compensation program paying its 50 salespeople a 4 percent commission on sales. In the first year after launch, salespeople made $100,000 to $150,000. As use of the new device caught on across the medical community, sales grew dramatically. Five years after launch, salespeople were earning an average of $650,000. Because the firm was incredibly profitable and leaders didn't want to risk any decline in sales force morale, they continued to "share the wealth" with the sales force. This caused some resentment among employees working in internal departments, such as Marketing and R&D, who felt it unfair for the sales force to be rewarded so generously. In addition, the market matured and more competitors entered, cutting into firm profits. It was clear that the firm could no longer afford its high sales force costs and that sales force income levels would need to come down. Yet changing the compensation plan would be devastating for sales force morale and would run counter to the current sales culture. The firm's salespeople were in high demand by competitors, and many jumped ship to seek the next big payoff.

Inefficiency in Scaling Independently

Companies can also get into trouble when they scale independently in different units of the organization. Although it may initially make sense for each team within a small company to decide what types of analytic capabilities it needs, failure to think about these capabilities strategically from an overall company perspective can lead to difficulties and inefficiencies later on.

Inefficiency Example — A Commercial Bank Suffers the Consequences of Independent Scaling of Analytic Capabilities

In the beginning, the business units of a commercial bank grew and developed independently. Leaders in each unit — mortgage loans, auto loans, credit cards, and savings — made decisions separately about sales analytics strategies and capabilities. Eventually, the bank had more than 10 customer data warehouses and dozens of reporting systems and decision support tools. This created duplication of effort and led to redundant overhead and high cost. More importantly, it led to poor customer service as turf wars raged and the business units were reluctant to share information with one another. This meant that a customer defaulting on his car payment could get a mortgage with the same bank, or a customer of the "high wealth" branch could be declined for a credit card.

Although the bank eventually centralized its customer information, many remnants of the legacy systems remained, creating strong inertia against change. Bringing all the disparate decision systems and tools into alignment required significant investments for all business units.

What Capabilities to Invest In?

New sales forces must determine the right sales analytics priorities and then create a road map for implementing the capabilities to support them.

Setting Priorities

Some capabilities are clear "must-haves"—for example, the firm needs a distribution system to deliver products; a sales strategy, organization, and team of salespeople to interact with customers; and a sales compensation plan and process to pay salespeople. But beyond the must-have capabilities, new sales forces need a structured process for prioritizing nice-to-have capabilities.

For example, leaders at a company starting a sales force in China faced a high-opportunity, moderate-certainty situation (see the "test" situation in quadrant 2 of the framework in Figure 13-2). They felt that a full-scale deployment of sales analytics capabilities was inadvisable because of the rapidly evolving nature of the Chinese marketplace. They used the framework shown in Figure 13-4 to prioritize the development of key sales data, reporting, and analytics capabilities.

This was the recommended course of action:

- **Phase 1:** Implement capabilities that have high business impact for moderate implementation effort (customer database, definition of metrics, and key performance indicators [KPIs]).

- **Phase 2:** Implement capabilities that have high business impact and require higher implementation effort (deployment management tool, promotional program tracking, dashboards, and integrated database).

- **Phase 3:** Reevaluate and, if valuable, implement capabilities requiring moderate effort to produce moderate business impact (strategic planning tools, reports, sales target-setting tool, and payout calculator).

- **Phase 4:** Reevaluate and likely drop plans for deploying capabilities requiring high effort for low business impact (sales force automation system).

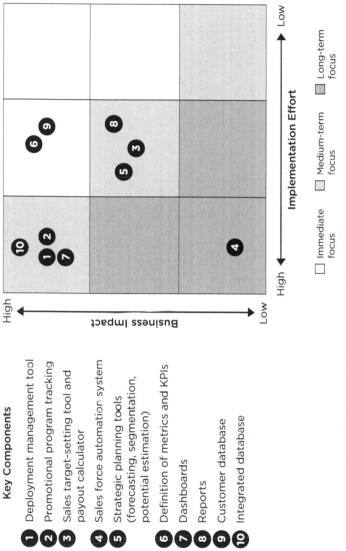

Key Components

1. Deployment management tool
2. Promotional program tracking
3. Sales target-setting tool and payout calculator
4. Sales force automation system
5. Strategic planning tools (forecasting, segmentation, potential estimation)
6. Definition of metrics and KPIs
7. Dashboards
8. Reports
9. Customer database
10. Integrated database

Figure 13-4. Prioritizing sales analytics capabilities for a new sales force in China

To create a prioritization matrix, do the following:

1. Make a list of all relevant sales analytics capabilities.

2. Gather input on two dimensions for each capability:

   - *Business impact*, which reflects the value that the capability creates for the company and its customers. This starts with profit impact but can also include factors such as increased employee morale, enhanced customer loyalty, greater competitive advantage and ability to respond to competitive threats, and improved efficiency by automating processes and reducing redundancy.
   - *Implementation effort*, which reflects the people, time, and costs necessary to develop the capability.

   When assessing impact and effort, include input from company sales and other leaders, in addition to consulting with outside experts.

3. Look at an effort-impact trade-off for each capability. Using a matrix (such as the one shown in Figure 13-4) helps to illuminate priorities.

Most new sales forces—even those with large, low-risk opportunities—have limited resources. Prioritizing the deployment of important capabilities is critical for creating the right implementation road map.

Creating a Road Map

A road map organizes the firm's sales analytics priorities; defines the people, data, applications, and processes needed to establish the capabilities; and sets a time line for development and launch. The example in Figure 13-5 shows an overview road map that the Chinese firm developed for the priorities identified in Figure 13-4. The road map covers four quarters before and four quarters following the product launch. The firm also had more detailed road maps for each specific capability specifying the required development phases, priorities, time lines, work streams, and release dates for meeting important deadlines.

The right road map depends on the situation. The road map for a new sales force facing an "invest" situation, for example, will include more capabilities and will involve a more aggressive time line than the road map for a firm facing a "test" situation.

Road maps can help all new sales forces guide priorities and work more efficiently to achieve goals on time. Road maps must be flexible enough to respond to the inevitable changes in goals and time lines that will occur as firm leaders learn about the market and adapt the sales strategy accordingly.

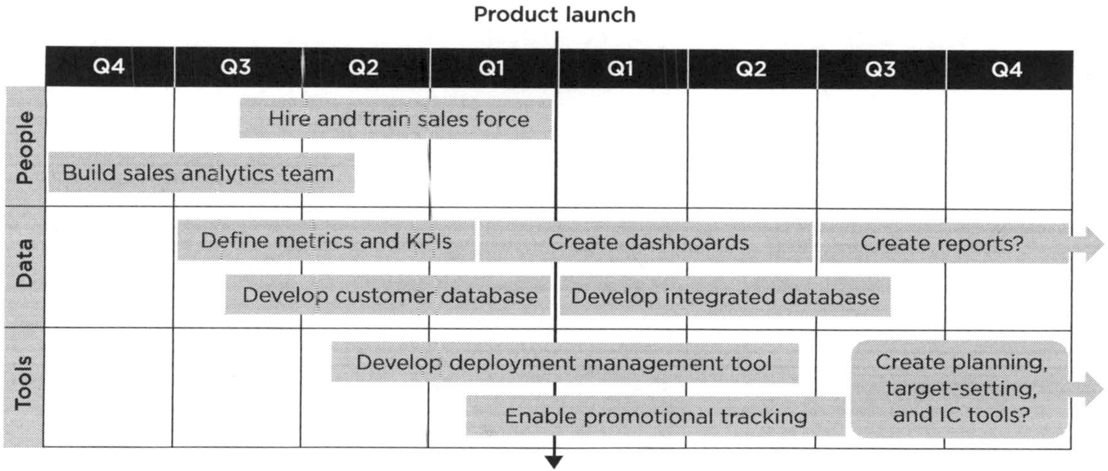

Figure 13-5. Road map for creating sales analytics capabilities for a new sales force in China

What Talent to Bring to Sales Analytics?

Three strategies can help new sales forces acquire the right sales analytics talent:

- **Hire the right person to lead the sales analytics initiative.** This individual should have the ability to envision the firm's analytics future, anticipate business needs, and work with leaders across the organization, as well as with external partners. A strong leader will recruit a strong team of individuals who have the inherent characteristics to succeed in their roles (see Chapter 6): "first class hires first class; second class hires third class." Hiring the wrong leader can cost a company years of advancement. It usually takes at least one to two years to discover the error and another one to two years to remedy it.

- **Build the internal team by adding the right people at the right time.** Team members should possess analytic skills, a passion for quality, and a strong customer-centric focus. By defining roles and responsibilities for team members, companies can develop hiring profiles for finding the right talent. Role definition also guides training and support needs, so team members develop the skills and knowledge they need to do their jobs.

    Timing is critical when building the internal sales analytics team. If too many people are hired too quickly and the product launch is delayed or demand is below forecast, the team will have too little to do. If too few people are hired too slowly, insufficient analysis and support will prevent the sales force from fully capitalizing on the opportunity. The effective use of external partners during the early stages, and in some cases for the long term, including offshore partners that can bring cost savings, can help companies manage these risks.

- **Leverage external partners.** In addition to providing flexible work capacity, outside advisers can bring functional and industry expertise to ensure that critical decisions are optimized from the start. Over time, as ongoing needs become more certain, the internal team can take increased ownership by learning from the partner and internalizing the capabilities. In some cases, it makes sense to hire a partner as a permanent employee for the internal team. In other cases, an ongoing outsourcing or offshoring arrangement is the best solution for providing the sales force with analytic support on an ongoing basis, especially as software as a service and cloud computing solutions become increasingly available for supporting sales force needs, such as sales performance reporting, customer relationship management, and incentive compensation. (Chapter 11 discusses how companies at the frontier of this movement use a network model to optimize their ongoing use of outside partners.)

Strategies for Working with External Partners

Companies launching new sales forces have used external partners to contribute in a wide range of areas, including guiding sales and go-to-market strategy, designing the sales force, hiring and training salespeople, developing sales information systems, and designing and implementing supporting programs such as sales incentive compensation and performance management. An experienced and objective partner can help determine how much and how quickly to invest, using analyses such as those shown in Figures 13-2, 13-3, and 13-4. Figure 13-6 lists several comments from leaders of new sales forces about the potential benefits and risks of working with external partners.

Companies can mitigate the risks of working with external partners by selecting advisers with a strong track record who are willing to partner with the internal team and train employees to leverage or eventually take over

Potential Benefits	Potential Risks
• **Expertise:** "We want the best solution based on industry experience, analytics expertise, and understanding our customers' needs." • **Cost efficiency:** "We want to leverage a solution that external partners can provide at lower cost due to their experience, technology, and/or expertise." • **Speed:** "We need a quicker solution than we can develop ourselves." • **Capacity flexibility:** "We can't take on the risk of hiring a large internal staff right now."	• **Dependence:** "We don't want to become dependent on consultants who know our processes better than we do. And the consultant could retire, take a job elsewhere, or his firm could go under." • **Lack of institutional knowledge:** "We need to develop this capability ourselves to create lasting competitive advantage." • **Coordination costs:** "We can't waste resources on coordinating with multiple consultants."

Figure 13-6. Comments from leaders of new sales forces about working with external partners for sales analytics

what they have developed. Several factors influence the decision to use external partners versus internal staff to meet the sales force's analytic needs:

- **Complexity of needs.** Internal staff may be well suited for meeting relatively simple needs, but as complexity increases, so does the potential value of going outside to buy expert advice.

- **Fit with existing external solution.** If external, outsourced, or hosted solutions already exist that are well matched to the company's needs, it is often cheaper to buy those solutions rather than re-creating them in-house.

- **Internal team strength and sustainability.** The stronger the internal team, the less likely the company will need to go outside to find the required expertise.

- **Certainty of success.** There is little risk in hiring permanent sales analytics employees if they are available in an "invest" situation. But in a "test" situation, companies can mitigate risk by working with external partners until sales force needs and the probability of success are more certain.

Conclusion

By investing early on to develop sales analytics capabilities, companies with new sales forces can avoid costly errors in sales force strategy, design, and implementation that jeopardize the success of their products. Sales analytics capabilities also provide salespeople in new sales forces with the support they need to work effectively and efficiently, allowing them to devote more time to serving customers.

Building the best sales analytics capabilities for a new sales force requires the right people and competencies, processes, data, and tools. These capabilities enable sales analytics to be a strategic partner with company leaders in driving commercial success. The best return on an investment in sales analytics comes when leaders:

- Match the investment in sales analytics to the size of the opportunity and the likelihood of success.

- Prioritize analytic needs and develop a strategic road map to maximize the use of limited resources over time.

- Tap into the best sales analytics talent by hiring the right people, partnering with external experts, or both.

Acknowledgments

Editing a book authored by 22 of the finest (and busiest) consultants and businesspeople in the world has been an incredible journey. We are greatly indebted to all of the authors, whom we thank collectively here, and whose names, photographs, and biographies appear at the start of each chapter. The authors are all members of the leadership team at the consulting firm we founded in 1983, ZS Associates. ZS employs more than 2,500 people in 21 offices across North America, South America, Europe, and Asia. Despite the many challenges and demands the authors face in their roles at ZS, they have put forth tremendous effort and shown great patience in writing this book. They spent countless hours collaborating with us and sharing their wisdom, writing and rewriting drafts, and responding to our all-too-often unrealistic demands and deadlines. Three of the authors—Doug Oettinger, Scott Shimamoto, and Dharmendra Sahay—acted as an advisory board during the book's earliest stages of development, helping us define and organize content so as to make it most valuable to sales and analytics leaders. We deeply appreciate the effort that all of the book's 22 authors have put forth.

As consultants, we have worked personally with executives, sales managers, and salespeople at hundreds of companies all over the world. Collectively, the authors of this book have had an impact on more than a thousand companies. The clients of ZS Associates have helped us and the authors discover, cultivate, test, and refine many of the concepts described in the book. Because of confidentiality, many of the people and companies must remain anonymous, but we owe a great deal of gratitude to all those who have helped us develop and enhance our ideas over the years. Special contributions to this book came from Chris Ahearn, John Barb, Chris Hartman, Bill Lister, Ken Revenaugh, and Bob Sanguedolce.

In addition, many colleagues at ZS contributed to the book directly and indirectly. Some of the authors acknowledge the contributions of specific individuals on the first page of their chapter. In addition, several people played key roles in bringing the entire project to fruition. ZS principals Brian Chapman and Michael Howes each read the entire manuscript and made suggestions for enhancing the book's clarity and value based on their years of experience working with clients. ZS associates David Vinca and

Nick Nazareno were our outstanding project managers, helping us keep the writing process organized and synchronized across 13 author teams. Shelley Gabel was instrumental in coordinating the meetings and ongoing communications between the editors and the author teams. Lisa Davis led the book's production and marketing efforts, reviewing the manuscript multiple times for clarity, and keeping us on track to meet every publishing deadline.

We would also like to thank the ZS marketing team, including Neil Warner who designed the book's cover and provided guidance for designing page layouts and graphics, as well as ZS publishing partner Books By Design, including Nancy Benjamin and her talented team.

Without the efforts of these hardworking collaborators, this book would not be in your hands today.

Andris A. Zoltners
Prabhakant Sinha
Sally E. Lorimer

Index

ability, 161
accounting functions, 126, 128
account planning, 166–68
account potential. *See also* customer
    potential; sales potential; territory
    sales potential
  data integration for, 170
  estimating, 25–27
  initial estimates of, 29–33
account profile tools, 54
AccuData, 28
activities
  as sales force effectiveness (SFE)
    drivers, 11
  in sales process, 39–40, 44
administrative costs, 200
advertising, 124
agile development approach, 233
airplane parts suppliers, 53
Albrecht, Chad, 123
Allied Signal, 53
analysis/design experts, 198
analytic concierge services, 171
analytics creep, 192
apartment rentals companies, 42
apparel companies
  customer potential data, 34
  natural experiments on sales force
    size and structure, 65–66
applicant tracking systems, 107–8,
  110
asset management industry, 90
auditing, sales process, 51

Austin-Tetra, 28

balanced scorecard, 178–79
Barb, John, 171
behavioral criteria, for customer
  segmentation, 30
behavioral interview questions, for
  sales force candidates, 108
best practice sharing, 168
biopharmaceutical companies, 240
Boston Scientific, 178
bottom-up forecasting goal-setting
  methodology, 151
Brown, Jason, 83
building materials industry, 29
business logistics providers, 54
business review tools, 54
business services outsourcing
  companies, 93
busy work, 85
buying patterns, 152
buying process, 47, 48

candidates
  analyzing backgrounds of, 108
  improving applicant pool, 109
  psychological test validity, 111
  recruiting, 107–11
  selection of, 109, 111
capabilities. *See* sales analytics capabilities; sales force capabilities
capacity flexibility, 253
capital equipment sales, 44

sales force decisions and, 12–13
of sales force resource plan, 59
of success profiles, 102–7
in support-diagnose-design-partner framework, 5, 9
territory alignment and, 88, 95–96, 100
desirable turnover, 118–19
development programs. *See* learning and development programs
diagnosis
customer potential and, 25
of data and tools, 185
goal setting, 142, 145–49, 150
of incentive compensation (IC) programs, 18, 125, 129–34
of learning and development programs, 112–16
of management, 101, 121
of people and competencies, 185
of performance management, 162, 170–76
of processes, 185
of recruiting process, 108–11
sales analytics and, 14–16
sales force decisions and, 12–13
of sales force issues, 59, 60–67
of sales force retention, 117–21
of sales process, 49–51
of success profiles, 102–7
in support-diagnose-design-partner framework, 5, 8–9
of targeting effectiveness, 34–36
territory alignment and, 88, 92–94, 100
diagnostic tests, for incentive compensation (IC) programs, 129–33
differentiation
ranking and, 179
sales success, 106

distribution companies
sales incentive compensation (IC) in, 124
supporting lead generation in, 52
district goals, 156
diversity
in data and tools, 196–97
managing diverse people and competencies, 197–99
in sales analytics capabilities, 196–201
work style differences, 196
downsizing, 213
draft territory alignment, 95–96
Dun & Bradstreet, 28, 34

early experience teams, 48
eBay, 244
economies of scale, outsourcing and, 209
education/educational products industry
customer potential estimates, 31–32
customer segmentation, 31
market potential measures, 29
efficiency
generalists and, 86
of sales force, 61–62, 158
specialists and, 86
territory alignment and, 86, 88
80/20 rule, 24, 31
empathy development, 231–32
enablers, in sales process, 39–40
episodic sales force needs, 20
excellence ratio, 131
executive sales leadership
network models and, 218–19
supporting, 126, 128
expectations
for outsourcing partners, 213
supporting with analytics, 165

Also written by the co-founders of ZS Associates, a global leader in sales and marketing consulting, are the following titles, which can be purchased on Amazon.com.

Building a Winning Sales Force

This practical guidebook shares a proven framework for assessing how good your sales force is and finding ways to improve it through better decisions about key sales effectiveness drivers, such as sales force design, hiring, training, incentive compensation, and performance management.

Building a Winning Sales Management Team

Written with input from 19 successful sales executives from leading companies, this book highlights the pivotal role of the first-line sales manager and demonstrates how by investing in the sales management team, your company can drive profitable growth in an ever-changing business environment.

Sales Force Incentive Compensation

This detailed guide is packed with hundreds of real-life examples of what works and what doesn't when it comes to creating a sales incentive compensation program that drives results, including how to design and implement a program that aligns with your company's goals and culture, while avoiding the common trap of overusing incentives to solve too many sales management problems.

Sales Force Design for Strategic Advantage

This book demonstrates how a well-designed sales force gives you a competitive edge in today's changing world. Learn how to assess a current sales force design and how to implement improvements through more effective customer segmentation, go-to-market strategy, sales roles, structuring and sizing, and territory design.

Accelerating Sales Force Performance

Packed with valuable insights and real-world examples, this book shares an innovative framework for evaluating and improving the performance of any sales force, and includes ideas for improving such "sales force success drivers" as culture, sales force structure, hiring, training, compensation, sales territory design, goal setting, and performance management.

40333387R00165

Made in the USA
Lexington, KY
01 April 2015